Alex was in the kitchen fixing himself some breakfast. I could hear the splash of running water, the clink of silverware, the clatter of dishes and a high, thin voice saying, "I'm going to kill myself."

A top drawer in the cabinet was open and there was a sharp, gleaming butcher knife in his right hand. He held it over his left wrist so the point was touching the pulsing blue artery. "I'm going to kill myself," he repeated gleefully in the manner of a small child who had made a delightful discovery.

I saw blood oozing from the white skin. I turned to the phone on the kitchen wall. All I could do was call the police station. As I was talking to the dispatcher, whoever it was that stood before me gave a contemptuous laugh. The voice changed, became deeper, more resonant, "The police can't touch me," he said.

"What is your name?"

"I am old. I am very old."

"How old were you when you first came?"

"I was always old."

"How old was Alex?"

"He was seven."

"What did you do for him?"

"I kept him from committing suicide. I kept him from killing himself."

The Magic Castle

A Mother's Harrowing True Story
of Her Adoptive Son's Multiple Personalities—
and the Triumph of Healing

CAROLE SMITH

St. Martin's Paperbacks

THE MAGIC CASTLE

Copyright © 1998 by Carole Smith.

Cover photograph courtesy of Morin's Studio.

Library of Congress Catalog Card Number: 97-36513

ISBN: 0-312-96820-5

Printed in the United States of America

St. Martin's Press hardcover edition / March 1998
St. Martin's Paperbacks edition / January 1999

10   9   8   7   6   5   4   3   2   1

To my husband—
without his love,
patience, and support,
there would have been no story to tell.

CONTENTS

ILLUSTRATIONS

ACKNOWLEDGMENTS

This book never would have been finished if it weren't for one of my son's personalities. His name was Brian, he was fourteen years old, and he was created to handle the need for revenge. His idea of revenge was to kill, and I can still hear that deep, guttural voice in Dr. Kingsbury's office. "Death! Death to Christine!" After a lot of communication with the doctor and my son, Brian was willing to settle for the book. If everyone could know what Christine and the other perpetrators had done, he would agree to become integrated.

Brian put the pressure on. Sometimes the rewriting and revisions took longer than he thought they should, so he would take over and cause a great deal of trouble. When it was finally done, Brian kept his promise. He was the last of the personalities.

I am especially grateful to Bill Conti, our therapist. When the project was more wishful thinking than reality, he would read those first drafts, and his praiseful words helped me to believe in my ability to actually write the book. Dr. Steven J. Kingsbury also read the manuscript and provided helpful technical advice. I would like to thank my agent, Ken Atchity, for his unwavering faith, and Jennifer Enderlin, my editor at St. Martin's Press, for her invaluable criticism. In addition, I would like to express my appreciation to Sue McDonald, for handling the much-detested chore of typing, and to Nancy Bland for managing to get printable copies from dog-eared originals of predisclosure drawings.

AUTHOR'S NOTE

This is a true account of my experiences in successfully raising a child who suffered from multiple personality disorder. In writing the book, I have made extensive use of notes I took during therapy sessions and directly after encounters with alters, mental health personnel, a child placement organization, and the office of the district attorney. Occasionally, I have combined several similar events to avoid repetition.

I was not present at the original incidents but I did observe many revivifications of the actual events. My belief in the truth of the personalities' revelations is based upon physical and circumstantial evidence and also occasional verification from witnesses. All of my encounters with the alters, including revivifications, have been accurately depicted and have not been exaggerated in any way.

Many names, locations, and identifying details, including those of my family, have been changed or modified. The only names used in this book that have not been altered are those of Bill Conti, Dr. Steven J. Kingbury, Dr. Nina Fish-Murray, Marie Parente, and Dr. Van der Kolk. The names of places and institutions that have not been changed are Boston Children's Hospital; Camp Wedicko; County District Attorney's Office; Massachusetts Department of Social Services; Massachusetts Mental Health Center; Mount Auburn Hospital; Northboro, Massachusetts; Robert F. Kennedy Residential School; and University of Massachusetts Acute Adolescent Psychiatric Unit at Westboro.

As a final note, when he was thirteen years old, my son wanted to sever all connections to the perpetrators and asked to have his first, middle, and last names legally changed. I gave him an old family name of mine, my husband's middle name, and, of course, our last name. It is important that the reader know of these changes. However, throughout this book I have simply called him Alex.

I

July to August 1984

Alex

My husband, Sam, and I were sitting across from each other at the scarred trestle table in the kitchen. Shafts of morning sunlight were coming through a window and my eyes idly followed the bright rays as they played across the pine-paneled walls. For two weeks now, we had been considering the option of taking a special-needs foster child into our home, and Sam was waiting for me to make a decision. Peering at me inquiringly, he had his elbows on the table and his blue coffee mug clasped in both hands. "So what do you think, Carole?" he said, lifting the mug to his lips. "Do you want to give it a try? Would you like to work for these people?"

He was referring to an agency that handled state contracts for the placement of emotionally disturbed children. "I—I'm not sure," I answered with a touch of hesitation and a lot of concern. "These kids have got some severe problems. Many of them have been institutionalized. Maybe I should go back to teaching."

A smile flickered across Sam's handsome features. A lock of gray-streaked hair fell across his forehead and he brushed it aside with a casual, absentminded gesture. "Is that what you really want?"

As Sam was well aware, teaching English to seventh- and eighth-graders was not very high on my job appeal agenda. I had not forgotten the frustrations of discipline and piles of paperwork. "No," I acknowledged. But I knew I had to do something. My husband, a masonry contractor, had injured his back in a fall last May. It was now midsummer, the bills had been piling up, and it would be December or January before he could resume the necessary lifting and climbing.

"At thirty-three thousand a year, this pays more than teaching," said Sam, tuning into my thoughts. "I think you'd find a hell of a lot more satisfaction in dealing with only one kid at a time. And Carole, it's not as though we don't have the place for it."

Sipping my coffee, I nodded in agreement. We did have the place for it. A sprawling ranch house. Twenty acres of oak, maple, and white pine bounded by a river and lichen-covered stone walls. Beyond the gnarled oak tree on the front lawn and down a gently sloping hill, there was a barn. It had a gambrel roof and it was stained a dark, almost black, brown to match the house. Inside were stalls for my horses, a generous hayloft, and more than enough room for Sam's pet rabbits.

Sam and I had raised four children here on this land in this small Massachusetts town of West River. We seldom saw the older three. Scott, an electronics engineer, was married and lived in California. Matt was a long-distance truck driver and lived in northern Maine, and Corey was in the navy.

I wouldn't have dreamed of bringing in a foster child if one of my own was still at home, but our youngest son, Eddie, had gone off to college, and there was a void, an emptiness. We did have a beagle puppy named Bailey and an orange angora cat named Rusty. "I don't know, Sam. I suppose it might be a good thing to have a child around again."

"And as for problems, Carole, look here," he said, waving his hand toward a stack of literature I'd brought home from the preliminary interview.

"Yes, I know. I've read it." I reached to the end of the table, picked up a booklet, and flipped through the glossy pages. I'd read about the complete support services and the twenty-four-hour emergency backup. I'd read about the supervision by trained experts and the clinical staff of psychiatrists, psychologists, and other professionals who could be contacted at any time to help in crisis situations. I'd also read about the respite procedure. If the care of the child became too stressful, the child would be temporarily placed elsewhere. Every possible contingency, every conceivable drawback, seemed to be covered. "Okay," I said to my husband. "Let's do it. But I won't be just giving it a try. You know how I am. If I start something, I stick with it. I am not a quitter."

The call came in August. My instructions were to stop at the agency and then go to pick up a boy at the foster home of a Mrs. Fisher. When I arrived at the office, a glamorous redhead with upswept hair and meticulous makeup handed me a manila folder. "I'm Cheryl, and you can go over the background information in here," she said as she ushered me into a comfortably furnished sitting room. "I must warn you. You'll have to watch this one. He's very manipulative and aggressive, and I've heard he steals."

She probably felt it her duty to warn me, but I'd hardly expected an angel. I tried to reassure myself with some positive thinking about successful people like salesmen and politicians who had to be manipulative and aggressive.

Opening the folder, I sat down to review the record written by the state social worker. The client's name was Alex. He was just past his tenth birthday and had lived in Bainbridge, Massachusetts, with his mother, Christine, and his stepfather, Albert Mercer, until he was five years of age. At this time the mother became unable to care for her children because of alcohol-related issues. Two older half sisters, Donna and Debra, had been given up for adoption. Alex, the product of an extramarital affair, had been taken by George Slade, the man purported to be his biological father. George, also an alcoholic, was married to a young girl named Sandra. Reports of neglect and physical abuse had led to the removal of the child from the home. At the age of seven he had been placed in the Robert F. Kennedy Residential School, an institution for children in Lancaster, Massachusetts. Although allowed to spend weekends with George and Sandra, he had remained at RFK until June 15 of this year. After leaving the school, he had gone to a summer camp in New Hampshire, Camp Wedicko. He had stayed there for six weeks and then had gone to Mrs. Fisher.

Another paragraph related how the Massachusetts Department of Social Services (DSS) had put much effort into working with the family so ultimately Alex could return to his father and stepmother. An additional note said that his intelligence tested slightly below normal. In the whole perfunctory account, there was nothing to give any indication of extraordinary trauma. The only item at all that triggered a nagging question in my mind was at the beginning of the report. The maternal grandmother, a woman identified as a former prostitute, had twice called the child's condition to the attention of the Department of Social Services while he was with his mother and stepfather.

What had happened? What could possibly have caused this woman, herself certainly no paragon of morality, no model of exemplary behavior, to take such a step? One could easily imagine that she lived in some fear of the law and might have felt threatened by the power of a system that could intrude into people's lives and take their children away. What had she seen? What did she know? Why had she been compelled to report her own daughter to these same frightening authorities?

I was several houses away when I first spotted him. He was sitting near the sidewalk on the edge of a front lawn, and beside him were two green plastic rubbish bags. The toe of a sneaker and the leg of a pair of jeans protruded from one of them. He did not look at me as I parked my car but stared straight ahead, impassive and aloof.

A thin, frowzy woman emerged from the house. She was obviously distraught. "You Carole Smith?" she asked.

"Yes, yes, I am," I said, leaving the car and walking toward her. "You must be—" I consulted the piece of paper I'd been given—"Mrs. Fisher."

"Thank the Lord!" she replied with much emphasis. "I've been waiting for you. Here, you'll be needing this." She thrust a folded card into my hand.

"Oh, yes, his Medicaid. Is there anything else?"

"No, the rest of his stuff's in them bags. I tell you I never been so glad to see anyone go as I am this one. I kept him two weeks and it was the longest two weeks of my entire life!"

After casting a scathing look in Alex's direction, Mrs. Fisher went on with an account of the crimes Alex had almost committed and would have if someone hadn't stopped him. In conclusion, she related what had happened when a man named Peter from the agency had come to her home to see Alex. "The kid was using a baseball bat to hit rocks," she said, "and Peter couldn't get near him. If you ask me, the guy was scared of him."

Alex sat quietly during Mrs. Fisher's tirade and regarded the woman with what seemed to be amused contempt. He was a sturdily built child with brown hair cut below his ears and long-lashed green eyes. He had a small, turned-up nose, a slightly cleft chin, and a barely noticeable scar on his left cheek. I guessed that he weighed close to sixty pounds.

"Hi," I said to him, swallowing hard and giving him a smile in spite of my growing dismay. Peter was supposed to be my supervisor on the case. If he was, as the woman claimed, afraid of this child, what had I gotten into? I reminded myself of the brave speech I'd made to Sam about not being a quitter.

"Hi," I said again in a firmer, more positive voice. "My name is Carole, and the people at the agency said you're to come with me." He didn't answer. His eyes warily examined me from head to toe like some kind of electronic scanning device. I had a feeling every detail was being recorded for future reference, and I experienced a vague discomfort. There was something about those cool, green eyes. They were out of place in the rounded, prepubescent features. They did not seem like the eyes of a child.

Alex picked up his possessions and wedged them into the floor space in front of the passenger seat. After I said good-bye to Mrs. Fisher and made my way onto the turnpike, he was still trying to maneuver his legs protectively around them. "My father's got a new Cadillac," he announced. I did not miss the condescending implication that my Ford was inferior. "My father owns two of them trucks," he added, nonchalantly referring to a shiny white eighteen-wheeler that was heading in the opposite direction. "A red one and a blue one."

I didn't believe a word of it, and I almost asked him if the new Cadillac and the two trucks weren't a bit of an exaggeration. But there was so much pride in his voice, and if his fabrications made him feel any better, what did it matter? It was all he had. "That's nice," I replied with as much enthusiasm as I could muster. "I guess your father makes a lot of money."

"Oh, yes. He makes a thousand a week. I seen him bring it home. He got twenty guys working for him. And you should see my stepmother! She's so beautiful. She's real awesome."

"I'm sure she is," I agreed.

We left the highway and drove through one of the wealthier suburbs of the area. Two white-pillared mansions were set well back from the road, and Alex proclaimed each to be not nearly so grand as his father's house. Soon after that, he began to fidget. His hands were constantly twisting, turning, and pulling anything and everything within reach. I said nothing when he replaced the easy-listening music I preferred with the dissonant sounds of hard rock, but when the maps, keys, and other contents of the glove compartment were strewn about and my automobile registration was being mutilated, I responded sharply. "Don't!" I snapped at him. "Put those away."

He stiffened visibly and recoiled against the seat. His face was a frozen mask of fear, and he watched me closely out of the corner of his eye while he returned the objects to the compartment. "You can't tear up my registration," I said apologetically. "We'd be in trouble if we got stopped by the police."

It was ten o'clock that night before I could get Alex into bed. My every attempt to have him undress and take a bath had been met with a screaming tantrum accompanied by every filthy word I'd ever heard and a few I hadn't. In the end we made a compromise. He agreed to let me wash his face and hands if he could keep on the same clothes he'd worn all day.

"At least he fell right to sleep," I said to Sam as I let out a sigh of relief and slumped into the antique Boston rocker by the living-room fireplace.

My husband settled himself into the black leather sofa in front of the picture window. He eyed me intently with a slightly raised brow. "Why do you think he insisted on wearing his clothes to bed?"

"I don't have a clue. He wouldn't unpack those plastic bags either. He said he hadn't decided if he was going to stay here or not. And there's another thing. He has this spontaneous, fearful reaction if I say 'no' or 'don't' to him. It happened in the car and again tonight. He literally cringes as though he expects to be hit."

"Maybe he was. They probably belted him every time they said it."

I inwardly flinched at the mental picture evoked by Sam's statement but I knew it must be true. It was the only logical explanation. Alex was conditioned to expect a blow. But it did seem he should be past that by now. He'd been in state custody for two and a half years. Pausing reflectively for a moment, I said, "You know, Sam, I need some kind of a plan. I need to figure out how to handle this child."

"What about this supervisor, Peter? He'll be able to tell you."

I told my husband what Mrs. Fisher had said about Peter's apparent fear of Alex and that I wasn't sure he would be of much help.

"Well, what are you going to do then?" asked Sam. "He's as bad as a two-year-old. He wasn't in the house an hour before he broke two dishes and a lamp. He didn't do it on purpose, but he doesn't seem to have any control. He'll drive you crazy."

"That might be it, Sam," I said tentatively as I rocked back and forth.

"What? He'll drive you crazy?"

"I suppose it's a possibility," I agreed with a wry smile. "But, no, it's about him acting like a two-year-old. I've been trying to think what his behavior reminded me of and I couldn't put my finger on it. He does. He acts like our boys did when they were at the terrible twos. Into something every minute. Demanding constant attention."

"Carole, he's not two. He's ten."

For a few minutes the only sound in the room was the creaking of the old chair. "Sam, I read this book once for one of those psychology courses I had in college. I remember it was by a doctor, Carl Rogers. He claimed you can't force a person to change and the only way people will change is if you accept them as they are. I'm sure there are arguments and disagreements about it, but here we're saying Alex is acting like a two-year-old. Well, what would happen, Sam, if we treated him like a two-year-old? If we accepted him on that level, I could give him the same kind of care and attention I would give a toddler. No expectations. No negative commands."

"I don't know," said Sam doubtfully. Then with a nod and an assenting shrug, "Hey, what the hell. You might as well try. You don't have anything to lose. The kid is a disaster."

Sam's candid assessment of Alex hung in the air between us as he put his feet up on the couch and leaned his head back against a pile of red and beige pillows. There was a contemplative note in his voice when he spoke again. "There is something about him. You know, Carole, I'll bet Alex has had a rough life, but he's got one thing going for him. He's a fighter. He's a survivor."

. . .

For the fourth time during breakfast the next morning, Alex jammed a handful of scrambled eggs into his mouth, snatched a piece of toast, and ran around the room leaving a trail of scattered food in his wake. His extremities seemed to have a will of their own that was separate from his mind and the rest of his body. His hands continually touched, rapped, or twisted while his feet kicked, tapped, or banged. I took a deep breath and counted to ten to keep from crying out, "Stop it. No! Don't!" as he raced from the kitchen into the dining room, kicked at the wall, and streaked greasy fingers across one of the windows. Returning to the table, he grabbed another handful of egg, went back to the dining room, and proceeded to rummage through some bureau drawers. His impulse control was virtually nonexistent. To feel was to react; to think was to do. There was nothing in between.

There were similarities between Alex's behavior and that of many curious, high-energy youngsters, but the causes appeared to be vastly different. A two-year-old is exploring his environment and learning about his world. In Alex's case, I suspected the hyperactivity was a protective device, a defense mechanism designed to keep at bay fears and feelings that were unknown and unnamed. Perpetual motion was a way to build a barrier against a multitude of unacceptable realities and to keep them from intruding into conscious thought. I listened to his talk, to the incessant chatter about everything and about nothing. It was as though the words, along with the nonstop movement, gave a reality to his being. They were, in effect, a confirmation of his existence.

On Friday, the third day, Sam walked in and surveyed the chaotic condition of the house. "I see you haven't been saying no," he said with a shake of his head and a chuckle. "Where is he?"

"Watching television. His attention span will last all of five minutes." I busied myself with scrubbing some dried cereal from the trestle table while Sam opened the refrigerator door and took out a can of soda. "I feel so sorry for that child," I said. "I can't imagine what's going on inside his mind. There is nothing, absolutely nothing, in him of peace and calm."

Serious now, Sam sighed and gave me a look of sympathy. "Doesn't look like there's much for you either," he said.

I gave the table a final swipe with the dishcloth. "I don't let myself get pulled into it. I have to stand back and distance myself from his acting out. It—it's all I can do."

This distancing I was telling Sam about was to become one of my most important strategies. It would enable me to protect my feelings and keep my focus. Caring for Alex was a job. It was simply a job. But even so, getting through those first days was a monumental struggle.

Later, on that same Friday, Alex decided to unpack his clothes and settle into the bedroom I had given him. "Can I move the furniture?" he asked as he dumped the contents of his plastic bags into bureau drawers.

"Yes," I said readily.

"Can I hammer nails in the walls?"

"Yes," I said not quite so readily. But this room, the smallest of the six bedrooms in my home, had a stucco finish. Any holes could be easily fixed, so what was the harm? I felt it was important for him to have control of his space.

I soon discovered the only way to save my sanity was to channel Alex's excessive energy into a daily routine of structured activity filling every waking moment. One of these activities was archery practice. I had found a toy bow and some arrows that had belonged to my son Eddie, and we set up a target against some bales of hay. On the first attempt, he missed both the target and the hay. His face grew livid and his small frame stiffened. "I can't do it," he screamed as he threw himself on the ground kicking and pounding the grass with feet and fists. "I can't do it!"

"Sure you can, Alex. You can do it. I know you can," I said by way of encouragement.

He jumped up and faced me. His teeth were clenched grimly together, and with every word his lips became thinner and more rigid. "No, I can't! I can't do nothing. I'm stupid. I'm no good. I'm garbage. Why don't you throw me away? Why don't you throw me in the dump?"

Going to the target, he grabbed the circled paper and ripped it to shreds. Then he retrieved the arrow, called it a few choice names, and snapped it in half. I watched in silence while he attacked the hay, shoving and pushing the bales until the fury of his tantrum subsided. I went over to him. I put my arms about him and held him close. "Come on, Alex. Let's make another target and try again. The real losers are the people who never try, and Alex, you're not a loser. So what do you say?"

We did make another target, and with each shot, the arrow came closer and closer to the bull's-eye. I was ecstatic. I clapped and cheered as though he had won an Olympic medal. "I knew you could do it. Look! It's great. It's wonderful!" I exclaimed. In most families, the first smile, word, step, or any of the many other things babies do as a normal part of the growth process is met with extravagant expressions of approval. That was how I responded to Alex. Each success was greeted with an abundance of praise.

But his sense of worthlessness was so deeply ingrained that success was verbally negated as it was physically achieved. The arrow could be right near the center of the target and he would still deny the visual evidence and cry out, "I can't. I'm just no good. I'm stupid."

At the end of our archery session, after he actually hit the bull's-eye, he handed me the bow and said, "Here, Carole, you do it." Only when my arrow completely missed was he able to reflect my pleasure in his own accomplishment. "See!" he cried out triumphantly. "I can do it. I can do it and you can't."

Aware of the fact that surpassing my performance held a special significance for him, I went along with it. "You are much better at this than I am," I said as I picked up another arrow and placed it against the bowstring. I let it fly wide of its mark, and Alex almost smiled.

The next project of our day was fishing. We carried a fishing pole and a freshly dug can of worms down the hill and through the woods to the river. My little beagle, running on ahead of us with his nose to the ground, let out a howl and dashed off into the underbrush. "I guess Bailey is after a rabbit," I commented. "Do you think he'll catch it?"

Alex was so wrapped up in his egocentric perspective he was unable to respond to anything I had said except for the one word he could relate to himself. "I can't catch nothing. Them worms ain't no good, and that dumb pole you got ain't no good either. I hope you don't expect me to get a fish with it," he continued in a disparaging tone. In between his condemnations of the bait and tackle, he loudly cursed the branches that brushed against him and the rocks that tripped him. He seemed to feel everything in his environment was making a deliberate effort to injure him.

We found a spot where overhanging branches of willow and swamp maple were mirrored in the water below. Hummingbirds hovered above the brilliant cardinal flowers, a bullfrog was sitting on a partially submerged log in the middle of the stream, and two mallard ducks were feeding in the shallows. The tranquillity of the scene did not last long. Charging up and down the muddy riverbank, Alex screamed at the top of his lungs if a dragonfly came within three feet of him. The hummingbirds disappeared in an iridescent flash, the frog dived to the safety of the river bottom, and the ducks flew heavenward with a raucous quacking.

When Alex quieted down, I baited the hook with one of the squirming earthworms and gave him the pole. His cast was clumsy, and the line became entangled in a branch. The inanimate object bore the brunt of his anger and he flung the pole into the river. Since the line was still held fast by the branch, I was able to retrieve it and return it to him. He made another cast, but the fish did not bite immediately, so he jerked the line out of the water. "This place sucks," he yelled. "There ain't no fish here. I hate this place!"

By some minor miracle the fish eventually did bite in the

brief moments that the hook was submerged, and Alex caught a trout and three smallmouth bass. We trudged up the hill with the tangible evidence of what I proclaimed to be his excellent fishing ability. Back at the house, I cooked the fish and served them for lunch. "Are you sure you want to eat it?" he questioned as he viewed the pan-fried bass on my plate.

I swallowed a mouthful of the fish and said, "Of course I do. Go ahead. Try some. It's really good."

Alex poked his fork into his portion and glared at me venomously from across the table. "You're just saying that. It's got bones in it. It stinks!" He threw his plate on the floor, ran into his room, and proceeded to have a second tantrum.

Forcing myself to ignore the screams and racket coming from down the hall, I finished my meal. With every bite I reminded myself of my plan and my goal. I'm dealing with a baby and I'm going to accept him as such. That is his room. Those are his things. If it's not dangerous, he can do what he likes to them.

I picked up the plate from the floor, cleared off the table, and waited.

I thought about what had preceded this outburst. The fish he had caught was less than perfect. It had bones in it. That was enough to trigger a raging fit of temper. By the time his anger had run its course, his bedding was ripped from the mattress, the posters and pictures were torn from the walls, and the contents of the bureau drawers were dumped in the middle of the rug.

I led him into the living room to the rocking chair, and he curled up on my lap, tight and tense, head, arms, and legs drawn together. I rocked back and forth. I stroked his tousled hair. I comforted him until his body softened and relaxed and he was ready to go on with the afternoon activities. These consisted of games of hide-and-seek, batting practice, catch, swimming, and making cookies. At any lull in the schedule—usually from exhaustion on my part—Alex became extremely agitated and I could see the fear leap into his eyes. "But there's nothing to do. There's nothing to do," he would cry out in panic as he searched frantically for something to fill what was evidently to him a real and horrible void.

On Sunday, the fifth day, a heavy rain prevented us from pursuing our usual program. Alex became quite alarmed at this turn of events and surveyed his room with glittering eyes. "I need stuff to make shelves. I gotta have shelves," he said, his voice betraying his tension. "You got any old boards around here?"

"I might be able to find some down by the barn."

"Well, get them. I gotta have them. Get them right this minute!" he ordered with all the authority of a five-star general. "And while you're at it, get me a hammer and some nails."

"I couldn't believe I was doing it," I told Sam that evening. "There I was tramping around in the pouring rain and mud and carrying wet boards into the house."

Sam shook his head dubiously. "Why do you let him order you around? Jesus, Carole! He could have at least helped you."

"It did keep him busy," I replied, ignoring Sam's objections. I knew perfectly well that had I requested help from Alex, his indignant retort would have been, "What? I hope you don't expect me to go out there and get my feet wet." I figured it would be better not to mention this.

"He pounded and hammered all morning," I said. "He's got one wall covered with lopsided shelves."

"He showed them to me. I don't see what the hell they'll hold. And I'd sure like to know why you let him get away with this stuff."

The question made me feel uncomfortable and defensive. "We've already talked about it. The first night. Remember? We were going to accept him as a two-year-old."

A confused expression came over Sam's face, and I realized the day-to-day reality of what was involved in this job was more than he had bargained for. "Sam, the truth of the matter is I think he's even younger in some ways. When I listen to his orders and to his constant demands, do you know what I hear? I hear a baby. I hear the endless, unanswered cries of a helpless baby. I can't ignore those cries, Sam. I can't."

"That's fine, Carole," he argued. "But babies don't swear at you and talk back. They only need to be fed and changed."

"And held, too, don't forget," I said, trying to get my husband away from the subject of Alex's outrageously disrespectful behavior. "Every time I sit down in the rocking chair by the fireplace, he comes and climbs up on my lap. He's getting very attached to me. If I have to leave him alone for more than ten minutes, he gets sick to his stomach and soils his pants." Recalling yesterday's archery contest, I told Sam about Alex's almost positive response when I missed the target and he didn't. "He's beginning to mirror my expressions, Sam. He's beginning to show some pleasure when he does well."

Sam did not look impressed. It was hard on him to watch this kid treat me as his personal slave, but I needed his support or there was no way I could continue working with Alex. I made another attempt to explain. "We agreed I would do this job. It's only been five days. I know what he does isn't right. I also know if I make one critical or negative comment, it will kill the whole process. I've just got this gut feeling that he has to have some legitimate control of his own before I can take away any of this rotten conduct. So far he's in charge of his own room, and Wednesday I'm going to start him in karate lessons."

"Don't you have to get permission from the agency?"

"I don't think so. The manual says we can use our own child-rearing practices. When my supervisor shows up, I'll explain how important this control is and how the advantages far outweigh any concerns he might have. And tomorrow," I added, "I'm going to try to put him on one of the horses. Maybe Roxy. She's small and she's gentle."

"He'll have to sit still for more than five seconds," was Sam's slightly sarcastic observation.

"Yes, but the biggest problem is going to be getting him on a horse, and I might not be able to do it. He's scared to death of them. The only time he'll go near them is if they're on the other side of the fence. It'll probably take weeks for him to get over his fear. And I'm worried he might be dumped. That would only make him worse."

"Carole," said Sam, "he couldn't possibly be any worse."

On the following morning I tried to show Alex there was no reason for him to be afraid of the horse. Tacking up the mare, I led her over to where he was crouched in the tall grass on the other side of the weathered post-and-rail fence. I stroked her velvety nose and her reddish-brown coat. I walked her back and forth and I mounted and dismounted. It did not help. I could not coax him to come into the paddock. Ready to give up, I reached in my pocket for a piece of carrot and held it out to him. "Here, Alex," I said, "would you like to give this to her? She won't hurt you."

He stared at me in wide-eyed terror and ran to hide behind a clump of scrub oak at the edge of the woods. What happened next was completely unexpected. He came out of the brush. He marched boldly toward me. And he begged to ride the horse. "Can I ride, Carole?" he asked. "When can I ride? I want to ride right now."

I couldn't believe it! How could he have lost his fear so quickly? I was puzzled by this unaccountable switch but nevertheless took advantage of it. "Sure, Alex," I said. "Of course you can ride," and I boosted him into the saddle. As soon as he was astride Roxy, I could see that my worries about his falling off were groundless. His sense of balance and his coordination were so good there was little danger.

Although on every day of the first few weeks we went through the same transformation from cowering fearfulness to self-assured confidence, Alex progressed rapidly. Our two fifteen-minute sessions became the highlights of his schedule. Once he learned how to hold the reins and sit properly, I snapped a twenty-foot rope called a longe line onto the halter Roxy wore under her bridle. With the other end in my hand, I directed him to walk her around me in a large circle. "That's fine, Alex. Keep her going forward. She's looking real good. Now pick up your reins and ask for a trot. Remember, you're in charge. You are in control."

He pressed his legs lightly against the mare, and she moved into a trot. An expression of awe and wonder came into his eyes. Being in command of a horse was obviously an incredibly heady sensation, and he couldn't get enough of it.

Roxy began drifting into the center of the circle. "You have to use your inside leg, the one toward me, and outside rein. There, that's right. Very good, Alex. See, she's obeying you. She's doing what you want," I said as the mare responded to his aids.

Our sessions had to be kept short, because it was painfully difficult for him to resist the impulse to drop the reins and swat a fly or scratch at an itch. Nor could he scream out at will or squirm around in the saddle or let his feet and legs move without purpose. If he wanted to ride, he had to concentrate on staying in the correct position and on using the right aids and signals. Alex did want to ride, and the motivation generated by that tremendous sense of power gave him the will to keep his hyperactivity in check.

It wasn't long before he was far enough advanced to begin learning to post to the trot. Since rising up and down in rhythm to the horse's movement is more complicated, I got into the saddle to demonstrate how it was supposed to be done. He stood in the center of the ring and watched attentively. "See, Alex, it's up, down, up, down, like this. You just go with the horse. I'll put the longe line on and you can try it."

I rode toward him, and he looked up at me with an expression of solemn determination. "Someday," he said, "I'm going to be a better rider than you are."

There it was again, this intense desire to do something better than I could. What was going on? Did Alex believe that by being superior to me he would be able to gain control over me? Why did he need this kind of power? Why was it so important to him? Whatever the reason, the only way he could get what he wanted was to make some changes in his behavior. And that was what I wanted. It was a trade-off.

I thought I might be able to use this new insight to introduce Alex to the idea of obeying some basic rules. Although he was generally accepting of discipline meted out by his karate instructors, most restrictions really meant nothing to him. They were not to be tolerated and were flouted at every opportunity. To take him out in a public place was a catastrophe. In the department store, the merchandise became war missiles, and in the supermarket the shopping cart became a destructive tank. Removing him from either store entailed a scene rivaling a television chase sequence.

My plan consisted of using a Scrabble game to practice acceptable conduct. If Alex wanted to play he would have to follow the directions. He could use only a prescribed number of letters, and these letters had to be chosen sight unseen. They had to correctly spell a real word, and each letter was worth a certain number that had to be multiplied and added as indicated by the board. He also had to patiently wait his turn.

I carefully manipulated my scores so he almost won most of the time and did win some of the time, and Alex's wish to beat me, to be better than I was, forced him to go by the rules. It was frustrating for him, and more often than not the game board and pieces were dashed to the floor. But he kept at it and he became surprisingly good. Not only was he able to think several plays ahead, he seemed always to know what letters were still available.

We had just finished a game one day when Sam came into the kitchen. Alex had run outside and I was morosely picking up the Scrabble pieces from the trestle table. "Carole, what's wrong?" he asked, instantly knowing that something was.

"Sam, I just did an awful—oh, Sam, I'm too ashamed!"

"What are you talking about? What did you do?"

I dropped the wooden letters into the box, folded the game board, and placed it over them.

"Well?"

"I cheated at Scrabble!"

My husband made a halfhearted and unsuccessful attempt to keep from laughing.

"He was winning, Sam. On his own! He gets so obnoxious when he beats me. I can usually handle it if I let him, but today . . . Sam, I'm supposed to be an English teacher, for God's sake. And, according to the record, he's had minimal education and isn't very bright. I certainly have some doubts about that! Anyway, I'm sorry I did it. It won't happen again."

The Scrabble game was not my only mistake. There were times during those early weeks when my efforts to see Alex as a baby failed miserably. Babies are cute and cuddly; Alex was usually hateful and hostile. Babies take naps; Alex slept only if totally exhausted. There was one incident in particular when he called me a fucking bitch before I'd had a cup of coffee. I lost it. I lost my temper and hurled the cup that was in my hand in his direction. It bounced off the wall and fell harmlessly to the floor, but when I saw the shock and fear in his eyes, I knew it was a setback.

On the whole, however, the acceptance of this child on a primitive developmental level was, for Alex, a second chance. It was a chance for him to begin to redefine his self-image. It was a chance for him to build a healthy self-esteem based on his own skills and his own competence. This would eventually give him the strength to explore the brutish forms and monstrous shapes that lay buried in the black, hidden recesses of a negated past.

II

September 1984

A Matter of Control

Two days after that embarrassing Scrabble game, I took the broom and went outside to sweep off the front steps. I was about finished when I caught sight of Alex. He was over near the fireplace chimney at the end of the house, and he made no attempt to hide the fact that he held a rock in each hand. Stealing a look at me, he yelled, "I'm going to kill the friggin' cat!" My heart leaped to my mouth. From where I was standing, I couldn't see the base of the chimney, but I knew it was a favorite lounging spot for Rusty, my angora cat. Alex drew back his right arm and hurled one of the rocks with all his might. "There, you stinkin' cat. Take that!" he cried as the other rock resoundingly hit the foundation.

The broom fell to the ground and I raced to Rusty's rescue. Halfway there, I noticed the familiar orange form sunning himself on a stone wall at the other side of the driveway. I stopped in my tracks. It was a prank. It was a deliberate trick to get me worked into a frenzy. And I had fallen for it. I didn't know if I was more angry at him or at myself. "Keep calm, keep calm," I said under my breath. "This is a job. Distance. Keep the distance."

Alex had disappeared into the woods, so I returned to the house to consider the other stunts he had pulled. Like climbing up on the roof and walking precariously along the ridgepole while I tearfully begged him to come down. I remembered how Mrs. Fisher's tale of woe was sprinkled with the words "if" and "almost." What he had actually done was to create a chaotic situation that forced her to react. Was this another way Alex could fulfill his need for control over women, especially women who were mother figures? It was beginning to look like it.

But lately it seemed his more successful manipulations were resulting in deteriorating behavior and culminating in destructive tantrums. Although he may have found a certain security in having this power, it was possible too much of it was frightening to him. If he, a child, could so easily outsmart an adult, whom could he trust and depend upon for safety and protection?

As I had told Sam, Alex needed to have his own legitimate controls in place before I could put a stop to any unacceptable conduct. Now that he did, now that he was riding Roxy without the longe line and mastering the basics of self-defense, I felt he was ready for me to take something away. I had no idea what that something would be until one afternoon when I was at the kitchen sink peeling potatoes for supper. To my right, on a cutting board built into the countertop, was a sharp carving knife. Alex came in, picked up the knife, and brought it down forcefully. This got no response from me, so he deliberately escalated the effect. He laid his free hand flat against the cutting board and raised the knife. I leaned against the sink and held my breath and went on peeling the potatoes. There was a whooshing sound and a loud, ringing whack. Out of the corner of my eye, I could see that the blade had come within a fraction of an inch of his fingertips. I still went on peeling the potatoes. Alex brought the knife down a third time. He gave an ear-shattering yell and threw himself to the floor. It took all of my willpower to keep from turning to see if the linoleum was covered with blood from his presumably amputated fingertips.

Leaping to his feet and grabbing the knife, he bellowed, "I'm going to kill those rabbits you got in the barn!" and ran outside. Should I go after him? I took a tentative step toward the kitchen door. Suppose he actually did kill the rabbits?

Sam's pet rabbits. No. I'd held up this far; I would see it through to the end. With visions of slaughtered rabbits in my head, I turned back to the sink, rinsed the potatoes—twice as many as I needed—and put them on the stove. In a few minutes I heard the door open. Alex walked quietly into the kitchen. His anger gone, bewildered and submissive, he carefully placed the knife on the counter and put his arms around me.

"It's okay," I said to him. "It's all right."

Following the knife incident, Alex was at last able to leave my side for brief intervals without becoming physically ill. This could be a mixed blessing, as on the day he walked to the pasture to dig some worms for fishing. A half hour later, I heard a shout from the living room: "Carole, come here! Come here! See what I've got!"

I went. I looked. There in the middle of my round oak coffee table, right on top of my magazines and falling off onto the rug, was a large pile of dirt alive with writhing, wriggling worms.

"Carole, Carole!" he said, pointing at the dirt pile. "I've got forty worms. See, count them. I've got forty!"

I once again reminded myself of the importance of absolute acceptance during this early stage of treatment. Under normal circumstances, I would have been irritated and annoyed at even a two-year-old for making such a mess. But the positive reinforcement of anything that improved Alex's self-image had to take precedence. Clapping enthusiastically, I echoed his joy over this grand achievement. "Forty worms? Wow! That's great. That's really fantastic!"

Alex was capable of seeing himself as someone who could do something well as long as I saw him do it. Since his concept of personhood was so damaged, his only perception of a good self was what was mirrored in my eyes and magnified by my words. It was especially important to him that I watch his karate lessons. From where I was sitting in the waiting room of the studio, I had a clear view of the twelve boys and girls inside the dojo. Barefoot and clad in loose-fitting white outfits, the children were practicing an exercise called the first pinion. One of the instructors was making her way through the group. Her name was Maria. Her cascading dark hair and sultry eyes were in unexpected contrast to the black belt in the martial arts she wore about her waist. Maria approached Alex and had him follow her lead as she demonstrated the flow, the sequential motion, of the pinion. I felt a tingle of pride. He had been taking karate for only four weeks but his natural grace and balance caused the moves to appear more like a dance than a mode of self-defense.

Later on in the lesson, Alex left the dojo to get a drink of water and neglected to make the mandatory bow to the American flag hanging on the wall at the end of the room. "That will be ten push-ups," snapped Maria.

Alex stared at her.

"Now!" she shouted.

I could not believe it. He dropped to the red-carpeted floor and, without any name-calling, sarcastic remarks, or so much as a dirty look, did the ten push-ups. He was actually obeying a direct order from Maria. Breathing a sigh of relief, I was encouraged to hope some moderation in Alex's macho attitude was taking place. Perhaps his relationship with this woman, a woman he respected and admired, would help him to modify his opinion that they were inferior creatures. He was firmly convinced the most pathetic male was superior to any female simply by virtue of his sex. To him, women were "people who cleaned up men's messes," a characterization with enough truth in it to rouse my indignation. He even went so far as to deny a woman was running for the office of vice president in the 1984 Democratic campaign. "No, no, she's Mondale's wife," he insisted. "She's got to be his wife!" Until he met Maria, he had been unable to acknowledge that a woman could be in a position of authority.

At the end of the lesson the children removed their belts, folded them, and placed them on the floor. Then they knelt with their foreheads touching the carpet and meditated for several minutes. After the meditation, another instructor, a heavyset man named Jack, entered the dojo. The lower part of his face was covered with a short, reddish beard, and around his head he wore a red bandanna that was tied behind his right ear. Jack was a former marine, a professional wrestler, and had a second-degree black belt in karate, but he looked like he'd just stepped off the deck of a pirate ship. "Tonight, for those of you who can stay, there will be sparring," he announced. "Everyone must wear protective headgear and boxing gloves."

Although normally in sparring no actual contact is allowed, Thursday night at this karate studio was known as Death Night. No-holds-barred contact was permitted, and Alex loved it. Here, within the security of the dojo, it was safe. It was safe to be aggressive. It was safe to let loose some of his anger. And if the aggression was controlled, Alex was praised and held up as an example to the others.

"Remember," continued Jack, "you are expected to use blocking systems. I want to see technique, not just wild flailing about. If you lose control of yourself, you won't be able to think clearly and, I guarantee, you will make mistakes. You can't afford to let emotion interfere with your ability to make sound decisions. If you do, you will accomplish nothing. You will simply waste your energy and your opponent will be victorious. Do you understand?"

"Yes," replied several of the students.

The color rose in Jack's face to blend with his beard and bandanna. He sucked in his breath and bellowed like an angry bull, "Yes, what?"

"Yes, sir," chorused the children.

"That's better. Okay, those of you who are staying be back in five minutes. Class dismissed."

In a corner of the room, a senior student named Delaney was working out on the punching bag. His long, sinewy muscles formed taut braids that bulged under his skin, and he moved with a catlike grace. Delaney was the only pupil to have earned his black belt, and nobody dared to mess with him. Nobody, that is, except Alex.

One of Alex's most annoying characteristics was his lack of awareness of body space. Continually intrusive into the space of others, he did not seem to know where his own boundaries ended and someone else's began. He picked up a pair of boxing gloves and, pulling them onto his hands, strutted toward the older boy with an air of pompous self-importance. The heavy bag was still shuddering from the full force of Delaney's spinning back kick. As he positioned himself for a second kick, Alex darted at the bag to give an ineffectual punch. Delaney's muscular arm shot out and sent him reeling backward. For the remainder of the break, he sat in a corner of the room gazing at Delaney with a black, palpable hatred.

This anger stayed with him during the sparring session, and the resulting loss of control cost him the match. One of the blows had caused a trickle of blood from his nose to drip onto his white sleeve, and Alex was terror-stricken at the sight of the red stain.

With legs outstretched and arms akimbo, Jack threw back his head and laughed uproariously. "What's the matter," he said, "haven't you ever seen blood?"

On the way home from the karate studio, Alex insisted on getting into the rear seat of the car. I got a glimpse of his face in the mirror. His lips were stretched taut over clenched teeth in an ugly grimace, and his eyes were wide gleaming pools of hate. His breath came in deep gasps, and the air made a roaring sound as it rushed through his nostrils. "I'm never going back!" he shouted. "I'm never going back to karate. And that bastard Delaney—I'm going to get Delaney if it's the last thing I do. I'll take a knife and slit his throat and laugh while the blood runs out. I'll kill him! I'll kill the bastard. I'll cut his heart out." Turning his anger on me, his voice rose to a shrill crescendo. "I hate you. Bitch! Fuckin' bitch!"

What I could not understand was that after this tirade of invectives had run its course, Alex emphatically denied ever having said any of these things. I could not understand how he could so blatantly lie when he knew I had heard them with my own ears.

Alex did return to the karate studio, where the lessons of the dojo were helping him to gain the power and control he would need to battle the fears threatening to engulf him. But Peter, my supervisor from the agency, did not want to hear about it. He was a small man with thick brows that accentuated the sparseness of hair on his head. His pale blue eyes, round and bespectacled, glanced warily about my living room. "So how is he doing?" he asked.

"Okay," I said, puzzled by the apprehension in his voice. "Alex is doing good."

A look of thinly disguised disbelief spread over Peter's face. "He is?"

"Yes. He's learning to ride a horse and he's taking karate."

"Karate! I don't approve. He'll use it to hurt people."

Somehow, I wasn't surprised by Peter's reaction. Had the boy been older and stronger, I might have agreed. He was, however, still a small child, and I found it a bit ludicrous that his beginner belt exercises could be considered dangerous. It wasn't as though we were talking about Bruce Lee or Chuck Norris. I tried to explain how the instructors gave Alex training in aggression control and how they also gave him the discipline that I, in my role of accepting mother figure, could not yet provide. I might as well have saved my breath. Peter just didn't get it, and when he kept asking me what kind of punishment I was using, I realized he was missing the whole point of my treatment.

To say I was disappointed would be a gross understatement. I had been looking forward to this meeting because during the past week there had been several exciting breakthroughs. I wanted to share them. I wanted information. But I didn't mention that Alex was frequently lapsing into a monosyllabic, incoherent, infantile way of expressing himself that was accompanied by sign language or that he had begun sucking his thumb while being rocked. If this marked a regression to an earlier, oral phase, I instinctively felt it was important to allow it to continue. I was afraid Peter would simply label it inappropriate and tell me to put a stop to it.

There was also the dream. It would be the first in a sequence of dreams. I was sitting at the trestle table hoping to fortify myself with a cup of coffee before Alex got out of bed. I didn't quite make it. Drowsily rubbing his eyes, he came over to me and climbed onto my lap. "I had a bad dream," he said. "A terrible dream. I was at a fair or carnival and I was running and I saw a girl lying on the ground. I kept on running as fast as I could, and as I jumped over her, I looked down. It was my mother. She was dead."

The bizarre behavior that occurred when Alex saw my husband washing dishes was another thing I wanted to discuss with Peter. If I'd been through a particularly exhausting day, it was not unusual for Sam to help me out. While he was cleaning up the supper dishes, Alex walked into the kitchen, gave him a startled look, and became hysterical. He ran around the house screaming, "No, no. You're turning into a woman! You're turning into a woman!" and ended up crouching in a corner with his hands covering his face.

Sam tried to comfort him, but to no avail. For a long time Alex cowered in that corner, peering at Sam through the bars of his fingers and crying out those same words over and over. Evidently, for a man to do what Alex considered woman's work was to him similar to castration.

And then there were the baby rabbits. We went to the barn to feed Sam's rabbits one chilly morning and found that the mother rabbit had given birth on the wire floor of the cage instead of the nest box. The cold had killed the babies. Alex gazed in horror at the naked babies and reached in to touch a limp body. Grasping the sides of the cage, he began shaking it as hard as he could. In a tormented voice he yelled, "Why did she do that? Why did she do that?" The movement of the cage stirred one of the supposedly dead babies to life, so we gathered them up and gently immersed them in warm water. After several hours of blankets and heating pads, Alex brought the resurrected rabbits back to their cage. As he placed them in the nest box, he gave the doe a lecture on the responsibilities of motherhood.

I wondered if he saw himself in those abandoned baby rabbits. Was his anguished, crying question really for the neglectful, uncaring mother rabbit or for his own mother? I wondered if all of these strange events were signs that Alex was beginning to trust and to have some sense of security, a sense that it was safe, at least on an unconscious level, to experience unspeakable feelings and to dare to ask why.

That night, as Sam and I sat talking in the living room, I vented my frustrations about Peter.

"The guy's an idiot," was Sam's angry response. "It's crazy to let him bother you. Whatever you're doing is working. Alex is a hell of a lot better. So forget Peter."

That was easy for Sam to say. He wasn't with Alex all day, every day. Yes, he was better. But at what cost? My husband couldn't fathom how this child was draining me dry, leaving me empty, physically and emotionally. Sam was a great help, and I had thought his support would be enough, but now I realized I needed more. I needed someone to give back a part of what the job was taking away. Without feedback and communication with a sensitive, caring person outside of my own family, all of my strategies, all of my work, would come to nothing. It did not appear to me that this someone was going to be Peter. In spite of my resolve—and I hate to admit it—there were times when I considered sending the boy away. Two things happened to keep me from giving up: getting Alex into school and finding Sarah.

III

Some Badly Needed Support

The guidance office was a cramped and crowded room that was squeezed between the hallway and the library. The guidance counselor, Miss Moffet, was a plain, no-nonsense woman in both appearance and approach. As I waited for her to pass judgment on my request to allow Alex to go to public school, she looked from me to the thick file on her desk and back again. "This is his record," she said with a shudder. "In all my twenty-two years as a counselor, it is the worst I've ever seen."

I winced. I knew some of what was in there. Ann, Alex's state social worker, had told me about his last school, the one he had attended before he was sent to RFK. She told me how he chased other students with scissors and how he climbed up on the roof so that the fire department had to come and get him down. And she told me about the special education teacher who had informed her principal that if he did not promptly remove Alex from the class, she would turn in her resignation. God only knew what else was in that record.

"Alex," I insisted, "needs to be in school. The agency has tried everywhere, and the only place willing to accept him doesn't have an opening until January."

"We are required by law to provide Alex with an education," she said. "This does not necessarily mean he has to be in school. A tutor could be sent to your home. Or we could supply the materials and it might be possible for you to teach him."

"It won't work," I replied, quickly rejecting both options. How could I explain that the intensity of Alex's hostility toward me was increasing in direct ratio to my becoming the maternal figure in his life? It was as though some other identity, some alien force, had taken over his body and was staring at me through cold, hate-filled eyes. "I'm asking for you to give him a chance. He's been with us for six weeks, and he's much better. He has more control. He's able to follow some rules. And most important, he's in a safe, stable environment. A lot of what's in the record is because he was being abused by his family."

"I hear what you're saying," she continued, "but we do not have separate special education classes in this school."

"Special education was part of the problem. In the last school, there was a stigma attached to that class. Alex says the kids called him a retard. His self-esteem is so low. To be labeled special ed—he couldn't handle it. I can give him the extra help at home. I promise I will."

Miss Moffet busied herself with picking up the incriminating folder and depositing it in a metal file cabinet. Checking to make sure the drawer was locked, she turned to me and cautiously nodded. "There is a fifth-grade teacher," she said. "His name is Don Sullivan, and he might be effective with a boy like Alex. I'll talk to the principal. I'll see what I can do."

Three interminable days later, Miss Moffet called. The school had decided to admit Alex. He would be in a classroom with normal children. He would be mainstreamed and would not have any special education classes. Although he was as excited about this as I was, breakfast turned out to be pure hell. "Would you like some Fruity Pebbles?" I asked him on the first morning.

"Fruity Pebbles?" replied Alex in a tone that suggested I'd just offered him rat poison. "I don't want Fruity Pebbles. I want Raisin Bran!"

"You said you wanted Fruity Pebbles, and I bought them

especially for you." I placed the box back on the shelf, took down the Raisin Bran, poured some in a bowl, and set it in front of Alex.

He stared at it incredulously. "Hey, lady, you got a hearing problem? What are you giving me that crap for? I don't want that. I want Cheerios."

Thinking it was just as well that Sam had already left for work, I bit my tongue, put the Raisin Bran back in the box, and offered him the Cheerios. "Friggin' bitch," he muttered. "You ain't got no good cereal in this dump. This place stinks! I want eggs."

I looked at the clock. Fifteen minutes. I had to survive fifteen more minutes. In fifteen minutes he would be gone. So I scrambled two eggs and toasted a slice of bread and set eggs and toast on the table.

Alex glowered at me and then at the eggs. "Did I say I wanted scrambled eggs? And I wanted two pieces of toast and I didn't want butter on it!" He threw the toast on the floor and began to eat the eggs. As he finished the last mouthful, he glanced out of the glass doors. A look of startled surprise crossed his features. His jaw fell open and his eyes grew wide. "Hey, Carole! Who's that strange man snooping around out there?"

"What man?" I asked, going to the door and peering out.

"Ha!" shouted Alex slapping his hand on the table in a paroxysm of glee. "I gotcha. I gotcha! Boy, are you dumb. Is it eight o'clock? I gotta get the bus." He snatched up his lunch money and ran from the house.

I poured a cup of coffee and collapsed into the nearest chair.

This outrageous behavior continued to occur on school days. When I participated and pretended to go along with him, the teacher reported good behavior. When I did not, the report was quite the opposite. My guess was that the mind-changing routine, tricks, and practical jokes were part of his repertoire of control mechanisms. If he could leave the house thinking he had gotten the best of me, he could get through the day. It was this that held him together and gave him the inner strength to function in a regular classroom. As I had learned, it was detrimental to allow him to have too much control. I could not upset the balance. But I could let him believe he had outwitted me often enough to enjoy the blessed relief of keeping him in school. Again it was a trade-off. And again I wondered why he found it necessary to have so much power over the mother.

With Alex away until three o'clock, I had the luxury of many hours of free time. Since I did not feel that I had been employed by the agency long enough to ask for a respite, it was time that I sorely needed. I soaked it into my being; I reveled in the renewal and sustenance of my spirit. I could also now attend the weekly support groups and share hardships and successes with other foster parents. It was encouraging to learn that Alex was doing better than a number of the clients. He was still in my home.

Dipping into reserves of patience I didn't know I had and determined to keep my promise to Miss Moffet, I began to help Alex fill in the gaps in his education. He was able to read and spell, but he could neither pronounce nor understand many of the words. Math, his best subject, suffered because he rushed through the tests and quizzes and made careless mistakes. "If I finish before the rest of the kids," he said, "they will think I am the smartest."

He found science to be the most baffling. There were questions at the end of the chapter that involved searching for information and formulating conclusions. The seeking out of knowledge seemed to hold special terrors for Alex, and lengthy, mutually exhausting tantrums preceded this kind of assignment.

His reaction was especially fearful when he learned that the earth was not the center of the solar system. This discovery dealt a severe blow to his egocentric worldview, and no sixteenth-century man was ever more threatened by Copernican theory than was Alex.

I refused to let the tantrums and threats to report me for child abuse deter me. Alex had never in his life gotten more than a D on a report card. But with the incentives of reward money and extra privileges, he received almost all B's for the first term. The only C was in science. "Did I really do that, Carole? Did I really?" he asked, his eyes shining with the pride of accomplishment as he studied the grades. The high self-esteem generated by this tangible proof of his success served as a stepping-stone toward internalizing his motivation so gradually he would become less dependent upon external rewards.

Don Sullivan, an unassuming man with a perennial boyish look, leaned against his desk in the fifth-grade classroom and explained to me what he was doing to cope with the problems. "That's his desk right there," he said, pointing to the first seat in the first row.

I shook my head in dismay. Alex's desk was stuffed with torn and crumpled sheets of paper overflowing onto the floor. "No wonder he can't find anything."

Mr. Sullivan gave me a reassuring smile, and I was relieved to know the messy desk didn't particularly bother him. "I can keep an eye on him there," he continued. "If I see that he is becoming tense or restless, I know trouble is brewing, so I find some excuse to send him on an errand to the office. This gives him a chance to cool off and talk to the secretary or the guidance counselor. As for his schoolwork, I'm afraid it's rather inconsistent. He can have an excellent command of the material in the morning and, oddly enough, not know it at all in the afternoon. I try to give him an opportunity to make up tests when he blanks out like that. When he does do well, I make it a point to compliment him in front of his classmates."

Delighted to hear what Mr. Sullivan was doing, I enthusiastically expressed my approval. Marks brought home on papers and report cards were important, but the self-image enhancement of praise given before an entire class was magnified a hundredfold.

I left the room with a feeling of immense gratitude for Don Sullivan. He was firm but not threatening, he never raised his voice, he was continuously aware of the child's frustration level, and he did not insist on arbitrary standards of perfection.

The greatest concern about school, however, was not academics. It was peer relations. Alex did not know what it was to have a friend. His fears caused him to be a bully, and his feelings of inadequacy caused him to be a braggart and a liar. Beyond provoking a response, real or imaginary, that would give him an excuse to fight, he had no idea how to relate to other children. He teased the girls and made disgusting comments about the mothers of the boys. Nobody liked him.

It was clear to me that Alex was not going to make it unless he learned some social skills. Since he very much wanted to have friends and was willing to do almost anything to get them, we set up some imaginary activities to be worked out with role-playing. It was one thing, though, to do this at home with me and quite another to behave appropriately with a peer. The interaction would be even more complicated because we had to begin with the few boys who themselves had no friends and were similarly lacking the requisites of polite society.

There was a boy named Joey who met our requirements and lived nearby. Joey's parents were more than happy to have their son spend some time at our home, and Alex was overjoyed to have someone to play with. Staying out of sight as much as possible, I carefully monitored the boys' games and conversations and wrote down my observations. After Joey left, Alex and I went over these notes and, interspersing lavish praise for proper behavior, I urged him to think of alternative ways to resolve conflicts and avoid arguments.

The most unsuccessful part of this approach was the attempt to help Alex to relate to or identify with the feelings of others. He was not yet ready for empathy. Gradually, if unevenly, he learned and changed and his circle of friends increased.

• • •

There was another improvement in my situation when I found a therapist for Alex. "I don't usually take clients myself," she said after introducing herself as Sarah Heywood, the director of our local youth counseling center, "but this case interests me. I think you have done some fine work with this child and I'd like to hear about it."

Sarah was a handsome woman of middle age and generous proportions, and she radiated a mothering, nurturing quality, a soothing warmth and comfort. Sipping the cup of coffee she had set before me, I basked in the glow of her healing words. I heard interest and approval and affirmation. I heard what I needed to hear.

"Peter won't say that," I said, fighting to hold back the tears. "He's my supervisor. All he does is find fault." I saw Sarah's eyes widen in sharp astonishment, and I was encouraged to continue. "I thought he would be so pleased when Alex was doing well in a regular classroom, but he only tried to find something he could criticize. I feel like no matter what I do, no matter what wonderful achievements we have, there is no praise, no feedback, just a deadpan look that never changes. Half the time I have the feeling he doesn't have any idea what I'm talking about."

Sarah drew her brows together in a disapproving frown. "It sounds like he's very threatened by your unorthodox approach and the fact that you're getting results is a severe blow to his ego. He can't accept these results because he wasn't responsible for them. And there's another thing. The people in human services see so much failure. They can't believe success."

What Sarah said made sense, and it helped to know why Peter acted the way he did, why he wasn't supportive. "It's still so hard," I said in an anguished tone.

"It is," she said, giving me a tranquil, reassuring smile. "I understand. But you're strong. I think you have the strength to do it."

And it was strange how the saying of it became the reality and whether it had been there or not, it now existed.

"The karate," I blurted out. "Peter's afraid he'll use it to hurt someone."

"Oh, no," said Sarah. "I don't agree."

After reiterating my beliefs about the importance of legitimate controls and the advantages of disciplined aggression, I added, "I think a lot of violence is born of powerlessness, and the more real power Alex has, the less violent he will become." There was an answering flash of recognition in Sarah's eyes. This was so heartening, to see a reaction, a positive response. The words tumbled over one another as I rushed to tell her about all that happened in the last three months.

"What you are doing is therapy, very effective therapy," she said when I had finished. "You can't take a child like this and expect to accomplish much in an hour a week. We don't have any magic, and there are no easy answers. The books that are written are mostly people's theories based on their observations of real life, and your observations and theories are as valid as anyone else's. They don't really know how the mind works." She regarded me with an alert, thoughtful expression. "I would say," she continued, "that you have good instincts and you should trust them. Go with them. I am going to call the agency and inform them I'm taking this case. Oh, and I'd like to suggest that you keep a diary, a notebook, and record Alex's progress. Someday you could show it to him and he will be able to see how far he has come."

Someday. Someday was the future. And Sarah was saying there would be a someday for Alex. I fervently hoped so. I was beginning to develop a deep admiration for this child's determination and courage as he labored to overcome his emotional handicaps. Sarah was right. There was a great deal of failure with these cases, but Alex was continuing to make gains both academically and socially. I remembered what Sam had said when he first came to us, about his being a fighter. In a flash of insight, I knew he was a lot like me in that respect. Was that part of the reason why I was doing so much to help him? A reason that had nothing to do with the money. Did I see in him something of myself? A kindred spirit?

"I'd like to meet Alex," Sarah said as she turned the pages of an appointment book. "Could you bring him in next Thursday at three?"

Thursday arrived along with unseasonal cold for early November and four inches of heavy, wet snow. "I ain't going! I ain't going!" screamed Alex while he simultaneously banged his head and fists against the wall.

"Not," I reminded him, since he himself had asked me to help with his atrocious grammar. "Not going."

"I'm not going," he repeated correctly if no less adamantly. "I'm not going to no shrink and you can't make me. Nobody's going to get inside my head!"

I explained the rules that said he had to be in therapy. I pleaded and cajoled and reasoned, but to no avail. In the end I had to insist. He fought me every inch of the way, hiding my car keys—I had an extra set—refusing to get in the car, refusing to get out of the car, and when we finally made it to the front porch of the counseling center, I had to peel him from one of the wooden columns supporting the roof.

Once inside Sarah's office, he folded his arms and stuck out his lower lip. "I'm not talking to nobody about nothing," he announced obstinately.

Sarah gave him an appraising glance and spoke to him in a well-modulated voice. "It's okay, Alex. You don't have to talk if you don't want to."

"You got that right, lady," he muttered, and with a taunting laugh, he proceeded to run around the room in a burst of hyperactivity. Taking some toys that were in a corner and throwing them in various directions, he climbed on the couch, tossed off the pillows, and tipped over an upholstered chair. Then he was at a china table lamp, spinning the shade and causing it to teeter precariously.

"Alex, please," I said in nervous embarrassment. "Come and sit down. You're going to break something." In answer to my warning, he dashed an ashtray to the floor and stared defiantly at me.

Both Sarah and I made an attempt to talk to him, but each word worsened his behavior until he stripped off his sneakers and socks and bolted from the room. "He hasn't been like this since the first week," I explained apologetically. "I didn't think it would be this bad. I was counting so much on getting Alex into therapy."

Reflective and preoccupied, Sarah tapped the eraser end of a pencil against her lower lip and gazed at the wall behind her desk. Leaning forward, she said in a decisive tone, "There is something you can do. It's called an Angry Book, and it doesn't work for all kids, but it can be very successful. Get a notebook, preferably a kind that can be locked. Have Alex keep the key. He can wear it on a chain around his neck if he likes. Have one page for each significant person in his life, including you and your husband. Everyone must have a page, even people he insists he loves. Each week have him choose a page and write something about that person that makes him angry. Tell him he may share it with you only if he feels comfortable talking about it. This . . ." A sharp insistent tapping interrupted her, and we turned to see Alex outside the window.

His face was framed in a circle of snow he had smeared on the glass, and again there was that fiendish smile and the cold, hard eyes. I felt an involuntary shiver go down my spine. "I thought he was in the waiting room," I said as I walked toward the window.

When I got there, Alex was gone. Looking out, I saw him about twenty feet away from the building. Barefoot and in his shirtsleeves, he was running backward. He stopped, scooped up a handful of snow, and with quick, vigorous motions, pressed it together. The snowball made a dull thudding sound as it smashed against the glass.

IV

December 1984

The Family

It was just before Christmas. The windows of the houses gleamed with candles, the doors were hung with brightly beribboned wreaths, and the lampposts were decorated with ropes of laurel. For weeks now, posters advertising an area ballet company's production of *The Nutcracker* had been seen in every storefront. I decided to take Alex. Sam didn't have a very high opinion of ballet and said he didn't think Alex would like it. But I took him anyway. And sure enough, he was entranced by the shimmering scenes and the magical transformation of an ugly nutcracker doll into the charming and handsome Prince.

At the end of Act I, the Prince lifted the gossamer-gowned child who danced the role of Clara onto his shoulder and carried her out into the audience. The pair came close to where we were sitting, so close I could almost touch them. The jewels in her tiara and the sequins of his costume sparkled in the spotlight. I stole a glance at Alex's face as he gazed in rapturous adoration at Clara and her Prince. It was as though he were looking into another world, a world that was far removed from the one he had known.

Later on, after we got home, he called me to his room to tuck him in. Still starry-eyed, he snuggled against his pillow. "I'm going to dream about her tonight," he said, an unaccustomed smile softening his features.

"Yes, Alex," I replied, giving him a hug. "Tonight and many other nights."

Leaving Alex to his visions of Clara and the Sugar Plum Fairy, I went into the living room, where I found Sam asleep in front of the television. He woke with a start when I turned it off. "Oh. You're back. So how did it go?"

"Sam, he loved it. He really did. You should have seen him."

"Alex actually sat through a ballet?" Sam rubbed his eyes, yawned, and raised himself to a sitting position. "I can't believe it. He's such a macho kid. Someone called while you were out. His stepmother—what's her name—Sandra. They want to make arrangements to pick him up on Christmas Day."

The news put an immediate damper on my spirits, and I sank dejectedly into the rocker before the fireplace. "I was hoping they wouldn't bother following through on that. They've shown so little interest in him. But Ann, the social worker, says they have permission to take him for the day. We talked about it during her last monthly visit."

"Does he want to spend Christmas with them?"

I let my breath out in a deep sigh and stared at the orange-and-blue flames curling around a maple log in the fireplace. "He says he does. They wouldn't force him if he didn't want to. And you know, Sam, he still goes on about how great they are and how many fancy cars and trucks they have. Social Services is obligated to try to reunite Alex with his family. The department has legal custody, but the judge said the family has to have one more chance."

"Chance? Chance to do what?" growled Sam. "Doesn't the judge know he was abused? And what's going to change? Ann told you the parents were supposed to get counseling and they haven't done a damn thing."

"She didn't use those exact words, but that's what she said. It doesn't seem to matter. Social Services has to obey the court."

"It's not right, Carole. Those phone calls upset him bad

enough. What in hell is a visit going to do?" What Sam said was true. The father, George, was allowed a single phone contact per week, and on Thursday, the day designated for this call, Alex's behavior deteriorated rapidly. Most of the time he would sit by the phone waiting for a call that never came, and then there would be the usual stress signals, the hyperactivity and the tantrums. He would also be very angry at me, as though I were somehow to blame. The strange thing was even when the call did come—and it was always the stepmother, never the father—the behavior wasn't any better. The fact that Sandra invariably ended her conversation with protestations of love for him did not appear to improve his frame of mind.

"What about this Angry Book you were telling me about?" asked Sam. "Has Alex written anything in it about those people?"

"Well, we haven't started it yet. I've been doing some preliminary work so he'd be motivated to write in the book. I began by asking him if he thought he had any problems. He told me there was one."

The corners of Sam's eyes crinkled in an amused smile. "Oh, only one," he said. "And which one did he come up with?"

Our eyes met and I smiled back. "The tantrums. He wants to stop wrecking his room. The loss of control scares him. And he doesn't want people to think he's crazy. But he does want to do something about it. And that's important. Alex wants it. Alex wants to change."

"Maybe he does, Carole, but just how is the book going to get rid of tantrums?" questioned Sam with more than a little disbelief.

"It isn't just the book," I retorted, my own doubts giving a flinty edge to my voice. "It's the karate and the esteem-building and feeling safe and secure. The book is simply a tool to help Alex to talk about some of the things that have happened to him. You see, Sam, angry thoughts can be scary to children, especially if they concern family members and caretakers. There's fear of retaliation; there's guilt. This is all very frightening. Now if these angry thoughts are locked in a book and Alex wears the key around his neck, they are symbolically safe and they can't hurt him."

Being a very pragmatic man, Sam's response was a look of pure skepticism.

"Here's what I've done," I said, and I went to get the imitation-leather-bound book with its brass lock from a table on the other side of the room. Sitting down next to Sam, I opened it. In the beginning, I had printed some basic guidelines:

It's okay to feel angry.
It's okay to feel angry at people you love.
You have the right to be angry at people who have phys-
    ically or verbally abused you.
You have the right to be angry at any parent or stepparent
    who has failed to protect you or has not taken proper
    care of you.

The remainder of the book was divided up into sections, one for each parent, stepparent, grandparent, sibling, and uncle. As Sarah had suggested, there were also sections for Sam and myself.

Sam leafed through the pages. "Who is Albert Mercer?" he asked.

"Alex's stepfather. He's been out of the picture for about five years. Alex has never mentioned him, but Sarah told me not to leave anyone out. Most of the names came from the social worker. I went over them with Alex, and there was one name he refused to let me keep in the book. In fact, he tore the page out. It was his half brother Georgie, George and Sandra's little boy. He's three years old. Alex said he loved Georgie very much and never had any angry feelings for him. He was so insistent that I got a bit suspicious. All kids get angry at a brother or sister once in a while."

Turning to another page, Sam read the name at the top. "Christine."

"The biological mother. She's only allowed to see him with supervision because he acts out after every visit. She was described in the case report as a dysfunctional woman who drifts from place to place. She has two daughters, Donna and Debra, who are several years older than Alex. They were given up for adoption, but they were seriously disturbed and it didn't work out. I understand they were sexually abused by their father."

"That would be Albert Mercer, Alex's stepfather?" Sam's voice was filled with disgust.

"Yes. He's the man she was married to when she was carrying on with George. And, of course, there's the ex-prostitute grandmother, and let's not forget Ralph and Harold."

"Who the hell are they?"

"Uncles. Christine's brothers. Ralph—I think it's Ralph—lives with the grandmother. Christine used to leave Alex with them when she went out."

Sam pushed the book away as though it were a distasteful object. "And you've also got an alcoholic biological father and his child bride. Some cast of characters!"

"It sure is," I agreed. "You know, I thought I had everyone's name in the book until Alex told me there was one that was missing. He said it was a baby, a baby brother. Christine's baby. He claims he held him and helped feed him, and he seemed genuinely puzzled as to why he had been left out."

"Well? Why was it?"

"Because there was no baby. I called Ann and asked her. She said Christine had no other children. Why would he invent this baby? Anyway, to get back to the book, I explained to Alex that when all the anger is kept inside with no outlet, it explodes into a tantrum, but if he could divide it into small parts and write what each person did to him, he would be less likely to blow up. Oh, my God, Sam, it does sound too easy to be of much help. There is so much rage in that boy."

"It could be worse if it does work," he replied cautiously. "Do you think you can handle hearing what this kid has been through?"

"I think I can as long as I have Sarah. I can talk to her about it. And I can write it down. She's having me keep my own book, a kind of diary of Alex's progress and my experiences with him." I got up and walked over to the fireplace. The logs had burned to a pile of glowing embers pulsating with red heat. I didn't want to think of the things that might have happened to Alex, the cruelties and abuses he might share with me. I changed the subject. "Did I tell you I ran into this man at the agency who was one of Alex's counselor's while he was at the institution, at RFK? He gave me this pitying look and said Alex was one of the worst they'd had. He said his arms still ached from holding him down. They kept him in solitary confinement half the time. Oh, and do you know what else? The camp he was at last summer. We thought it was just a regular boy's camp?"

"You mean Camp Wedicko?"

"Yes, that's it. I found out only kids with the very worst of psychiatric profiles are admitted. I was informed that every counselor has to have a master's degree in psychology."

"That's why this Peter, your supervisor, was so afraid of him," said Sam.

"But why couldn't he have told me?"

Getting up from the couch, Sam took the poker and pushed a stray ember back into the hearth. "Carole," he said "if you had known, if I had known, would we have taken Alex?"

It was a troubling, disturbing question. The answer was probably no, a painful acknowledgment that I was unable to put into words.

Three days later we were on our way to a Christmas party hosted by the office of the Department of Social Services. "We're going to drive right by my father's house," said Alex, hardly able to contain his excitement. "I think it's on the left."

"Well," I said casually, "let me know when we come to it." I didn't want to appear to be too curious.

He wriggled around in the seat and said, "Oh, I will, I will. And Carole, my father's van might be parked in the yard. I hope it is. Wait till you see it. It is awesome. It's the most awesome van you ever saw."

He was so positive. There was no question in my mind that Alex honestly believed what he was saying, and I found myself thinking there might be some truth to his tales about his father.

He was on the edge of his seat now and his face was aglow with anticipation. "It's right around this bend, Carole. Up that hill. Slow down, slow down! There!" he cried out exultantly. "There it is, that yellow house." His voice trembled and faded. "Right—right there. . . ."

The traffic was too heavy to see clearly which house Alex was referring to, so I pulled off to the side of the road. The only yellow house across the way was a large, older dwelling that had been divided up into several rental units. It was in need of paint; there was a broken window, and a rotted gutter hung at an angle over the front door. The place had an air of decay and neglect. A tricycle with a missing wheel lay on the lawn, and the van Alex wanted me to see was in the driveway. It was old and battered and featured multiple dents and terminal rust.

I felt my heart sink with sympathy and compassion for him as I eased back into the traffic. He was staring straight ahead, his eyes glazed and his posture rigid. Neither the party nor anything else cheered him up. For the next several days he was withdrawn and unusually quiet, speaking only when spoken to and sometimes not even then. At one point I offered, by way of consolation, the view that material things such as houses and cars were not really important. There was no reply.

I somehow knew that when Alex saw where his father lived, he became aware of a reality far beyond a run-down house and a rusty van. But there were no tears. I had never seen him cry. There was only a silent depression and an ineffable sadness. Until Christmas Eve.

Fragrant green boughs tied with big red bows decorated the house, and the aroma of fresh-baked pumpkin and mince pies wafted through the rooms. The Christmas tree was hung with fragile multicolored ornaments and draped with glistening tinsel. Under the tree were many gaily wrapped gifts to be opened before the father came to take him for the day. I had bought almost every toy and game I could think of, including a large teddy bear. Since Alex had passed his first karate test, the bear was dressed in a white outfit with an orange sash tied around the middle.

I was in the kitchen chopping celery and onions to make stuffing for the turkey when Alex, for no apparent reason, became agitated and bolted from the house. Hurrying to the window, I saw him speeding down the driveway on his bike. Something was wrong. I should go after him. I went to the kitchen to get my car keys. But sitting on the counter was the turkey: plump, pale, and unstuffed. It would roast all night at a low heat and be done to perfection by morning—if I ever got it in the oven. And there were the fruit bowls to be filled and last-minute gifts to be wrapped. Maybe it was nothing. Maybe he would come home. I returned to my work.

In half an hour, the call came. It was the mother of Alex's friend Joey. There had been an accident. "We told him he'd get hurt doing those crazy stunts on his bike," she said. "But he wouldn't listen. The more we warned him, the more daring he got. I think his leg is broken."

Alex's leg was broken, and later, in the emergency room, the orthopedic surgeon showed me the X rays. I could see the break, the sharp angle of black space where the femur was sheared in two. The doctor went on to explain what he was going to do and why, and I nodded in the right places as though I understood. My thoughts were with Alex, lying in pale terror on the table.

I stayed by him and held his hand throughout a painful procedure that involved the insertion of a metal pin from one side of his knee to the other. To minimize any risk that the injured right leg might become shorter than the left, it was immobilized by a traction device. This consisted of pulleys, weights, and bars that were attached to the pin. It was midnight before Alex was settled into the cheerfully decorated room with its wallpaper of brightly colored ascending balloons.

In the morning, Sam brought him all of his gifts. At noon, when I went to visit him, I was surprised to see them piled on top of three tables that had been placed in a row alongside his bed. The stacks of presents formed a kind of barricade, and crowning the uppermost box, the flag on this battlement of toys, was a card I had given him. On the card was a picture of a little boy holding a floppy-eared puppy, and it was opened so the message, "Merry Christmas to a Wonderful Boy," could easily be read. Walking farther into the room, I saw a man and a woman sitting on an empty bed across from Alex. They could be none other than George and Sandra, the father and the stepmother.

My initial impression of George was that he was trying to hide inside of himself. He was leaning over, looking at the floor, and his head was pulled down between hunched up shoulders. A scraggly beard and long, dark hair served to conceal his features. His arms were wrapped tightly around his tall, thin body as though he were trying to hold it together.

"You must be Alex's father," I said, resolved to be polite and nonjudgmental. After all, hadn't the social worker told me that, in spite of the abuse, there was a real bond between father and son? George continued to stare at the floor. He made no effort to respond; there was no acknowledgment of my presence. Extending my hand, I stepped closer. "I'm Carole, Alex's foster mother."

Much to my embarrassment, I stood there with my hand out as George lowered his head even more and Sandra busily avoided eye contact. With no word or warning, George leaped to his feet and ran from the room.

Sandra, shy and very young, seemed fearful and fidgeted uncomfortably. Her eyes darted repeatedly toward the door-

Barn Drawing, January 3, 1985

way. She mumbled something to Alex about coming back and she, too, was gone. He seemed relieved when they left, and they never did come back.

"I want to make you a picture," Alex announced shortly after New Year's Day of 1985. He chose a brown crayon and, pressing his lips together in intense concentration, proceeded to draw a sparse outline. "It's a barn," he said of the six unadorned markings that drifted off the edge of the paper. With the crayon poised over his pad, he examined the picture thoughtfully before adding a small, irregular shape beneath the line that represented the roof.

"Oh," I observed, "it has a window."

"Yes," he said, a proud smile lighting his face. "It has a window." Tearing the drawing from his pad, he held it out to me. "It's for you, Carole."

"Thank you very much, Alex," I replied sincerely. "I'll keep it always." As rudimentary and incomplete as the drawing was, it signified an important milestone in Alex's life. It was the first giving.

The next evening, as I walked by the pediatric nurse's station on my way to visit Alex, I heard someone call my name. I turned to see the head nurse rushing toward me. "Oh, Mrs.

Smith, I was hoping I could catch you before you saw Alex," she said somewhat breathlessly.

"What's wrong?" I asked, noting her distress. "His leg?" A flood of unspoken questions came to my mind. "What's happened?"

"Oh, no," she said, quickly reassuring me, "it's not his leg. It's just that he had some visitors earlier and he's been in a terrible state ever since. He's been throwing things at the nurses and yelling at them. I thought I should warn you."

My hands flew to my face in consternation. "Who were they? What did they do to him?"

"A woman called last night. Her speech was slurred and she sounded as though she had been drinking. She said she had seen in the paper that Alex was in the hospital. When I verified this, she said she was his mother. Today she showed up with the grandmother and an uncle in tow. We had to let them in. We don't have the authority to stop visitors unless there is a restraining order or they are creating a disturbance, and while they were here he seemed okay. It was after they left that the trouble began. Anyway, I must say they were odd-looking people, so we tried to keep an aide in the room all the time they were there. The mother promised Alex that when he was released from the hospital she had a beautiful home waiting for him and she would take him there and make everything up to him. She said she had a minibike she'd bought for him, and . . ."

I was unable to contain myself for another minute. "The— the mother is not supposed to see him unless a social worker is present. She does not have any visitation rights except under those conditions. Any contact with her has a devastating effect on him."

"Tell me about it," the nurse replied grimly.

I was so angry. How dare those people come here and wreak havoc like this with their false hopes and unfulfillable promises? How dare they come here and destroy the days and weeks and months of work we had done with this child?

I entered Alex's room for what was to be one of the worst

thirty minutes of my entire life. The rage I had seen before
was nothing in comparison to what awaited me. As I approached his bed, I was greeted by a stream of expletives, a
shrill, unearthly screaming of names exploding from an inner
core of white-hot hate. It was hard to believe this loathsome,
hellish creature glaring at me through narrowed, reddened
eyes was the same smiling boy who had given me that drawing yesterday. His lips curled back in an ugly grimace and his
fingers clawed at the air, reaching for me. I stepped back instinctively. I hadn't the slightest doubt that could Alex have
gotten to me, he would have tried to kill me. Any feeling of
warmth or affection he ever had for me was negated by this
consuming, malevolent hatred and lost in the depths of blind-
ing fury.

A plastic bottle of lotion sailed over my head and hit the
opposite wall. Then he grabbed a set of checkers and hurled
them at me, one by one. The checkers glanced harmlessly
off my face and arms and fell to the floor. They were too
small to physically hurt. After throwing the checkerboard
and his teddy bear, he began to search for more missiles in the
drawer of his bedside table. I pulled the table away.

"Filthy whore," he shouted, sucking in his breath and letting it out with a tortured roaring sound. "Fucking slut! I hate
you. I hate everything about you. If I had a knife, I'd cut your
heart out!"

Trying to hide my trembling, I sank into a chair on the
other side of the room. I had to think. I had to separate myself from this onslaught and figure out what was going on.
Christine had just left. Was there a connection between
Alex's behavior and the visit from his mother? There had to
be. But what? I had no way to tell.

Another wave of fury came over him, and he glared at me
with baleful green eyes. His voice was hoarse now from
screaming. "I hate your guts," he hissed. "Rotten bitch. I wish
you were dead! I don't want you near me. Get out of here.
Get away from me. Don't come near me!"

I wanted to leave. It would have been easy to leave. Something told me, though, that it was important to stay. It was important for Alex to know that his blackest, worst rage would not drive me away.

He lay back on his pillows, the terrible words still pouring out in what was by this time a mechanical monotone. Drained and exhausted, his body racked by dry, shuddering sobs, he drifted off into a fitful sleep.

I got up from my chair and walked closer to him. His dark hair fell across his forehead and a fringe of lashes curled against the soft curve of his cheek. Automatically, my hand reached out to him. But I drew it back. I could not reconcile this image of childhood innocence with the demonic creature of a few moments ago. I could not touch him. Not now.

V

Talking Times

Sam lifted his eyes from his plate and looked at me intently. "It's been five days, Carole. Are you going to visit him?"

"Not yet," I said. "I can't. I've never seen anything like that. And he's saying to you he doesn't remember? He's lying! How could he not remember?"

"I don't know. When I go to the hospital, he acts like nothing happened. I bet he's too ashamed to admit it."

"Well, he's got to," I said somewhat testily. "He has to at least apologize. There's more of the meat loaf, Sam, if you want. Oh, I did speak to the head nurse. They haven't seen or heard anything from Christine. She never tried to go back. You know what I think? I think he feels safer giving me his anger." Anger. Such an innocuous word, I thought, to describe what I had experienced. "Sam, it was so awful. He was like—he was like a cornered beast. His eyes. That murderous rage. It was for Christine. It had to be for Christine. Not me."

My husband stabbed his fork into a boiled potato. "Why the hell would he have that kind of hatred for his own mother?"

"Why would he have that kind of hatred for me? I don't know what she did to him. I do know what I haven't done."

I went to see Alex. Even though I was a bit uncomfortable, I wanted to go. I wanted to see him. I bought him a blue quilt. He had been needing a new one for some time, and I took it up to the hospital with me. The room was warm and the quilt was thick, but he wrapped it protectively around his body. He was reserved at first and his conversation was strained and polite. Was it cold outside? How was Bailey? And Roxy? He missed Roxy. With pleading eyes, he reached out and laid his hand in mine. "I want to come home, Carole. All I want is to come home."

"Are you sure?" I asked with my throat tightening and the question sounding stiff and thin in my ears. I was still feeling the unhealed edges of pain. "What about last week? Why did you . . . ?"

"I didn't mean it, Carole. I'm sorry. I'm sorry, I swear I didn't mean it!"

"Well, I'm glad you're owning up to it," I said with some satisfaction. "It's okay, Alex. We want you to come home."

After Alex had been in the hospital for almost three weeks, the doctor told me he was ready to be released. But first, he explained, a body cast had to be put on him so that the leg would heal properly.

"Will it hurt?" asked Alex when I gave him the news.

"No, the doctor said he would give you an anesthetic. He'll put you to sleep so you don't feel anything."

Alex's reaction to this information took me by surprise. He gave a cry of distress and shrank back against his pillows. "No, no, Carole. Don't let them. Please! I don't want them to put me to sleep. Don't let them. I'm afraid, Carole. I'm afraid."

"The doctor isn't going to hurt you. He's there to help you. He wants you to get better. Alex, what's wrong? Why are you so afraid?"

"He'll stick things in me. I'm afraid he'll stick things in me."

The cast, heavy and cumbersome, enclosed Alex from his chest to his toes. For five weeks, he was confined to bed, and caring for him was exhausting and overwhelming. Day and night, I was constantly responding to the calls of a virtually helpless child. Carole, I'm hungry. Get me something to eat. Carole, I'm thirsty. I need a drink. Carole, I spilled my drink. Carole, my back itches. Please come and scratch it. Carole, I have to go. I need the bedpan. Carole, change the station on the TV. Carole, come and play a game with me. Carole, I dropped my book. Come and pick it up. Carole, I'm cold. I need another blanket. Carole, Carole, Carole!

My ears rang with his cries and demands until I began to hate the sound of my own name.

In the midst of all this turmoil, a peculiar thing happened. It began with the bedpan. "I did it. I did it! Carole, come and see! Come and see!" Alex would shout after he had a bowel movement. His face fairly glowed with pride as he regarded the contents and his demeanor was open and frank. There was not the least hint that he thought there was anything unusual about a ten-year-old boy behaving as though his bowel movements were prized possessions and showing not a shred of embarrassment as he eagerly sought my admiration for this achievement. "Look, look! Did I do a lot? Did I do good? Did I?"

I knew immediately that something was out of sync, and I had a weird feeling of being in a time warp. I had been there before. I had heard this before. "Mommy, I did it. I did it! Did I do good, Mommy? Did I?"

Toilet training.

Such intense interest in the performance of this basic bodily function belonged to the toilet-training period. This was anal-stage behavior. I didn't even hesitate. The words I had so often spoken came easily to my lips. "Yes, Alex. You did great. Good boy. What a good boy!"

Sarah listened attentively when I related what had happened. She said Alex's early Oedipal stage had probably been disrupted and that sometimes, if a child feels safe and secure enough, he will regress to a previous stage. This particular aspect of the regression lasted for approximately a month before it gradually tapered off. But there would be more to come.

During the last two weeks in January, Alex began working with his Angry Book. He kept the book close at hand and wore the key around his neck on a silver chain. "I wrote about my stepmother," he said at the beginning of our first session.

"Do you want to tell me about it?" I asked. "You don't have to talk about it unless you want to."

For a long while Alex seemed to be looking off into the distance. Then he said in a firm, resolute voice, "No, but I will read it. I will read it to you." Turning to Sandra's section of the book, he began: "My stepmother sent me to the bar to get my father. I couldn't find him. I searched everywhere but I couldn't find him. I went back to the house. My stepmother was gone. It was very cold out. I tried to get in but everything was locked. I waited and waited and finally my stepmother's sister drove by and saw me. She took me to her mother's house. My stepmother was there and when they asked her why she had left me, she said, 'Oh he didn't want to come with me.' "

"How old were you?" I asked.

"Five or six."

I had a fleeting impression of a cold, frightened little boy running around trying doorknobs, peering through windows, calling out for his stepmother. I tried to think of what Sarah had said. "Help him to label his feelings," she had told me. "Kids can't talk about feelings because they don't know the words." It made sense. If you can give a name to something, you can describe it, elaborate on it, and categorize it. If it has a name, it is no longer a diffuse, shadowy entity. If it has a name, it can be controlled.

"You must have felt abandoned and really afraid."

There was a glimmer of acknowledgment in Alex's eyes. "I did. Yes, I did," he agreed. "I was scared."

"I would be scared too if someone left me all alone when I was little. It's okay to be scared."

Alex's face became tense and flushed and he gripped the bedclothes with his fingers.

"Yes," I said, guessing at his feelings, "you have a right to

Barn Drawing, January 20, 1985

be angry about being locked out in the cold and left alone. We talked about that, remember? You have a right to be angry."

"Yes, I do, don't I? I do have a right." There was a sense of smug pride in his voice as he recognized this right. "And she lied," he shouted indignantly. "She lied!" Hitting the book with his fist and throwing it across the room, Alex was directing his anger at a legitimate source.

Suddenly he raised himself up on his elbows and his face assumed a shocked expression. I saw a look of awe and revelation spread slowly across his features. "Carole," he said, "I never talked like this before." He gave me a hug and he said it again, this time as though to himself rather than to me. "I never talked like this before."

Toward the end of the regressive period, he told me he wanted to draw me another picture. His crayon flew across the blank paper in quick, decisive strokes. I stared incredulously as the drawing grew before my eyes. He said it was a barn, but it was rich with detail and more like a house than a barn. A table and some chairs could be seen through a large window and circles of smoke came from a chimney. A walk led from double doors to a road, and beyond the walk, a horse looked out over a stone wall.

When Alex handed me the finished drawing, I mentally compared it to that first primitive sketch. How could this be possible? I asked myself. How could the same child draw two pictures that were developmentally years apart?

Our next Angry Book session was in early February. I sat close to him on his bed while he read what he had written. Opening the book to Christine's page, he spoke in a monotone. His voice was completely devoid of any feeling or emotion. "I was four, almost five," he said. "We were living with these people. There was a woman and she had a little boy I played with. One day the woman came in very angry and she said, 'Christine, Alex broke this toy truck,' and my mother took a belt and hit me fifty times. Every time she raised her arm she screamed, 'I'll kill you. I'll kill you.' I was bleeding and I went out and found the other kid and beat him up because he lied about me breaking the truck. I ran away because I knew I would get another beating."

Alex's stoic facade while telling his story did not lessen the impact of his words. The "fifty times" may have been an exaggeration, but I could still see the enraged mother brutally beating her small and defenseless child. "How could she do that? No child deserves that. It wasn't your fault."

He regarded me with astonishment, as though this were some new and radical idea. Through a blur of tears, I saw his face crumble and his own tears, so long denied, roll freely down his cheeks. "I was too little. I was too little," he sobbed repeatedly. "I was too little for her to hit me so hard." Then he was in my arms and I was holding him and we were both crying for a boy who was too little.

One morning a few days later, I heard Alex excitedly calling my name. I rushed into his room to see Bailey, the beagle, cowering on the edge of Alex's bed. Bailey was petrified of any kind of height and had always been fearful of getting down off the bed. Since Alex never seemed to be aware of this, he invariably shoved the dog onto the floor. Today was different. Very different. As he watched Bailey, he was full of compassion and concern. "Look, Carole, Bailey is afraid," he said sympathetically.

"He's always been afraid."

"No he hasn't," Alex insisted. "He's never been like this. Poor Bailey. Are you scared? Here, I'll help you, Bailey. I'll help you." The dog wagged his tail beseechingly as Alex reached over and gently assisted his descent.

I was elated. This was the second important event in three weeks. There had been the beginnings of his ability to focus his anger, and now the empathy. It was only after he had ac-knowledged and cried for a part of his own pain that he was able to relate to the feelings of another being. It was signs of progress like this, to be joyfully shared with Sarah over steaming cups of morning coffee, that kept me going.

During the fourth week of Alex's convalescence, I finally got around to unpacking the bag he had brought home from the hospital. Under an assortment of crayons and games, there were several photographs and an iridescent-blue butterfly-shaped barrette. That night, sitting next to Sam at the trestle table, I showed these things to him. "Someone must have brought an instant camera when the relatives came to the hospital," I said. "And this barrette must be some kind of memento. I remember the nurse saying that Christine left it on his bedside table."

The first of the snapshots was a picture of a pretty woman in her early thirties. She was dressed in clothes more appro-priate to a young teenager and was smiling the way children often do for the camera—pasted-on and automatic.

"Christine?" said Sam.

"Who else? It has to be."

With Alex's permission, I had shared his disclosure about the beating with Sam. I looked again at the picture, and the unspoken question was there between us. Could that be enough? Enough to spawn so terrible a hatred?

Placing a photograph facedown on the table, I picked up another. It was of an older woman, and she was not smiling. Her lips were set in a grim line, and her eyes, half closed, looked wary and suspicious. Her arms were folded across her ample chest as though to ward off unseen danger. "The grandmother," I said.

"Jesus!" remarked Sam.

I examined the picture carefully, trying to find some sign of tenderness underneath the hard-as-nails exterior. It was difficult to believe this was the same person who had once tried to protect Alex and had probably provided some degree of early nurturing. "And here is Uncle Harold," I said, holding up the last picture.

It wasn't what was in the photo that was so horrifying. It was what wasn't. The eyes in the face of the hollow-cheeked young man who leaned forward and stared straight into the camera were devoid of human expression or emotion. They were completely blank, blank and empty. Sam fell silent as he studied the zombie-like image, and when he did speak it was of something else.

"Did you ask the nurse about the bleeding?" he said without looking at me.

He was referring to the blood that had sometimes appeared in the bedpan when Alex moved his bowels. "Yes, I did. She recommended a stool softener. I haven't seen any results yet, but it's only been three days. It—it bothers me, though, Sam," I said hesitantly. "I don't understand why he should be bleeding."

"Carole, like I've told you, you worry too much. The kid is simply constipated from lying around in bed all this time. The cast comes off in another week and he'll be fine. You wait and see."

The matter-of-fact common sense of Sam's words calmed my fears and set my mind at ease. It was a logical explanation, and after all, what else could it be?

.   .   .

The treatment for the bleeding did seem to be effective. For the next two weeks, there was no sign of it. There was, however, a recurrence in mid-February. It was on the day Alex and I had our last session of talking time, as we had come to call it, before the removal of the cast. "I don't need my book today," he announced. "I just want to talk. I want to talk about my mother, but everything comes at once. There's so much. I can't tell about one thing."

So much. There's so much. I wouldn't think of that now. I couldn't think of that. "Alex, maybe if you really concentrate, you can do it. It doesn't have to be anything big. Maybe one small incident."

He moved closer to me on the bed. He felt safer talking about what people had done to him, he had explained, if I was sitting next to him. His smooth brow knitted in thought and he lifted grave eyes to my face as he began to speak. "It was an awesome hot day and my mother sent me to the store to get her an ice-cream cone. Strawberry. She wanted a strawberry cone. When I got back with the ice cream, it was melted. My mother started screaming, 'What did you do? Eat it?' and she took a belt and she beat me with the belt. She beat me for a . . ." Alex left the sentence unfinished, and an abrupt change came over him. An uncontrollable agitation, like a convulsion, seemed to seize the upper part of his body. There was a twitching and jerking of the arms and head, but this was quickly followed by a longer, more sustained twisting and thrashing. "His name," he said, his voice hissing through almost closed lips. "What was his name? My stepfather? I don't know his name."

Frightened by this sudden metamorphosis, I jumped up from the bed. "Albert Mercer," I said. "It's in the record. His name was Albert."

"Yes! Albert. Bert. Get me my book. And a pencil!" he ordered with the most extreme urgency.

My eyes hastily swept the room. The Angry Book. Where was it? There on the bureau. I grabbed the book and the pencil alongside it and held them out to him. "The key," he cried.

And tearing the silver chain that held the key from around his neck, he thrust it at me. My hands were shaking as I fumbled with the tiny key but somehow I managed to unlock the book.

Snatching the book and pencil from my hands, Alex frantically turned the pages. He came to one with "Albert" printed across the top, and he wrote on it in slashing strokes. When he finished he raised the pencil high over his head and brought it down in a violent, stabbing motion that ripped the page from the binding.

At this point his body stiffened and became rigid. Glaring fixedly at a spot near the door of the room, some ten feet from where I was standing, he began to speak. Shivers went up my arms and the back of my neck. The symbolism of a page in an angry book was more than we had bargained for. Alex was seeing Albert Mercer. He was talking to Albert Mercer. "You suck, Bert," he said. "You suck! I hate you. I hate you!"

The spell was brief, and after it was over I said in a low voice, "Why do you hate Albert Mercer, Alex? What did he do to you?"

Alex shifted his gaze back in my direction. Beads of perspiration rolled down his reddened face. "None of your business!" he snapped.

"Okay," I replied. I would stick to our agreement. "You don't have to talk about it if you don't want to."

"Nobody's going to know," he said with fierce determination. "Nobody! He did something to me." His white-knuckled hands gripped and clawed at the bedclothes, and his speech was slow and carefully enunciated. "He did something to me. And it isn't in the record."

That night I found the torn page and I took it to the counseling center to show Sarah. " 'Bert sucks,' " she said, reading the scrawled message. "That's probably exactly what he did," she concluded without elaborating.

"What was going on?" I inquired anxiously. "What was happening? It was all so strange."

A slightly perplexed look crossed Sarah's features as she

leaned back in her chair and pondered my question. "The only similar experience I've had was while working with a Vietnam veteran."

I sensed Sarah was thinking more than she was saying. But in 1985 the label "post-traumatic stress syndrome" was reserved for war veterans who had been through unimaginable suffering. Who wanted to believe that children could display the same symptoms?

Alex would have no memory of what he had said about Albert Mercer. I did not know why. I did not know how he could forget so vivid an episode. I did not understand that it wasn't time, that he wasn't ready.

The removal of the cast in mid-March precipitated a spell of unusual behavior. "What the hell is wrong with him?" Sam exclaimed in exasperation. "He screams bloody murder the minute you're out of his sight."

My husband was referring to Alex's reaction if he became separated from me at the supermarket, department store, or anyplace else. He stood rooted to the floor, opened his mouth, and screamed at the top of his lungs. At home, he followed me from room to room, clinging to me and wanting to be held and rocked. He even tried to come into the bathroom with me. And when I locked him out he huddled miserably against the door until I reappeared.

"What's wrong with him?" Sam repeated impatiently. "And why are you smiling? What's so funny?"

"Can't you see? It's more of that two-year-old stuff, more regression. Sam, trust me. It's a good sign. It means he's feeling more secure. He acts that way if he can't see me because he can't recall what I look like and he thinks I'm gone forever. Have you forgotten going through this when the boys were two and three?"

Sam gave me a despairing glance. "Carole, it is so damned hard to look at a ten-year-old and think two."

Yes, it was. But Alex still had to learn as any small child does that if I went away, I would come back. This would take practice. Sam had recently returned to work, but I knew he planned to be home on Friday. I made arrangements to visit a friend, painstakingly prepared Alex for my three-hour absence, and left him in Sam's care.

"He held together for about thirty minutes," said Sam, when I came home. "But he just—Carole, I've never seen anything like it. He sat by the window for about half an hour after you left and then he disintegrated right before my eyes. He became incoherent and irrational—saying all kinds of weird things. He wrecked his room, tore the curtains down, and ripped up his poster. The furniture is piled in the middle of the floor. You can use his bureau drawers for kindling! It was hell, Carole. I'm telling you, it was hell."

For days Alex's attitude toward me was hostile and obnoxious, but in spite of his obvious anger over my leaving him, my page in the book remained blank. I decided to use our talking time to work on this. "Alex," I began, "I know you are angry with me because I went to see my friend. It's hard to talk about that, isn't it?"

He hung his head and gave an affirmative nod.

"You've been doing a great job talking about the anger you have for many of the other people in your book."

"I know. But talking about them—it isn't the same."

"What do you mean?" He made no response, so I patiently persisted. "How is it not the same, Alex? Can you tell me?"

"I shouldn't have been mad. It wasn't right. You should be able to go out with your friends if you want."

"Yes, Alex, I certainly should. But your feelings about it aren't right or wrong. They exist. If you feel it, it's real. It has to be dealt with. And how do we deal with feelings?"

"We talk about them." This was followed by "Another thing is, I was afraid."

"Afraid of what?"

"Afraid!" he cried out, and giving me an imploring, helpless look, he burst into tears and buried his head in my shoulder. "With them, I d-don't have anything t-to lose," he explained haltingly. "But I'm afraid you'll get m-mad at me."

Oh, my God, I thought, as I hastened to reassure Alex that I would not get mad at him if he told me about any angry feelings he might have because I left him.

What Alex had said about not having anything to lose was true. For all practical purposes his family had already rejected him. Three months had passed since Christmas and his father had not cared enough to make one phone call to see how he was doing. And his mother had made no attempt to contact the social worker to arrange visitation.

Alex's anger toward me was so intertwined with his anger and hatred for Christine and Sandra that it would become the goal of much of our work in the time to come. And as the emotional bond between us strengthened and deepened, it would also become the source of much of my own heartbreak.

VI

March to July 1985

Turning Points

Alex's family may have rejected him, but the painful and sorrowful process of rejecting them caused him to suffer from conflicting emotions. The following week, before beginning his homework assignment, he asked, "Was Benedict Arnold really a traitor?"

There was something in his eyes, something in his voice, that told me the question did not really relate to his history lesson. "I have an idea," I said, "that you feel as though you're being torn between two worlds. Our ways are not the same as the ways of your family. Do you think you're being disloyal to them when you do things our way, when you like doing things our way?"

His answer, a quick, anguished "Yes," sounded as though it had been wrenched from his deepest, innermost self and had escaped his lips against his will. It was followed by rambling accounts of children who had been stolen. Was this another conflict? Was he afraid his family might, indeed, take him away, and was he feeling guilty about this fear?

By the end of March, the specter of Christine Mercer's visit to the hospital had faded considerably. We still worked on behavior modification and we still practiced social skills with Joey, but on the whole, life was more normal. He was even able to tolerate a minor punishment, such as the loss of a television program. "I no longer feel like I'm walking on eggshells," I said to Sarah.

On the last day of the month, there was a phone call. I was

outside hanging clothes on the line behind the house when I saw Alex at the back door. "Carole! Carole!" he said gesturing wildly. "It's a girl. It's her. It's a girl! She's on the phone."

Wrestling with the wind for a sheet, I clamped a clothespin on one end and said with some impatience, "Who, Alex? What girl?"

"A girl," he repeated. "Her. My mother!"

A sensation of dread, a cold, gripping, heavy feeling, settled in the pit of my stomach. Pictures flashed through my mind. The contorted features. The fiendlike eyes. The raging hatred. It was a phone call, I said to myself, only a phone call.

"Please, Carole," he begged. "Please come in with me while I talk to her."

"In a minute," I said as I pinned the other end of the sheet. He made no move to leave the doorway. What was wrong with him? Why was he so anxious and worried? My mind denied the evidence of my senses, but I left the clothes and went into the house with Alex. As incredible as it seemed, he was afraid to be alone while he talked to a mother who was miles away.

Signaling me to stay close to him, he went over to the phone on the kitchen wall. "Hi, it's me," he said. "I'm back." And after a short pause, "No, you have to talk to Ann. You can't see me without talking to Ann first." He spoke slowly and patiently in the same tone an adult might use with a small child. "No," he insisted, "you're not supposed to do that. I can't. I told you. You have to talk to Ann." There was another pause and, putting his hand over the receiver, he said in a nervous whisper, "She won't listen to me. You tell her."

Reluctantly I took the phone from his hand and said as pleasantly as I possibly could, "Mrs. Mercer? This is Carole Smith. What seems to be the problem?"

The voice on the other end of the line was coarse and harsh, and the words were worse. "What do you mean, what's the problem? You got my kid, don'tcha?"

"Listen, Mrs. Mercer, if you want to see Alex, you have to call the caseworker and a visit will be arranged."

"Fuck those bastards! I want to see my Alex." The rough speech grated against my ear.

"Mrs. Mercer," I began again, "I am sorry, but I don't make the rules. My understanding is that you have to call Ann."

"Fuck you," came the reply. "You're all alike. Fuck all you bastards!"

The phone call precipitated three days of stress-related behavior, the hyperactivity, the excessive need for nurturing, and an especially violent tantrum. But this time, there was something new. Alex walked from room to room touching various objects and saying, "This is my chair. This is my table. This is my bed. This is my dog," and so on until he had proclaimed ownership of practically everything in the house. I could only guess at the meaning of this odd behavior. Did it signify an attempt to take one more step into the safety and security of our world and, beyond that, the world he had glimpsed at *The Nutcracker*?

On the night after Alex talked to his mother, the second dream came. "I was in a canoe," he told me as he sat on my lap and put his arms around my neck. "It was on the ocean and there was water for miles around. My grandfather and grandmother were in one end of the canoe and my stepmother and father were in the other end and I was in the middle. The canoe tipped over and I was under the water. I was struggling and struggling to get to the surface. And then I woke up."

Feelings, Sarah had said. Ask him what feelings were associated with the dream. "Can you tell me, Alex, can you remember how you felt while you were under the water?"

"I was dying," he said. "I felt like I was dying."

Shortly after the beginning of April, Alex called from the center of town to tell me he had found an envelope containing twenty-five one-dollar bills. It turned out that the money had been lost by a ten-year-old girl who had been collecting for the multiple sclerosis fund drive. When Alex gave her every cent of the money, the story of his honesty spread rapidly around town. The local newspaper got hold of it and sent a photographer to take pictures of a smiling Alex holding out a fistful of dollar bills. The picture, along with the story, appeared right in the middle of the front page of the paper.

Alex was a hero.

Everywhere he went he was met with praise and admiration. At his school, the picture was on the bulletin board in his classroom, and Don Sullivan gave a brief talk on the rewards of ethical behavior. At the karate studio, the picture was hung on the wall of the waiting room, and Delaney, the very same young man who had sent Alex flying across the studio last November, approached him and shook his hand. "I lost my wallet two weeks ago," he said, "and I wish someone had returned it. You're okay in my book, Alex." Coming from Delaney, that was quite a compliment.

This experience generated so much self-esteem that it proved to be a major turning point in Alex's life. He basked in the approval of his classmates. "It's so great," he said, radiating happiness. "Everybody in my class likes me. Timmy says I'm not a jerk like I used to be."

The more he had of this blossoming social acceptance, the more he wanted and the harder he worked to get it. It was a tremendous relief when this extended to his academic efforts and our battles over homework came to an end. Alex eagerly and independently attacked his studies. "When I really know what I'm talking about in class," he explained, "the kids treat me different. They treat me with respect."

The aftereffects of the incident continued to snowball. Alex not only got up enough courage to attend a church-sponsored dance for fifth and sixth grades, he actually danced with a girl. "I did it," he shouted on the way home. "I really did it. Carole, I asked her and she said yes and I did it!"

He also became a member of the Little League baseball

team and wore his uniform with great pride and as often as possible. Sam shared Alex's love for the game and, sitting with the other parents in mosquito-bitten discomfort, we dutifully cheered the team's every effort.

And there was the earning of the purple belt in karate. This involved an examination designed to test the stamina, knowledge, and control of the candidates. An impressive ceremony accompanied the awarding of the belt to those who were successful, and Alex was happily among them. It was another step in the slow and painstaking process that had begun almost a year ago, the process of rebuilding a child's severely damaged self-concept.

Alex and I continued with our talking times, and it was during one of these that he made a painful admission. "Before—before I came here," he said, "I really thought I was crazy."

On a hunch, I asked, "Did anybody ever say that you were?"

"Yes, yes!" he screamed. "All the time! My father. I can hear him. I can hear him now. I can hear him say it. I hear it before I go to sleep at night, over and over. 'You're crazy. You're crazy!' " Sobbing piteously, he rushed to a corner of the room and lay in a crumpled heap with his hands against his ears.

I was trying to keep my own emotions intact. Barely able to speak, I said, "That must have been so awful for you, Alex. Do you ever think you're crazy now?"

"No, not now," he said wiping his tears away with the back of his hand.

"Why?"

"Because of my marks in school and my baseball and karate. If I was crazy I couldn't do the stuff I do." Getting to his feet, Alex faced me with squared shoulders and a proud tilt to his chin. "And because of my friends," he continued. "I wouldn't have any if I was crazy."

"You're right, Alex. You're not crazy."

"Another thing he did. He gave my dog away. My dog

Spunky. He was the only thing I loved, and he gave him away."

"You know, Alex, I've never criticized your father, but I can't help feeling angry when I hear things like this."

He came to me and gave me a hug. "It's okay," he said. "I don't like him anymore anyway."

As for Christine, Alex remained steadfast in his hope that she would call again. When the phone rang, he would run to it shouting, "Maybe that's for me!" and when it wasn't, his grieving was almost unbearable. This was something I could not comprehend. I could not reconcile the longing for his mother with the fear and fury so clearly associated with her.

"Why doesn't she call?" he asked, his eyes wide and luminous with unshed tears. He was sitting on the floor with the dog and he was waiting for an answer. And I didn't know what to say. I was torn between Alex's pain and my own selfish needs. After what I had gone through every time he had any contact with this woman, I was quite frankly hoping she wouldn't call. But I couldn't tell him that. How could I explain why his mother was incapable of being responsible for him, incapable of meeting his needs, and incapable of providing him with the love and care that is every child's birthright?

I took a deep breath and made an attempt. "Sometimes people have so many problems they—well, they just can't cope. They get overwhelmed by life. So overwhelmed, in fact, they are unable to sustain a relationship."

I expected to hear screaming denials or perhaps a tantrum. At the very least I thought I would be called a liar. There was nothing. Alex was perfectly calm. He already knows this, I said to myself. He already knows. The only thing he did was to press his hands tightly against Bailey's floppy ears. "Bailey wouldn't like me if he knew that."

"I know, and I like you very much," I said.

At the end of the week, he told me about the third dream. "I was in a canoe on the ocean again," he said as he crawled onto my lap and rubbed the sleep from his eyes. "My mother was on the shore. I was waving goodbye to her and she threw her arms up in the air and screamed. Then the canoe sinks and I'm on the bottom. I'm on the bottom of the ocean and there are a lot of dead bodies around and you come and carry me out."

Not knowing how to deal with the fact that I found Alex's account of his dream strangely disturbing, I smiled and said casually, "Well, it's good that it has a happy ending anyway."

"No," he said, shaking his head with an air of infinite sadness. "I'm dead."

"Dreams involving water," said Sarah when I told her of it, "are often associated with birth. This may well signify a separation from the mother and a rebirth."

Sarah was right. But this rebirth, this renewal and regeneration, would turn out to be a lengthy, piecemeal process that would take many shapes and many forms.

At about this time, Sarah regretfully told me she was leaving. She had taken another position, and although she expressed an interest in continuing to see me, it involved traveling some distance and did not appear to be a practical alternative.

I had one final session with her. "I'll miss you," I said, and thinking of the prospect of being left with only Peter for support, I added, "I don't know how I'll manage without you."

Sarah gave me a warm embrace. "You can do it. You have the strength to do it." Standing back, she gave me an appraising look. "The counseling center is trying to find someone for you and Alex. It may take a while. All I can tell you is, when you have a problem, go with your instincts. They are good."

I would think of those words in the years to come. They would give me the confidence and courage I needed to do whatever was necessary for Alex's survival—and my own.

By July of 1985, Alex had been with us for almost a year and the early treatment plan of absolute acceptance was no longer either appropriate or necessary. Sam and I decided to begin the transition to responsibility by having him take a close look at his objectionable behavior. In order to change this behavior, he had to admit that it existed. To this end, we sat him down at the trestle table every night and asked him to own up to the day's transgressions. That was all he had to do. There was no punishment and no scolding, although we often did have to point out how his responses were habitual ways of dealing with a past environment. The first time we tried this reality check, Alex's admissions were preceded by kicking, screaming, fist-pounding tantrums. But when we came to the most serious incident, one that involved the smashing of toys and a threat to slap me in the face, there was a different reaction.

"I didn't do it. I didn't say that," he replied, not with the angry denial of before but with a combination of sincerity and confusion.

"It's right here," I said as I held up my list. "I wrote it all down exactly as it happened."

"Oh. Okay. I remember. I didn't mean it. I swear I didn't mean it. I'm sorry."

What was wrong with this quick confession? I couldn't quite put my finger on it. He had faced up to everything else. These violent actions would not be easily forgotten. If he was trying to evade responsibility, why did the admission come so quickly? The episode in the hospital had been similar—initial loss of memory followed by abject apology. And what about the rageful outpouring after the run-in with Delaney? He hadn't been able to remember that either. I turned my attention back to Alex. "You know the rules," I said. "Excuses like 'I didn't mean it' or 'I was just kidding' are not acceptable."

For three weeks, the confrontation took place every night. And, except for riding lessons and reading, there were no diversions. There were no television programs, no activities, no friends. There was nothing to distract him from taking an honest look at what he was saying and doing. Even though he sometimes opposed the process, Alex himself did want to give up this obnoxious conduct.

By the end of the three weeks there was a marked improvement. But he would always revert to his old ways during periods of severe stress. One of these was the time of the full moon. Month after month, it was always the same: the agitation, the excessive lying, the meaningless talk, the screaming nightmares that tortured his sleep. And the bleeding. That, too, seemed to coincide with the full moon. Constipation might originally have had something to do with this, but the more recent incidents were accompanied by abdominal pain and diarrhea. Our pediatrician could find no physical cause and recommended a specialist.

It was in July when I first became aware of a connection between these manifestations and the phase of the moon. The symptoms were at their peak and I had gone into the kitchen to take some aspirin. I happened to glance at the calendar on the wall, and there it was. The white circle designating a full moon. I looked back. June. Yes. And May. Definitely in May. By the end of the summer, I would dread the coming of that moon.

Another stressful time was the twenty-sixth of July, Alex's birthday. Ann had told me that for as long as she had been on the case, this had been extremely traumatic for him. Since it was now the twenty-fifth, the day before his eleventh birthday, we were about to find out just how traumatic.

The trouble began in the morning. He had taken his new fishing pole and new tackle box to a pond down the road to do some fishing. An hour later he returned empty-handed. "What happened?" I asked somewhat indignantly. "Did someone steal them?"

"No," announced Alex in a matter-of-fact tone. "I gave them away."

"What do you mean, you gave them away?"

"You got a hearing problem? I meant exactly what I said. I gave them to some kid who was walking by."

"Sam just bought that fishing pole and tackle box for you. You were so pleased. How could you give them away?"

"So I did. So what?"

I felt the muscles tighten in the back of my neck and the rising nausea in the pit of my stomach. Warning signals went off in my mind. Alex had given away two recently acquired and highly prized possessions. This was irrational and uncharacteristic behavior. Within seconds he was out of control. Letting loose with a stream of terrible obscenities, he ran outside and began throwing rocks at the windows. I heard the sound of breaking glass coming from the rear of the house, and I rushed to a back bedroom to find that one window was shattered. There was nothing I could do, and I felt helpless.

A loud thumping noise from up above told me he was on the roof. Alex spent the next hour finding a dangerous balance on the steep angles and teetering precariously on the ridge. Going from window to window, I anxiously tried to catch a glimpse of him. Minutes seemed like forever, and when I did see him, he was speeding down the driveway on his bicycle. He veered recklessly to the left so he could go over a piece of ledge and I held my breath as the bicycle flew into the air. Somehow it landed upright and he continued on his way.

I spent a nerve-racking afternoon, wondering and worrying. Where could he be? I got in the car and drove around the streets searching for him, knowing all the while that if I found him, he would just run and I wouldn't be able to catch him. But it was something to do.

At four o'clock, there was still no trace of him. At five o'clock, Sam called. "You know what that kid did?" he fumed. "I'm here at the variety store and they tell me he charged a whole bunch of stuff to me so he could treat his friends. He also went out and begged perfect strangers for money. Jesus, Carole, what's got into him?"

"I don't know, Sam. It could be the birthday. Ann warned me about that. His behavior has been outrageous all day, and he took off hours ago. I have no idea where he is."

Although Sam was far too upset to be interested in the reasons behind Alex's actions, he promised to go look for him. Two hours later, my still disgruntled husband arrived home with the boy in tow. "I went all over town," he complained. "He was up near the lake."

Keeping my mixed feelings of relief and anger in check, I said, "Why did you do these things, Alex? Do you want to talk about it?"

He gave me a black, surly look and answered with his own questions. "Am I going to get any punishment? Am I going to get any birthday presents?"

"Why not? A birthday has nothing to do with punishment. A birthday celebration is an affirmation of life."

Alex dropped his lower jaw and stared at me as though I had made a shocking statement. He called me a particularly offensive name, and the filthy language and the destructive tantrums began all over again.

Afterward, when it was over and I'd gotten him into bed, he lay with his eyes wide open. "I'm afraid to sleep," he said. "Please stay with me."

I did. I stayed close to give him what protection I could from these inexplicable fears and terrors. But what was the connection to the birthday? There had to be a connection. There had to be.

During the following evening, while Alex was in the living room watching television, I brought some clean laundry into his room. The floor was littered with what appeared to be scraps of shiny paper. I picked them up and I saw they were Polaroid snapshots that had been cut up into little pieces. They were the photographs of Alex's family he had brought home from the hospital. A picture taken of Alex and Christine had been slashed through and through with scissors, but Christine's face was still intact. I took that tiny section, and although I had no idea why, I put it away and I saved it.

VII

A Foiled Kidnapping

In spite of the loss of Sarah and the birthday trauma, Alex had been steadily improving his riding skills. Once I was sure he had learned the basics, I brought him to a local stable for professional instruction. By the end of October, he was ready to compete in the Junior Walk Trot Division of the West River Fair Horse Show.

Sam and I stood by the ringside on that crisp autumn morning to watch Alex ride in his first class. He was dressed in a dark blue jacket with brass buttons, beige jod pants, gleaming black boots, and black gloves. Posting effortlessly to the rhythm of Roxy's trot, he kept an eye on the judge and the twenty-one other horses and ponies in the ring. "He looks good, doesn't he?" commented Sam as Alex circled to avoid getting too close to another horse.

I was trying to give Alex's performance a critical and unbiased appraisal, and I was proud to see he was one of the best riders in the group. "He's not as polished as the girl on the flashy palomino," I observed, "but she's been showing for several years."

At last the class ended and the horses and ponies were lined up before the ringmaster. I wanted with all my heart for Alex to win a ribbon—any ribbon. It would mean so much to him, and he did deserve it. A round of applause greeted the not unexpected announcement that the girl on the palomino had taken the blue. A boy riding western-style complete with cowboy hat, fringed shirt, and chaps was second, and a girl on a white Welsh pony came in third. More clapping. A long delay. Alex's name. The announcer was saying Alex's name. He had won fourth place! The ringmaster pinned the white rosette onto Roxy's bridle, and once again applause filled the air.

After the last class of the day was finished and he had added two more ribbons, a third and a sixth, to his earlier win, he threw his arms around the mare's neck and pressed his cheek against her silky coat. "Oh, Roxy," he said, "you are the best, most wonderfullest horse in the whole world."

Sam's eyes sought mine and we both looked at Alex, and in the midst of the noise and confusion of the throngs of people, there was a connection and closeness, a feeling of family. "Alex," said Sam, "you did a real good job today. If you want to stay here while we trailer Roxy home, it's okay."

He jumped at the chance to remain at the fair and bask in the admiration of his friends. "Be sure and be careful of my ribbons," he called out as he ran off with two of his classmates.

It took less than an hour to bring Roxy to our barn and return to the fairgrounds. When we located Alex, he was no longer the carefree, joyful child we had left. He was hiding around the corner of a booth, peering at us with fear-glazed eyes and screaming terrible names. In that brief period, he had become transformed into a cold and primitive being.

I was bewildered by the unaccountable switch, and I couldn't bear to see the hurt and disappointment on Sam's face. What could possibly have gone wrong? I did not know, and Alex, our Alex, locked away in some dark, impenetrable dungeon of fear and hatred, was not going to tell. "Sam," I said, reaching for straws, for any shred of explanation, "do you think winning those ribbons was too much for him? Evidently it's the greatest thing that's ever happened to him and perhaps he feels he doesn't deserve it."

"Maybe," replied Sam in a manner indicating his complete lack of interest.

Alex was somehow able to regain enough semblance of control to go to school on Monday morning. But it didn't last, and his conduct soon worsened. Teachers complained that he was attacking other students for no apparent reason, insulting staff, and destroying property. The principal was forced to suspend him for Wednesday and Thursday. It didn't help. His behavior was no better by Friday. And Friday, just before Halloween, he did not come home.

I could not imagine where he could be, and within an hour I was driving all over town. I checked the houses of every friend he had, and I checked the variety store, and I checked the school. No one had seen him.

By dark the only option left was to go to the police. "What was he wearing?" they asked.

A numbing fear clutched at my throat and paralyzed my mind. Pressing my fingers against my forehead and closing my eyes, I tried to think. "A blue jacket," I said slowly, "brown pants and . . . I don't know. I don't know what else. Oh, sneakers, blue-and-white Nike sneakers."

"Where would he go?"

"I've been all over."

"What about relatives? Foster kids often try to run away to relatives."

George and Sandra? Not likely. And besides, he was terrified of hitchhiking. He would never get in a car with a stranger. They wrote down George's name and address anyway.

I returned home to find Sam pacing the floor with a nervous, restless energy. He had already heard the news. He asked me if I'd looked in the barn and I said I hadn't, so we took a flashlight and searched the stalls and hayloft. Alex was not there. When we got back to the house, the school principal called to say he had questioned the bus drivers and Alex had not taken his own bus but had gotten on the bus that went to the town beach area at the lake. I relayed this information to the police, and I made some coffee, and we waited.

That was where they found him. He was hiding in the bottom of a rowboat near the shoreline of the lake. A young officer, holding Alex by the hand, brought him to our front door. While Sam and I were thanking the policeman, the boy pulled away and bolted past us. Excusing myself, I followed him into his room. He had crawled under his bed, and I got down on my hands and knees to try to coax him out. "Please, Alex," I said, "everything's okay. You're home. You're safe. We were so worried. Why don't you go in the bathroom and wash up and get ready for bed. And if you're hungry—you must be hungry—there's cookies and milk."

He made no sound. His arms were straight down, close to his body. His face was staring upward. He was rigid and motionless. Like something dead. "Come on, Alex. Nothing's going to happen to you." I stretched my arm under the bed to touch his cheek. It was cold from the night chill of the lake. Forcing him out might do more harm than good, I thought, so I took his blue quilt and, pushing it over and around him, I covered him as best I could.

For the rest of the weekend, he remained in a faraway, unreachable place, and I sensed that if anything were to penetrate that protective brittleness, he might break into a thousand pieces. I had to be patient. Whatever was going on had to take its own time.

It happened on Monday. The anger emerged in full force. Alex went on a rampage and threw, slammed, or destroyed everything in his path. He hurled the dining-room chairs against the wall. He demolished the wrought-iron lamp on the post at the end of the driveway. He smashed his bicycle by repeatedly dropping heavy rocks on it. He scratched and gouged the paint on the car before he locked himself in it and proceeded to tear up my registration and other papers.

That was it! That was enough! Alex had never before been so destructive, and again, since we were beyond absolute acceptance, this outrageous behavior could not be tolerated. I felt I needed a temporary separation from Alex, a few days at most. I went to the phone and called the office. Peter was in, thank God, and I told him what had happened. "Peter," I said in desperation, "when I took this job, I was assured an emergency respite was one of the services provided. I need that respite."

"Of course it's part of the program," said Peter, "but this may not be that much of an emergency, and, uh, besides, we just don't have a place right now. Perhaps there's someone, maybe a friend, you could leave him with for a while."

"Oh, my God," I said through clenched teeth. "Am I to understand you want me to take this out-of-control kid who has just done several hundred dollars' worth of damage and dump him on a friend?"

Alex had come inside and was listening to this conversation. When he realized there would be no respite, his eyes gleamed with a malicious triumph and he began another round of destruction.

"No," I said resolutely, "you are not going to do that."

He gave me a look of undisguised defiance, threw back his head, and laughed. "Who's going to stop me?" he chortled gleefully.

"I am!" I shouted. And breaking every agency rule about laying hands on clients, I made a lunge for him. He ducked, ran for the front door, and was halfway out of it when I grabbed his right shoulder. Spinning him around, I yanked him back into the room and knocked him to the floor. He fell on his back, and by pinning his arms down and straddling his body with my legs, I was able to keep him from getting up.

It was like holding on to a wild animal. Alex arched his back, made violent twisting motions, and repeatedly flung his legs upward in a strenuous but futile attempt to dislodge my 135 pounds.

"Let me up," he said, drawing his lips back from his teeth.

I was panting from the exertion and gulping in breaths of air. "I'll let you up, Alex, after you tell me who's the boss. Who is it, Alex? Who's in charge here?"

"Never," he vowed. His head was quivering in rage. "I'll never say it. Never!"

"Who's the boss, Alex?"

"Let me up. I'll kill you, you fuckin' bitch. When I get my hands on you, I'm going to kill you. I swear it."

"Who's the boss, Alex?"

"Not you, that's for sure."

He tried to spit in my face, and I tightened my grip on his wrists. I felt my fingers digging into his flesh.

"You're hurting me," he cried as he renewed his efforts to free himself. "You're hurting me."

"You know something, Alex? I don't feel the slightest remorse. I'm not one bit sorry. Now tell me who's the boss?"

"No, I won't say it. I hate you! I'll use my karate on you!"

"Who's the boss, Alex?" I kept on asking the same monotonous question and I kept on getting the same steadfast refusals, threats of bloody retribution, and charges of child abuse. At the end of half an hour of this, my voice was hoarse and grating. I was beginning to tire. Then Sam came home, and when he walked into the room, Alex knew it was over.

The maniacal rigidity of his features softened and his body relaxed and became still. The cries of hatred and rage became the tearful sobs of a frightened, hurting little boy. "You're the boss," he said clearly. "You and Sam, you're the boss. You're in charge."

Afterward, after we had gotten him fed and bathed and in his pajamas, I said to him, "Now, Alex, now do you want to tell us what this is all about?"

Taking my hand, he led me to the rocking chair by the fireplace. "Will you hold me?" he asked.

"Of course," I said wondering at the tremulous fear in his voice as I sat down on the chair and gathered him close to me.

"She tried to take me. My mother. She was there on the day of the horse show, the day I won my ribbons. She—she said she wanted to take me trick-or-treating on Halloween."

Here it was again—the mother.

"She was going to take me to a cabin way in the woods," continued Alex, "where nobody'd be able to find me. She wanted to get me without being seen. But you and Sam came, so she said she'd pick me up near the lake at five o'clock on

Friday. I don't know why I went. I was afraid to go. I was afraid not to go. I took the school bus to the lake and waited, but she didn't come. It got dark and I didn't dare come home so I hid in the boat."

"You shouldn't ever be afraid to come home," said Sam.

I rocked Alex slowly back and forth and patted his shoulder comfortingly. "Sam's right," I said. "And what she did was completely illegal. It was attempted kidnapping."

Abruptly Alex jumped up and began running in circles around the room. "There's something else. She said something else!"

"What, Alex? What is it? Can you tell us?"

"No," he said crying and running faster as though to escape those unspoken words. "No, I can't. I can't say it. I can't say it."

Snatching a piece of paper and a pencil from my desk, I placed them on the coffee table. "Can you write it?" I asked, and my fears of yet another period of dangerous behavior lent great urgency to my voice. "Alex, can you write it? Can you write it down?"

Alex stopped running. His face was ashen and his eyes were squeezed almost shut. With shaking hands, he grasped the pencil and wrote across the paper. When he finished he pushed the paper away from him and ran from the room. Across the top of the sheet, printed in a childish scrawl, were the words "Things a retard mother said to do." Under this line there was a list of the following four objectives:

> BURN DOWN THE HOUSE
> POISON THE HORSES
> SABOTAGE THE VEHICLES
> BEAT PEOPLE UP

VIII

The Death Threats

Nothing in our experience had ever prepared us for coping with someone like this, someone who did not seem to have a conscience or normal boundaries. I looked out the window at the woods and fields that surrounded the barn and dared not voice my thoughts of darkness and fire and the horses. "I did what I could," I said to Sam. "I followed Ann's advice and went to the courthouse to take out a restraining order against Christine. She is to stay away from Alex wherever he may be for one year."

"It might backfire," replied Sam. "Suppose she goes out of control and tries to get revenge? She must be crazy. She's capable of anything."

My breath quickened with dawning recognition. "Oh, my God, Sam," I said. "If you and I are afraid of this woman, what in the name of heaven is Alex feeling?"

We talked about that, about Alex's fears and the conflicts he must be having. Did he believe he was a traitor because he had told on his mother? Did he believe he had betrayed us by going with her? And why had he wanted to meet Christine when he was clearly so afraid of her? This was something we could not understand. After some discussion, we came up with a plan to help Alex separate his feelings of betrayal, guilt, love, and hate. A little creative guesswork resulted in a list of five sets of first-person sentences stating opposing emotions like "I hate my mother for abusing me. I feel guilty because I hate my mother."

I instructed Alex to mark each of the sentences true or false. If I had guessed wrong and Alex marked a statement as false, no harm was done. If he marked it true, he was essentially saying, "Yes, this is a problem for me." These problems were now externalized and they were no longer a formidable, formless chaos. The elusive, frightening emotions were captured and individually caged in written words, each to wait its turn to be poked and prodded. This task would be accomplished in counseling sessions.

We once again had a therapist. When Sam and I heard that the counseling center had found a replacement for Sarah, we did have some anxious moments. Suppose the center had come up with someone who was incompetent? Our fears turned out to be groundless. The new counselor was of medium height and athletic build, and, although his wavy hair and mustache were streaked with gray, I guessed him to be in his midthirties. His casual manner and friendly smile were reassuring, but most of all it was his eyes. Dark and liquid and gently probing, they bespoke a quiet, inner strength that had nothing of arrogance or pretentiousness. Most important, as I would soon learn, he was not locked into any particular school of psychological thought or weighed down with preconceived theories. His name was Bill. Bill Conti. And he had been well chosen. By coming to the house and meeting the boy in his own territory, by working with slow and careful patience, Bill began to establish the groundwork for a relationship of consistent friendship and trust. But Alex was still uneasy about the prospect of someone getting into his mind and refused to go to Bill's office for therapy unless I promised to stay in there with him.

Contending with the conflicts triggered by Christine's attempt to kidnap him would be our first major undertaking. The true/false statements were given to Alex soon after he was forcibly restrained. The timing of this was important. It had to be done while he was feeling the effects of the restraint and was most aware of the seriousness of his behavior. If he had been allowed to recoup and hide behind a

protective wall of denial mechanisms he would not have co-
operated. He also signed a contract wherein he agreed to
choose one statement each week and talk about it in therapy.

It was not enough. At the first session Bill and I both
sensed our progress was being blocked. Something was missing. The clue to what it was came in the form of a phone call
from Ann. "You have to remember," she said during our conversation, "that part of him loves his mother. We see it every
day. No matter how abusive the parents are, the children remain bonded to them."

No! I could not hear this. I did not want to hear this.
Everything in me cried out against it. How could it be? But
deep inside, I knew that what Ann had said was true and this
was the most likely explanation for Alex's conflicting feelings. He felt guilty about hating his mother because some
part of him did love her. The declaration of his hate for Christine in the true/false statements and the verbal admissions
were words of the intellect masking the kind of hate I had
seen in his hospital room, the hate that lay buried beyond
conscious reach. Was he afraid to let himself feel this because it might destroy the small piece of love he still had for
his mother?

Bill and I talked it over, came up with what we hoped
might be a solution, and planned our strategy. Since Alex's
agreement to come to Bill's office most definitely did not include any willing involvement, this communication was often
essential to the success of the therapy. It is one thing to work
with an adult who is paying upward of fifty dollars an hour
to a professional. It is quite another to work with a belliger-
ent eleven-year-old. Although he did not trash Bill's office as
he had Sarah's, he had no intentions of cooperating while he
was there.

When we arrived for the next session, Alex emphatically
announced that he wasn't going to do any talking. Bill and I
dealt with this situation by having Alex listen while we spoke
to each other about whatever issues and concerns we had decided to tackle. I began the hour by telling Bill about a chart

Alex's teacher had hung on the classroom wall. If a student got 100 in math, a gold star was placed on the chart next to his name. Since Alex was now doing his math more slowly, he had more gold stars than anyone else.

"Nice work, Alex," said Bill, and in his voice and in his eyes there was such genuine warmth and enthusiasm that a simple compliment became a glowing approbation.

"I am so proud of him," I said.

"As well you should be," replied Bill. "It shows he has the control to go more slowly in order to achieve the real rewards."

"Exactly," I agreed. "And the other children can look at the chart and know Alex got those hundreds. The stars represent those grades. They are symbolic. You know what a symbol is, don't you, Alex? I think you had it in literature a few weeks ago."

Alex gave a short, derisive sneer to indicate his opinion of the intelligence of anybody who could doubt his knowledge of the subject. "Of course I do. It stands for something else."

"Right," I said. "The symbol you had in your book was the flag. The flag was a symbol of the country."

I took from my pocketbook the list of true/false statements and the contract Alex had signed. His features instantly chilled, and sliding down in his chair, he pulled his jacket up so that it hid his face. After reminding him of our agreement, I said, "It's really hard for you to talk about these things you have marked as true or even to listen to us talk about them, isn't it, Alex?"

A low grunt came from behind the jacket.

"Yes, and I know you tried. At the last session you did make an effort. But it seems to be difficult for you to deal with certain feelings like, for example, the hate you have for your mother, because, Alex—because part of you still loves her."

Alex's head emerged turtlelike from his jacket, and he jumped up from his chair. "No!" he objected forcefully. "No, I hate her! I wish she was dead!"

"God knows you have every right to hate her," said Bill in support and validation of Alex's feelings. "You have every right in the world. Any kid would hate someone who abused him like that. But as bad as your parents were, they did give you good genes. You're good-looking and healthy. The little part of you that loves Christine might be there for no other reason."

Alex slammed his body back into the chair and began fiddling with the dial of a radio that was on Bill's desk.

"You are a handsome boy," I added, "and those stars certainly prove you're intelligent. And you have an inner strength, a will to survive. You must have been born with it."

"A lot of kids," said Bill in a low, composed voice, "probably wouldn't have survived."

Alex stopped turning the radio dial. He was listening. He was receptive. "Alex, you've told me that you want to get better, that you want to be able to keep control," I said, reminding him of our goal. "You've already come a long way toward achieving this, but more needs to be done. Do you agree?"

Finding some encouragement in his lack of response, I pressed forward. "You know in order to get better you have to talk, and since you're having a problem with that now, what I have here might help."

I opened my pocketbook again and removed three small objects and a wooden box. It was a small box—it fit in the palm of my hand—but it was beautifully carved with intricate designs. I held the box out to Alex, and, curiosity overcoming reluctance, he took it from me and gave me a questioning look. "Alex," I said, "I also want you to take this butterfly barrette your mother left at the hospital, this piece of a picture of her that I saved, and this little stuffed heart that has the word 'love' embroidered on it. I want you to take them and put them in the box. These things represent whatever there is of love you have for your mother. They are symbolic of that love, and if you take the love and put it inside of this box, it will be safe and nothing you ever say or feel about her can hurt it or destroy it. Remember, Alex, the love will be safe and we will put it away and keep it for you until you are older."

He placed the items on his lap and carefully examined each one. He ran his fingers slowly across the carved designs on the box and lifted the tiny brass latch. I hardly dared to breathe. Suppose he said this was dumb and dashed everything to the floor?

Appearing to rouse himself from a reverie, Alex took the carved box and the iridescent-blue barrette and the picture of his mother and the little heart embroidered with the word "love" and walked a few steps to the corner of the room. He stood with his back to us, and somehow, at this moment of ceremonial separation of the most inviolable of bonds, it became a very private and shielded place. When he did turn around, his head was still bowed over the closed and latched box he held tightly clasped in both hands. As he reached out to give it to me, I could see that his face was flushed with emotion and his eyes were filled with tears.

Before we had a chance to see any results from this session, there was a terrible fear that came upon Alex. It seemed to be around him and about him like an invisible shroud, and he was powerless against it. If I touched him from behind or if he unexpectedly saw me in a room or hallway, he would leap into the air and land in a half-crouching stance as though ready to attack. He was constantly looking over his shoulder and insisted on keeping all the doors locked. He even went so far as to nail boards across some of the windows. It was like living with a robot programmed to react with a fearful response to virtually everything. He refused to tell me what was wrong and one night when Sam was out of town, that fear exploded in a violent tantrum.

It was getting past his bedtime and I was helping him pick up an assortment of colored markers he'd been using for a homework project when I heard a whistling sound of breath being quickly sucked in. I lifted my head to see that awful blackness in his eyes. He sprang away from the table, grabbed a wooden chair, and hit it against the wall until two of the legs were broken.

I could see no apparent reason for this destruction. Alex had been with us for fifteen months now, and such behavior was completely unacceptable. Shouting angrily, I ordered him to his room, and his bewildered denials of any wrongdoing only served to increase my displeasure.

The next afternoon, I was waiting for Ann. She had made an appointment to come out to the house for her regular monthly visit. Many state social workers did not contact clients once they were contracted to a private agency. But Ann, much to the annoyance of the agency, insisted on it. I often thought how lucky we were to have her support and involvement. She was an extraordinary woman who was somehow able to combine sincere caring with a sharp professionalism.

During her last visit, she had asked Sam and me if we would consider taking custody of Alex on a permanent basis. All efforts to return the child to George and Sandra had been halted, and Ann said she would like to see him stay with us. We told her we would think about it. And we did. We thought about it. We talked about it, up and down, back and forth. Doubts. Worries. Questions. We could. We couldn't. Yes. No. We were growing very attached to Alex, and he to us, but what about these spells he had? Would he get better? Would he get worse? I would have to tell Ann that we were not ready to make a decision. I took the chair he had broken and placed it in a corner of the dining room with its jagged stumps in full view.

She came a few minutes later. Giving me a hug, she ran her hand through her blond chrysanthemum-cut hair and sat down at the dining-room table. "How are things? How's Alex?" she asked as she slid her arms out of her coat and draped it behind her. She was wearing trimly tailored brown slacks and a flowered blouse and was attractive in a soft, natural way.

Ann followed my eyes to the broken chair in the corner. "Alex?"

"Yes," I said, pouring tea into my favorite rose-decorated china cups. "He's been very fearful. Really jumpy and nervous. Sam's been gone for a few days—he's worse if Sam's not here—and last night he just went berserk."

There was a sudden gravity behind Ann's eyes. "Oh, how awful!" she exclaimed. Before I could say anything else, she introduced the subject of Donna, one of Alex's half sisters. "You remember I told you she had been adopted but she was so badly damaged it didn't work out. The family was forced to return her to state custody."

I stirred sugar into my tea. "I remember."

"Donna is fifteen now, and the group home she was in just informed me she has run away."

I heard a half-stifled cry and turned to see Alex standing in the doorway to the kitchen. His hands were clapped over his mouth and his eyes were bulging with terror.

Immediately surmising the truth, Ann said in a resolute voice that was more statement of fact than inquiry, "Alex, has your sister contacted you? Has she called you?"

"No, no!" yelled Alex, running into the kitchen, where he could no longer see us but could hear what was said.

"You must be very frightened," continued Ann, her tone sympathetic but firm. "I know you must feel scared, but I think Donna has something to do with what's been going on. The people at the group home told me she had been making unauthorized toll calls before she left."

"Oh, my God, Ann," I said, setting my cup down so suddenly that some of the tea sloshed over into the saucer. "That's it! That's got to be it. For almost two weeks we've been getting these silent phone calls. She must have been calling for Alex, and if Sam or I answered, she hung up."

As Ann took a sip of tea and thoughtfully considered this, Alex dashed into the room, hurled a crumpled ball of paper on the table, and disappeared into his bedroom. Smoothing the paper out, we read the three words that were printed in small letters across the page:

Yes She Call

We could not get anything more out of him. He hid underneath his bed and would not speak to me or say good-bye to Ann.

When Sam returned home, I showed him the note Alex had written and filled him in on what had happened. "It's Christine," he said in a flash of anger. "How much do you want to bet? It's that goddam Christine who put the sister up to this! First she tries to kidnap him, and now . . . Where is he?"

"Under his bed. He won't come out."

Sam went to the door of Alex's room. "Alex, we aren't going to hurt you and we aren't going to let anybody else hurt you. So get out from under that bed."

Alex got out from under the bed.

"Okay," said Sam, and motioning toward the kitchen, "Go in there and sit down and you tell us what has been going on around here!"

Alex was still too upset to obey Sam's orders completely, and instead of going into the kitchen, he ran into the dining room. But as he reached the table, he stopped and turned to face us. "She called. My sister—she called about five or six times," he said in an agitated manner. His features, twisted in agony, betrayed the immense difficulty of what he was to tell us. "She said she was going to kill me. She said she knew where I lived and she was watching me. She was watching the house. She had a gun. She said I had to leave here and if I didn't leave, she was going to kill me, and—" He leaned on the table as if to gather the strength to continue. "She said she was going to kill both of you."

Sam swore under his breath. He struggled to gain composure. "Alex, listen to me. Nothing is going to happen to you.

And tomorrow morning I am calling the phone company and ordering a different number. It will be unlisted. They won't be able to get it. I can guarantee you they will not threaten you or us by telephone again. If you had told us about the calls when they first began, we could have had a trap put on the phone and pressed charges against this girl. You have to learn that you can trust us to keep you safe."

Trust. This was the most basic, most pervasive of issues, one we would go back to again and again. It was becoming clearly evident that during Alex's early childhood, his safety had been in constant jeopardy. Harm could have come to him from any quarter, for any reason. Or for no reason.

Sam was true to his word, and the threats were promptly stopped. Alex was once more feeling safe. As the holidays came upon us, he was making good progress in therapy. The symbolic putting away of any love he had for Christine proved to be another major turning point, and although he seldom contributed more than an occasional but significant yes while we were in the office, he was far more open and receptive to what Bill and I had to say to each other.

The results of the sessions came later. He carried the threads of our discourse out of the room with him, and, either in the privacy of the car or at home, he would throw himself into my arms and sobbingly admit the excruciatingly painful truths. I don't think we were really aware of it at the time, but for him to be able to reach into the core of his suffering and experience his emotions like this was ultimately every bit as necessary to his recovery as the talking. After Alex gave his consent, I would share these revelations with Bill, we would plan our strategy, and the new material would be brought into the next session. And so it went. Week after week, we related past to present to form a continual and healing cycle of pain and release.

Our second Christmas with Alex was a far happier occasion than the first. As a member of our church youth group, he was participating in the traditional candlelight service. At eleven o'clock on Christmas Eve, Sam and I, along with a few hundred other townspeople, braved the cold, wintry weather to go to the church. We took our seats in one of the narrow, horsehair-cushioned pews, and we sang the carols, and we listened to the young people tell the story of the Christ Child's birth and to the minister speaking from the green-garlanded pulpit. "We rejoice," he said. "We rejoice this night in the unquenchable and eternal light that lighteth every person that cometh into the world. We seek thy presence here, O Thou Most High, in the ways of all our doings until every child shall be brought out of darkness into thy marvelous light."

While the organist played "O Come, All Ye Faithful," Alex and a girl named Linda, the two children chosen to be the candlelighters, marched with a slow and measured pace down the center aisle. When they passed by us, I commented to my husband on how angelic Alex looked in his long, wine-colored robe with the white collar.

"Yeah," said Sam in a tone of dry cynicism that indicated a certain lack of agreement with my observation.

On reaching the end of the aisle, each child took a tall white candle and stood before the pulpit to wait in the hushed silence. The overhead lights became dimmer and dimmer until all that could be seen was the tiny flames of those two candles. The silence deepened, and the minister spoke again. "In this, the darkest season of the year, let there be light." As his voice faded, the congregation rose and, in customary and orderly fashion, began to bring their candles to Alex and Linda.

We were among the last to go, and I looked about me to see that those who had already lit their candles were standing in a large circle around the inside of the church and the church was filled with the glowing radiance and soft, wavering shadows of the candlelight. Step by step, we made our way toward the candlelighters to take part in this time-honored ritual.

Then it was my turn, and I paused before Alex to tilt my

candle into the flame he held out to me. His eyes, full of love and wonder and newly vulnerable, were riveted to mine, and that one brief moment, illumined by the flickering light of a Christmas candle, became crystallized in my memory. It was a moment I would come back to many times during the years ahead. It was hope and it was promise and it was my light in a deeper darkness.

After the holidays, in January 1986, I planned to take Alex on a trip to Washington, D.C. This trip was apparently a precipitating factor for some very disturbing behavior. A few days before our scheduled departure, he began to exhibit the obnoxious acting out that was associated with stress. I knew this was the prelude to painful disclosures of still more abuse, and there was nothing I could do but wait it out and see what developed. By late afternoon, I heard the cries coming from his room. I ran in to find Alex sitting cross-legged on the floor. His head was tilted slightly upward, his mouth was wide open, and his eyes were squeezed tightly shut. The cries were sharp and high-pitched and in such rapid sequence that he was gulping for air in an attempt to catch his breath. It was a scene of absolute panic.

"Alex, what's wrong? What's the matter?" I said, kneeling down beside him and putting my hands on his shoulders. My voice caught his attention, and he opened his eyes wide enough to see me, but he did not know who I was. There was no sign of recognition. I could have been a total stranger. Cringing at my touch, he pulled away from me, and the screams took on a new dimension of terror.

Puzzled and confused, I stood back. I remembered that other spell when he had gone into a trancelike state and seemed to be able to see his stepfather and tell him how much he hated him. Although there were certain similarities, this incident was much longer and more intense. As the screaming subsided into occasional hiccuping sobs, Alex fell forward with his knees tucked under him and his forehead against the floor. I tried once again to comfort him. This time he knew who I was. "Oh, Carole," he said, clinging to me. "It was so awful."

"What, Alex? What happened?"

"I was sitting on a sidewalk. It was in front of a store and there was grass growing out of the cracks in the cement. There was green paint that was all peeling and cracked on the storefront. A girl was in a car with a man. The car was red and it was parked in front of the store. The girl drove off with the man and left me. She left me there on the sidewalk."

"A girl?"

"My mother. The girl was my mother. She just left me on that sidewalk. And that's what I'm afraid you're going to do. Whenever you take me somewhere, I'm afraid you'll leave me." Convulsed in tears, Alex buried his head in my shoulder. "I'm—I'm afraid you'll leave me in Washington!"

We did not yet have a label for this odd occurrence. If the words "flashback" and "dissociation" were being used in connection with the effects of child abuse, we were not aware of it. I had a vague and imperfect realization that Alex had somehow gone back to a very early preverbal stage and had actually relived a traumatizing abandonment, but what it was and what it meant was lost in the frightening helplessness of the experience.

IX

Sacrifice Any Child

In May 1986, Alex passed the rigorous test of mind and body to earn his blue belt in karate. Along with the karate, he continued to play baseball with his Little League team. As far as I was concerned, being a spectator at these games was about as exciting as watching grass grow. Sam, on the other hand, thoroughly enjoyed them. Alex didn't hit the ball often, but when he did, it usually resulted in a home run. "I make believe the ball is Christine's head," he confided to me. "That's how I hit it so far." At the end of the season, the coaches picked the best players from each team for the All-Stars. Sam was the first to get the news Alex had been chosen. It was hard to tell which of the two was the more excited over this achievement.

Alex's relative stability over these past months was so encouraging that we told Ann we were prepared to begin the adoption process. Alex was overjoyed by our decision, but we immediately encountered opposition from the agency. First, Peter gave me a "poor to mediocre" job performance evaluation. On top of that, when I met with a director of the agency to voice my objections, he indicated his concern that I might cause him trouble by complaining to Ann about the evaluation, and then he made a threatening and ruthless statement. After explaining how the contract between the Department of Social Services and the agency gave him the right to take Alex from us and put him in another home, he actually said, "I will not hesitate to sacrifice any employee of this agency. Or any child!"

Within a week of our resolve to become Alex's parents, he began acting strangely. He was attempting to press himself against me and kiss me on the lips. He even took flowers from a bowl on the dining-room table and tried to put them in my hair. Once again I had a weird feeling of being in a time warp, of having been there before. I remembered a four-year-old boy's hugs and kisses, and I could hear him saying, "I love you, Mommy. I want to marry you when I grow up." Alex was caught in the throes of a full-blown Oedipal stage!

His overtly sexualized actions put me into a panic. He was not four years old. He was almost twelve. Neither Bill nor his supervisor had ever dealt with anything like this, and they could not tell me what to do. "Go with your instincts," Sarah had said, so I did, and I knew what I could not do was to reject Alex. I could not push him away and say, "No, stop it. Stay back!" Holding and hugging were a necessary part of our daily routine, and, Oedipal stage or not, he still needed an inordinate amount of affection. I also sensed this was a vital developmental phase, and although I had to be careful not to facilitate any sexual acting out, it was very important for Alex to be allowed to experience it as normally as possible. I did the best I could with an uncomfortable situation. I held him a few inches from me when he came for a hug and I moved my head so his kisses fell on my cheek.

We took the problem to Bill to see if we could help Alex understand what was happening to him. He still insisted that I accompany him to these sessions. It would be many years before he would be able to go in alone to face the terrifying thought of anyone getting into his mind. I was his safety and security, and sometimes even that wasn't enough.

In an attempt to normalize Alex's sexual feelings, Bill explained how every boy has a stage at about four or five years of age when he thinks he wants to marry his mother. "The difference is," he continued, "when you were that age something kept you from going through the phase the way you should have. I can remember feeling like that about my mother when I was a little boy. These feelings go underground into the unconscious and stay there until a boy gets older, until he is ready to have them for a girlfriend or wife."

Alex looked at him with revulsion and moved his chair as far away as he could. His eyes bulged and his features grew taut. Making a choking sound, he jumped up and rushed from the room.

Bill caught and held my glance. "I think," he said knowingly, "we have just hit a nerve."

So it was in this state of tinderbox explosiveness that Alex went into the Fourth of July weekend. He had been impossibly outrageous all week, and by Thursday, the second day of July, he was out of control. "Call Ann," he insisted. "Call Ann and tell her to get me out of here. I want to leave!" And with a fiendish laugh, he went on a rampage, smashing furniture, throwing potted plants off the porch, and terrorizing the horses by hurling rocks at them.

There was nothing I could do. I couldn't reason with him. He was too irrational. I couldn't reach Sam. There was no phone where he was working. I couldn't go there to get him. Sam had one set of keys to my car and Alex had the other. He had snatched them from the kitchen counter as he ran out of the house. And if I called the police, he would only hide out in the woods until they left. In the end, I locked the doors and the windows and stayed inside.

I heard the dull thud of rocks hitting the side of the barn. Then there was silence. Dead silence. What was he doing? What was he up to? A scrambling and thumping on the roof soon answered my question, and I pulled apart the living-room drapes to see him straddling the peak of the roof at one end of the house. He had a baseball bat in his hands and he was shouting obscenities at the sky. For the next hour, there was a banging on the roof, and when it was over, I saw his face pressed close against the outside of the window, leering at me with that ugly, mirthless smile and taunting eyes.

In desperation, with little hope he could actually help, I went to the phone and called Bill. My hand shook as I dialed the number, and my voice trembled as I described the events of the morning. "Right now," I added, "he's down in the basement. It sounds like he's using his bat on the furnace and water heater."

"It seems like he's going to escalate this behavior," said Bill, "until he forces you to do something. I don't see that you have any choice but to bring him in to the agency."

I called Cheryl. The line was busy. I dared not wait. The noise from downstairs was becoming increasingly louder. Hurriedly throwing some of Alex's clothes in a suitcase, I told him he was leaving. Since it was what he said he wanted, he gave me back the keys and agreed to get in the car and come with me.

All the way to the office, Alex's manner was one of calculated control, and his attitude toward me was distant and cold—almost as cold as the reception I received from Cheryl when I arrived at the agency. "You should have called first," she said haughtily.

Feeling suddenly ill at ease, I compared my tear-stained, disheveled appearance to Cheryl's impeccable dress and beautifully coiffed hair. "I couldn't get through," I said. "I need a respite. It's an emergency. He's running wild, destroying property, and terrorizing the horses. I feel like I'm being held hostage in my own home!"

"I'm sorry," said Cheryl in a tone that indicated quite the opposite. "Although we certainly do have emergency respite, I don't think this quite qualifies as an emergency. You can't use respite as a solution to every little problem. You are expected to deal with them yourself."

I couldn't believe what I was hearing. "But Cheryl, Bill Conti, our therapist, said I should bring him in."

Cheryl raised her perfectly arched eyebrows and examined

her long, polished nails. "That does not justify bringing a client into this office without permission from your clinical coordinator."

"Peter?" I said in amazement. "He's on vacation. How can I talk to him?"

Realizing there would be no respite, I walked out of the office and brought Alex back home with me.

My husband was not one to be easily upset. But this did it. When he heard what had happened, he was outraged. Pacing rapidly from one side of the living room to the other, he paused long enough to wave the agency manual under my nose. "This whole thing is nothing but a goddam crock," he said. "There's paragraph after paragraph in here that tells about how stressful this job is and how they have all this support and assistance and encouragement for you. You never would have taken the job in the first place if you hadn't been assured this help would be there if you needed it. Listen to this: 'Our foster parents have complete access to a staff of psychiatrists, psychologists, and psychiatric social workers. These people are on call twenty-four hours a day, every day, to give help and assistance in crisis situations.' Where are these people? And this. 'Living with these children can be emotionally draining, as it involves constant pressure.' They've sure got that right! 'Our program,' " continued Sam with bitter sarcasm, " 'includes respite care that can relieve these pressures.' What respite? This thing isn't worth the paper it's written on."

Sam was forced to stay home from work to help me with Alex. The boy seemed to be trapped in a turbulent whirlpool of frenzied emotions and conflicting needs. It was as if he were in the grip of a compelling obsession that forced him to do and say terrible things. Even though I knew his anger was for them and his acting out was because of what they had done to him, each hate-filled word was a piercing wound, a knife slash to the heart.

I can't say that there weren't moments when both Sam and I were tempted to give up, but we knew from past experience that Alex's spells were temporary and we strongly believed that the respite, if we ever got it, would alleviate the problem.

In the end, it was Ann who found us the respite we so sorely needed. She placed Alex in a DSS foster home, and on the day after the placement, her supervisor called Peter and me to a meeting at her office. While we waited for this meeting to begin, Peter told me he thought Alex's recent problems might be related to the transition to permanent custody. "It's unfortunate that we have no experience in helping people with this," he said.

I stared intently at the short, balding man leaning against a desk several feet away. Was this Peter talking? Was he actually admitting to me there was anything about the agency that was less than perfect?

"It could be," I acknowledged. "Or it may be the Oedipal thing. It's just so painful. It's impossible to remain clinically cool and detached." I closed my eyes against the sudden tears. "That is my child out there, Peter. It hurts."

"Yes, it does," he said, coming over to me and patting me on the shoulder.

When the meeting began, the DSS supervisor asked me why Alex was not presently in my home, and still distraught, I recounted the trauma of the past week. Appalled by what she heard, she riveted Peter with an unyielding stare and asked in a frigid tone, "Do you mean to tell me that your agency does not have emergency respite?"

I was prepared to hear the usual line, complete with coverups and stonewalling. It didn't happen. Peter's eyes rested on me for a moment, and in a clear, steady voice, he said, "No, we do not have emergency respite."

This was not the Peter I knew. This was not the critical, rigid, fearful man with the unfeeling, blank eyes and monotone speech I had been working with for most of the past two years. I do think I was at last seeing the real Peter. He was a decent, caring person who had allowed himself to be manip-

ulated into doing the bidding of people with a simplistic and
naive approach to serious and complex problems.

I also believe he finally realized the agency was making
him into someone he did not like very much. Peter's honesty
at the DSS meeting ended up costing him his job, and for his
own sake, I was glad he was leaving. I wished him well. The
empathy and understanding he gave me that day were the
first I'd ever really gotten from anyone in the organization.
And it was the last.

The condemning, harassing phone calls began on Tuesday. "Alex is a client," insisted Cheryl, "and has to be treated
as such. We can't allow emotional involvement to interfere
with case management. We have nothing to do with emotional involvement. Our people do not become emotionally
involved. You are a professional!"

I was confused. "How can you say this?" I asked. "It
doesn't make any sense. How is it possible to have a child for
two years and want to keep him, in spite of the many difficulties, without having any love for him? How can we want
to keep him without becoming emotionally involved? If this
causes your agency some inconvenience, isn't it worth it to
have a permanent, loving home for Alex? Isn't that, after all,
the long-term goal?"

We would soon discover the answer to my last question,
as incredible as it seems, was a resounding no.

Three days later I received a letter from the agency telling
me I had been placed on three months' probation. The
charges included poor communication with supervisors and
inappropriate clinical decisions. I was accused of never having asked for help, and my emotional involvement and
request for respite were treated as unforgivable crimes. A
final note stated I would not be allowed to talk to Bill about
any problems.

Sam laughed as he read the letter. "Look," he said, "they
spelled 'inappropriate' wrong. Ignore it. It's a joke! They
screwed up and they're trying to use some sneaky bureau-

cratic maneuver to shift the blame. They even admit right here in paragraph two that, no matter what has happened, you're supposed to put on a good act for funding agencies. The problem is that you didn't tell a bunch of lies to DSS to cover up for them."

I wished I possessed Sam's wonderful strength and self-confidence, but I didn't. The sensitivity that had played such a crucial part in my work with Alex now became a double-edged sword. I was devastated. I felt as if I were being plunged into a world of negative images where white was black and good was bad and right was wrong. It was a world where people said I didn't say what I said or do what I did, and whether I did it or not, it would be used against me. I felt they were trying to drive me crazy.

After Bill had worked with Alex and it was decided he was stable enough to be returned home, my new supervisor paid me a visit. Peter's replacement was a big-boned woman with curly, blond hair and chiseled, angular features. Her name was Laura Jordan, and she listened to my accounts of Alex's latest achievements with an enthusiasm that was a welcome change from Peter's deadpan noninteraction. We experienced an impassioned exchange of views and a sharing of common feministic interests. It pleased me to find she was intelligent, receptive, and sympathetic. Halfway through the meeting, however, I began to suspect Laura Jordan was not what she seemed.

Taking a compulsive drag on the cigarette she held between her fingers, she leveled her eyes calmly on me and said, "Why do you want to keep this baby? At your age, you and Sam should be enjoying yourselves. Do you really want to put such an unfair burden on your husband?"

I felt a sudden tenseness and shifted my weight uneasily in my chair. Why was she talking like this? I wondered. What was going on?

Laura flicked her cigarette into the ashtray I had set before her, took a gulp of black coffee, and continued questioning me pointedly. "Why do you want to go through with it? It's a big step, a big responsibility. Why do you want to be tied down to a child like Alex, a child who is so much trouble?"

I tried to convince Sam and myself that Laura only wanted us to know exactly what we were doing. "She wants us to be sure," I said.

"Bull!" said Sam. "I've figured it out. I know what's behind all this crap. The agency just signed a new contract for Alex with DSS. Right?"

"So?"

"If Alex is in state custody, the contract runs for two years. Think about it, Carole. The only way they can hold on to the contract and the bundle of money going with it is to screw up our plans to keep Alex. Or to get rid of us so he will have to stay in the agency. That's why they get so teed off when Ann interferes. I don't know why any of this should come as a surprise," he added when I expressed disbelief they could do such a thing. "Remember what you told me that guy said at that meeting you had with him?"

"Sacrifice any child," I said slowly. "He meant it, didn't he, Sam? He really meant it." I pressed my hands against my stomach to ease the feeling of cold weight that had settled there like a block of ice.

Throughout the month of September and into October, working under the black cloud of probation was a tremendous strain. On the last day of this trial, Laura arrived at the house to meet with Sam and me. She was all smiles as she sat down at the dining-room table to exchange pleasantries over freshly brewed cups of coffee. "How are you feeling?" she asked.

"I feel a whole lot better now the probation is over, but Laura, we've been thinking, been talking about it. I can't deal with this anymore. We want Alex back in DSS until we have custody."

"I'm sorry," she said. "You can't do that. Suppose something happened after he left. We could be responsible. They could say he should have been kept as a client. If you are sure you really want to keep the boy, maybe I can help. I could give you counseling."

The very thought of putting such a fox into the henhouse frightened me even more. "No. I want Alex under the jurisdiction of DSS."

Laura paled and gave me a thin, tight-lipped smile. "You can't. You can't do it. We have a contract. And besides, Alex has to stay in the agency because he still needs the services we provide."

"Services!" I cried out in resentment and indignation. "What services? You don't have respite. You can't help me through this transitional period because you don't allow for emotional involvement. In fact, all you do is put me under so much stress that it's a wonder Alex hasn't blown right out of here."

Laura replied that she didn't want that to happen and went on to deny she was the cause of my stress. While she was trying to persuade me to allow her to help me with this problem, Sam came into the room and stood over by the hutch. I glanced apprehensively at him while Laura pushed aside her cup, picked up her briefcase, and opened it. "Oh, there's one more thing I have on my agenda. Believe me, it's the least important." These words were delivered in a nonchalant, off-hand manner and gave no hint or clue to what was to follow. "I've extended your probation until December first."

"What?" I said, jolted by the impact of this wholly unexpected turn of events. And then, as the full effect of Laura's announcement hit me, I slammed down my cup onto the dining table with such force it shattered to pieces. "No!" I shouted, backing away from the formally printed notice of disciplinary action she held out to me. "No, I quit! I'm through!"

"Think of what you are doing," warned Laura. "Think of Alex. If you quit, he would have to leave."

I was crying now. "How can you do this?"

"Because you're not in control," she answered coolly.

I looked at the broken cup and at the coffee that had

splashed on the tablecloth and the floor, and I felt the tears streaming down my face. How could I have been so stupid? I had walked straight into her trap. She was right. I was not in control.

"She'll take Alex," I said to Sam.

"Yes," agreed Laura. "I can take Alex as soon as he gets home from school. But I'll give you a few hours."

"You're not taking Alex anywhere," said Sam. "Carole, get hold of Ann."

"I'll pick him up at five o'clock," said Laura. "Have him packed and ready."

"You get out of here!" Sam thundered. "Get out of here before I throw you out. Get off my property!"

He advanced menacingly toward her, his head lowered and his brows knit in a threatening scowl. Fear replaced the gleam of triumph in Laura's eyes as she retreated hastily toward the door, let herself out, and hurried to her car.

Ann was gone for the day, so we left a message for her supervisor and made preparations to hide Alex rather than surrender him to the tender mercies of Laura. At four o'clock the phone rang. It was the DSS area director. Alex was not going anywhere. Alex was to stay with us. What they did or how they did it, I don't know, but the next day, with a touch of a key on a computer, he was no longer an agency client.

X

Flashbacks

It was during the afternoon on the last day of that October.
I knew something was wrong. It was quiet. Too quiet. The
heavy, dead silence was inconsistent with the presence of an
active boy like Alex. Where was he? What was he doing?
I went through the rooms of the house. They were empty. I
looked out the front door and walked down the hill. As
I approached the barn, I heard a rustling sound coming from
around the back. I turned the corner of the building. In the
bright sunlight, on a pile of dry leaves, a sickening scene
met my eyes. Alex had a large, squirming frog in one hand
and a razor knife in the other. On the ground nearby were
the scattered remains of several other frogs. Far too horrified
to notice that they had been carefully dissected with a surgi-
cal precision, I let out a sharp cry.

Releasing the frog unharmed, Alex jumped up and ran to
the edge of the woods. "Please, don't tell Sam! Please!" he
begged desperately. "I'll kill myself. I swear, I'll kill myself
if you tell Sam."

"Come with me!" I ordered. "You're going to see Bill."

"Don't tell him either. I won't go if you do."

"I won't tell," I lied. "Just get in the car." I had to get him
to Bill any way I could. Whatever was going on, it was something I couldn't even begin to comprehend.

At the counseling center, Alex did talk about what he had
done. He said that while it was happening, he felt dead inside
and it was like watching someone else. Bill had some con-

cerns about the suicide threats and tried to make him feel better by telling him he wasn't alone and it wasn't unusual for children who have been cruelly treated to treat animals the same way.

At the end of the session, Bill sent Alex outside, and his eyes held a melancholy sadness as he informed me that the mutilation could be an indication of sexual abuse. This was no astonishing revelation. It was the unthinkable and dreaded knowledge that had been nudging against my thoughts in the early morning hours before I could waken up enough to gather my protective resources and seal out the growing suspicions. There was his terror of taking off his clothes when he first came. There was the Angry Book session: "You suck, Bert! I hate you! He did something to me. Nobody's going to know!" And his fear of the doctor when I told him they would anesthetize him to put on the cast: "He'll stick things in me!" And most of all, there was the bleeding. It would go away but it always came back.

I did not want to think of the cause, and for a while I did not have to. In spite of the growing evidence, sexual abuse was still in the realm of conjecture and supposition, because Alex could not remember. At one point, Bill came right out and asked him about it. Alex rested his chin on his hands, and with furrowed brow and half-closed eyes, he made a futile effort to recall what had happened to him. "Would you tell us if you did remember?" asked Bill.

"Yes," replied Alex in a voice so forthright we could not doubt his sincerity. We did not mention the matter again. That was an end to it for now.

If anything positive came of the affair with the frogs, it was a reinforcement of Alex's sense of security as he became more aware of the essentially unconditional nature of our love for him. During the past Oedipal crisis, I had come to realize that my feelings, like those of most mothers, were not dependent upon his behavior. Parents do not normally stop loving a child because he has problems. This was an important factor in his healing. No matter what awful things he had been forced to do or had been done to him, he would not be rejected. Although Sam wasn't one to talk about such matters, his reaction was similar to my own. In fact, some time later, when Alex discovered I had immediately told Sam about what had happened, his astonished reaction was, "You mean he knew and he still treated me the same? He still treated me the same?"

In every other way, Alex appeared to be thriving. His riding skills were coming along so well that I allowed him to compete with Blaze, a gelding I had recently purchased. Blaze was a talented young horse, and the pair won a championship at their first show. The trophy, a shining silver plate, was placed on the mantel over the fireplace for all to admire, and the tricolor ribbon was hung on a nearby wall. These were soon joined by other trophies and ribbons and they made a colorful display.

In karate, he was preparing for his green-belt test, but in a surprising turn of events, he announced he wanted to give up his lessons. I could not believe my ears when he said he wanted to take ballet instead. It seemed that he had watched a football game on television in which a player named Willie Gault made a fantastic game-winning leap. Willie Gault was also a ballet dancer, and since Alex had an absolute passion for football, he wanted ballet lessons.

My mind balked at an attempt to reconcile the macho, feral child of a few months ago with the world of ballet, but I said yes anyway and promptly enrolled Alex in Miss Delia's School of Dance. It was Miss Delia's ballet company that had put on the production of *The Nutcracker* we had attended two years ago. She was somewhere in the vicinity of seventy years of age and was a stickler for old-fashioned deportment. Along with the dancing lessons, students were taught the manners and decorum of well-bred young ladies and gentlemen, and they were expected to carry themselves with pride. "Walk like you are somebody!" she directed emphatically. "Head high, back straight. Show the world that you are special. Walk like you are somebody."

"Miss Delia," observed Alex with the kind of reverent awe he had previously reserved for his black-belt karate instructors, "is really tough."

The following spring, in as festive a ceremony as Ann could manage, complete with beribboned roses, picture-taking, and presents, we went to the county courthouse to finalize the adoption. "Can I call you Mom?" Alex asked me when it was over.

"Of course," I said. "Of course you can." And he did, and it felt like the most natural thing in the world. Soon after that, Sam became Dad.

All of this, all of these esteem-enhancing, ego-strengthening events, coupled with the knowledge he was safe and secure and loved, created a fertile ground for those strange occurrences we now knew to be flashbacks. It was as though a voice inside of him were saying, "It's okay. You are older and stronger. You are no longer a helpless child. You are ready to survive it." Through observing a number of such spells, I learned there was almost always one other precondition. There was a triggering factor that initiated the process. This could be an incident in some way similar to the original, or it could be a date, an anniversary of the abuse.

As far as Alex was concerned, the flashbacks had nothing to do with remembering or reliving a trauma. For Alex, these things had never happened, and he was experiencing the images and feelings for the first time. The episodes he had not yet experienced were in the future even though they had actually taken place years ago. During integration, or the process of coming into his conscious mind, they would become the present. Only after integration would they become the past and a part of normal memory. Knowing all this did not make it any easier. To watch Alex lose his identity, to stand by and helplessly watch him suffer, was very frightening.

A fight in school proved to be the triggering factor for the first of the June flashbacks. Alex had been roughhousing with another boy and had gotten caught in a headlock that momentarily cut off his breath. His angry reaction was far out of proportion to the reality of the situation, and he was suspended for two days. On the second day of the suspension, I heard strange, guttural sounds coming from his room. I went in and found him sitting on the floor. With a hand gripping each leg of a pair of my nylon stockings, he ripped them in half and cast them aside. Tumbling backward, he struggled as if to free himself from some unseen force. At the sight of his beet-red face and terror-stricken eyes, fearful questions ran through my mind. Should I attempt the Heimlich maneuver? Should I call for help? He began to gag, and his movements became more violent. Suddenly, his arms and legs fell limp against the brown shag rug and he lay quietly. The rise and fall of his chest told me he was breathing, but he did not answer when I called his name and appeared to be in a deep sleep.

Four or five minutes passed before he awakened. Staring at me as if surprised to see me, he said, "I couldn't breathe. It was awful. I couldn't breathe."

"What happened, Alex? I was so worried. I thought you were choking. Are you sure you're all right?"

"My father—George brought home a blue-eyed, blonde woman," he said in a tone of earnest indignation. "Sandra, my stepmother, was out shopping, and they went in the bedroom"—here he faltered and dropped his eyes—"to do you-know-what," he finished wryly. "I got mad and I called him a name and threatened to tell on him. He grabbed some nylons and stuffed them down my throat and he swore he would kill me. I couldn't breathe. I saw stars and I guess I passed out." Snatching up the mangled remnants of my nylons, he threw them as far as he could. "I hate them! I hate it when you wear them. I always want to tear them up. I hate them!"

This particular flashback opened up a whole Pandora's box of disclosures that were as painful to me as they were to him. "Sandra would hold me down on the bed while George beat me," he said. "I hurt so much I couldn't sit down in school. The teacher thought I was being bad. She didn't know I really couldn't."

"Why didn't you tell them? Oh, my God, Alex, why didn't you tell?"

"Some of it, like what he did to me with the nylons, I didn't know. Not until the flashback."

"What about the beatings?"

"I couldn't tell. I was afraid he would kill me. Even now. When I wait for the school bus, if a van goes by, I'm afraid it's him. I think he would have killed me if it wasn't for Ann. She came and took me away when the school nurse pulled my pants down and saw the marks. Ann saved my life. Mom, why do you think I broke my leg?"

"What are you talking about?"

"My leg. Christmas Eve. The night before I was supposed to go back there."

"Oh, Alex! You mean it wasn't an accident?"

"It wasn't an accident. It was the only way I knew how to get out of going. I couldn't just say I didn't want to go because I thought he would get revenge on me." Alex closed his eyes, and tears crowded against the sealed lids to trickle unheeded down his cheeks and the sides of his nostrils. "And another thing is I was ashamed."

"Ashamed?"

"Yes. I always thought they treated me like that because there was something wrong with me. If I told what they did, everyone would know about me."

Then there were the bullets. A friend of Sam's was buying a house and needed to temporarily store some of his possessions in our barn. Alex knew he wasn't supposed to get into this stuff, but nevertheless he did. He found a box of shotgun shells and proceeded to run about the yard, whipping them in every direction. "He threw bullets at me," he shouted in a frenzied outcry. "That's what he used to do. He threw bullets at me. He threw bullets at me!"

Sam and I stood by until Alex had exhausted both himself and his supply of bullets. I could see my husband was angry.

"Why did you take the bullets?" he asked when we'd gotten him inside of the house.

Alex's eyes glittered with a malignant hatred and his voice was racked with despair. He was on the couch in the living room, and he accentuated his words by beating against the pillows. "George threw bullets at me every time he got mad. He picked them up in his hands and he threw them at me. And Sandra. And Georgie. He threw bullets at them. Sandra would hold Georgie and use him for a shield. At night I used to wake up and find him standing over me with a gun pointing at my head."

Sam shut his eyes and pressed his lips together, and I could see how hard this was for him. I thought of the night he had asked me if I could handle hearing what had happened to Alex. But it was Sam who couldn't bear to know these things and sometimes tried to protect his feelings with the question "How do you know he's telling the truth?"

It was difficult to explain this to my husband, but to witness a flashback was so close to watching the actual event that I could not doubt it had occurred. Alex was not a delusional schizophrenic or psychotic, and I could not believe these spells were some kind of act.

I turned my attention back to Alex. He was still talking about the gun. "George had a funny smile on his face," he said, and here he broke into uncontrollable sobbing and buried his head in the pillows. "I never knew when I went to bed at night," he cried, "I never knew if I would be alive in the morning."

> Now I lay me down to sleep
> And pray the Lord my soul to keep.
> If I should die before I wake,
> I pray the Lord my soul to take.

The old children's prayer went through my mind, and I remembered how I had hated being forced to say it every night. I remembered how I had hated going to sleep thinking I might not wake up in the morning. But there was no time to dwell on how much worse it must have been for Alex, because the tale of the bullets paled in comparison with what was to follow.

It was on the next day. Again he was on the couch. He was squirming restlessly about and no position seemed to give him any comfort for more than a few seconds. His face had the appearance of being swollen, although he had not been crying.

I looked away from him and stared out of the window. The summer sun, coming through the leaves of the oak tree, punctuated the shade with scalloped patches of light. There was no breeze. Except for a flash of bright orange as an oriole flew from limb to limb, everything was still. "What's the matter?" I said.

"Do you remember I told you about my dog, Spunky?"

"Yes, I do. You said you really loved him and that they gave him away."

"They didn't give him away."

My eyes scanned the treetops as I tried to get another glimpse of the oriole. I could hear his rich, trilling song but I could not see him.

"George was drunk. He had these huge firecrackers like little sticks of dynamite. He took Spunky and locked him in a box with the firecrackers. There was a long fuse and he lit it and blew up the box. Spunky was all bloody on top and black on the bottom. He was dead."

Shock. Outrage. Questions. In that order. How could these things have happened? How could this abuse have been allowed to continue on weekends while Alex was in state custody and under the care and protection of a state-sanctioned institution? I was not angry at Ann. Ann was a dedicated and caring social worker. I knew she had done her best and more than most, and I firmly believed Alex was right when he said she had saved his life. I also knew these revelations—I had called her and told her about the choking with nylons and the throwing of bullets—were causing her a great deal of suffering and soul-searching. She had thought there was a caring relationship between father and son. But Ann was the only human link I had to a vast void of officialism, and it was to her that I cried out my anguish and frustration. "Why didn't they do something, Ann? Why didn't someone do something?"

"We had no choice," she explained. "We had to go along with the court's order to keep the family together."

"What about the beatings?" I asked. "Why didn't someone from RFK check under his pants for signs of abuse? He says there were welts and bruises."

"He never told anyone!" she said in a defensive manner. "I would take him out to lunch to give him the opportunity. I asked him questions about abuse, but he didn't tell."

He didn't tell. I had heard it before and I would hear it again. He didn't tell.

How does a child tell about mindless violence threatening him with complete annihilation?

How does a child tell when the perpetrators of that violence are the same people he must depend upon to feed him and clothe him and keep a roof over his head?

How does a child tell about parents who are repeatedly trying to injure him?

I thought of the counselor from the institution I had met at the agency office three years ago: "Alex? He was one of the worst we had. My arms still ache from holding him down."

And the guidance counselor from the middle school: "Alex's school record is the worst I've ever seen."

And Ann: "We kept getting calls from the principal saying that Alex was chasing kids down the corridor with scissors or that they had to call the fire department to get him off the roof of the school. The special education teacher threatened to quit if they didn't get him out of her classroom."

And there was the primitive psychiatric profile qualifying him for the select admission to Camp Wedicko.

How does a child tell?

•   •   •

The triggering factor for the worst of the flashbacks occurred on June twenty-seventh of 1987, when Alex was almost thirteen years old. He had accompanied me to the home of a friend who had an adopted daughter. This young girl was known to have been sexually abused prior to the adoption, but the boldness of her behavior took me by surprise. Jumping on top of Alex's stomach and making thrusting motions with her body, she chanted, "Put your blood into mine, Alex. Put your blood into mine."

It took two days for the flashback to emerge. It began with a rapid fluctuation between love and hate. One minute he would be asking for a hug and the next he would be calling me names. And there was the laughter, weird and inappropriate and never touching his eyes. Toward evening, he ran past me with such a look of terror that I followed him to his room. He was on his bed, frantically rolling his body right to left, left to right, while low, agonized moans escaped from his lips. His face was red and contorted and his eyes were squeezed tightly together as though to shut out some awful vision. Periodically his writhing form became rigid and his limbs jerked convulsively. His eyes were wide open, white, blank, and staring.

The moans became increasingly louder and more frequent, and he hurled himself from one end of the bed to the other. There were shouts of "No, no, it's not happening. It's not happening. It can't be true. It's coming. It's coming!" and he began banging his head against the wall with a violent force. I tried to restrain him. I pulled him away from the wall, and he fought to free himself, arching his back and struggling mightily. Sometimes I managed to hang on to him long enough to lessen the impact of the self-inflicted blows to his head. But he kept breaking loose and lunging at the wall. His breath was rushing through his throat in hoarse, ragged gasps. And then I heard a scream that seemed to come from the frozen depths of hell, a scream so primitive it was scarcely human.

As the scream echoed in my ears, he appeared to go into

a trancelike state. He could respond to my voice but did not seem to be aware of my presence. "You're safe now," I assured him, sensing he'd gone back into time. "You're safe. I won't let them hurt you. They can't hurt you anymore." Sitting on the edge of the bed, I brushed the damp hair from his forehead with my hand. "You're safe now," I repeated softly. "They can never hurt you again." The comforting words reached through to him, and his sweat-drenched figure lay quietly on the tangle of blankets and sheets.

I did not want to ask. I did not want to know. But I had to. "What is it?" I said. "What is happening to you?"

He whimpered fearfully. "I'm four," he answered. "I'm four years old."

"Who's doing this? Bert? Is it Bert?"

"No, no," he said, turning his head from side to side. "It's a girl. It's a girl! She's on top of me. I can't breathe. I'm dying. I feel like I'm dying."

A girl.

"I was running, I saw this girl lying on the ground."

"It's a girl. It's her. It's a girl! She's on the phone."

"A girl was in a car with a man. My mother. The girl was my mother."

Christine!

I stood up and took a step away from the bedside. A numbing paralysis swept over me. Light-headed. Dizzy. Plunging downward in an elevator. Fast. Too fast. Maybe I was mistaken. Maybe it was someone else. My mind tried to reject what I'd heard. Mothers don't do that. As bad as Christine might be, she couldn't have done that.

But she did. I knew she did. I could not deny what I had just witnessed. Wouldn't it explain some of the behavior, such as the extreme reaction to the Oedipal phase, the need for control over the mother, and the acting out after any contact with her? And didn't it also shed some light on what was behind the grandmother's reports to DSS?

"Don't look at me," he said when it was over. "I don't want anyone to see me. Please! Don't look at me! I'm dirty.

I'm disgusting. I'm so ashamed!" Covering his face with his hands, he ran into the bathroom, filled the tub with cold water, and jumped in fully clothed.

Alex spent most of the next two days sitting in corners with his entire body shrouded in a blanket. On the second day after the flashback, he asked to be held. I sat down on the couch and put my arms around him so his head was nestled in the hollow of my shoulder, and I held him for a long time before he began to talk. "There were four people who did it to me," he said in words that were wrenched from abysmal depths. "Christine, my sister Donna, Bert, and another man—I don't know his name. I can't remember what the men did to me, but Christine did it one or two times a week. She did it even after I went to live with George. She was living with some friends. Their name was Henderson, Howard and Patsy Henderson. They had a little boy who was four years old. George would take me to stay with her on weekends, and it kept happening. Every weekend." Lifting his head from my shoulder, he looked at me and asked if he could be tested for AIDS. "She was doing it with other people too, and I'm worried that I might have AIDS."

Why was all of this so hard to hear? I'd known it was coming. I'd thought I was prepared. He hadn't gone into the details. But still, it was so incomprehensible. I'd read it could be detrimental to show too much emotion. The child might stop talking to protect the feelings of the listener. "I'm sorry," I said, trying to stem the flow of tears.

"No, it's okay. It helps me if you cry. It does. It helps."

"What else, Alex? What else can I do to help you?"

"Give me what I missed," he said, hanging on to me as if for his very life.

"How?" I asked Bill afterward. "How could anyone do that to their own child? Their own baby?"

"They did it to your baby, too," he said. "That was your baby."

Exactly. Ever since the last flashback, I had been overwhelmed by strong feelings of tenderness and fierce, protective love for Alex. They were the same as those a mother has for her newborn baby. Bill was right. They had done this to my baby, and I felt as though I were trapped in a swelling bubble of pain that was expanding and pressing down on me at the same time. Sitting on my bed, I wrapped my arms around my legs and I cried and I cried and the tears spilled onto my knees. How could she? The question seemed to come at me from all directions. How could she? Like rifle shots. Wounding, splitting, killing. How could she? I hugged myself and I rocked back and forth and I cried for Alex, for his childhood. Lost. Lost forever. And I cried for myself. To know this. To know a mother could do this broke my world into pieces. Had Christine been in the room, I believe I would have murdered her.

The flashback was similarly a birthing process for Alex, and the excruciating pain of getting in touch with having been sexually abused marked the real beginning of his healing. Given the knowledge that Christine had not only physically abused him but had sexually abused him as well, none of us could bear to have his birthday on the actual date of July twenty-sixth. Alex was determined to sever every link, every connection, to the perpetrators, and from this time forward we would celebrate his birthday on the twenty-ninth of June, the anniversary of the flashback.

The celebration for Alex's thirteenth birthday was a bit late, but nothing was spared to make the day an unforgettable rite of passage. Sam and I lavished gifts upon him and took him, along with one of his friends, to an amusement park. At one of the games of chance, Alex won a stuffed red plush heart. "I want to give this to you, Mom," he said proudly. "I won it for you."

I was quite touched by his gift, and thanking him, I slipped the heart into my pocketbook.

Unfortunately, it was the day after the celebration that was unforgettable. It began with him smashing his hand into the mirror on his bedroom wall and went downhill from there. I'd heard them all before, the names and the insults delivered in a caustic voice. But in the state of maternal vulnerability following the flashback, the pain of the sudden shift from love to hate seemed more than I could bear.

Some skillful therapy on Bill's part brought out the sobbing admission from Alex that he didn't feel he deserved it when good things happened to him. "I'm afraid," he said. "I'm afraid it's all a dream and it will be snatched away. I can't believe all these good things are happening to me. When the good things happen, I feel like a different person. But I look in the mirror and I see the same bad, stupid me, and I want to just smash my fist through the mirror. That's why I broke the mirror this morning. I felt bad and stupid and I acted bad and stupid."

Bill's face was grave and filled with compassion. "You were told for years how you were bad, stupid, crazy—all the stuff. And it's not true. You didn't deserve the bad things. You do deserve the good things. Every single one of them."

In July, I took Alex and Blaze to a regional horse show. On the second day of the competition, a sudden deterioration in his behavior sent me flying to the nearest phone. "Sam, Sam," I said, breathing a heartfelt sigh of relief as I heard the familiar voice on the other end of the line. "Can you get away? Can you come down here? Something's wrong with Alex."

"What's the matter? What's going on?"

"I'm a hundred miles from home with a horse and an out-of-control kid. That's what's going on. He won his class this morning and this afternoon he went berserk. And he's bleeding. The bleeding started up again."

"Damn!" said Sam. "Can you get him to take those pills?"

Sam was referring to a medication called Atarax. It had been prescribed by the psychiatrist at the counseling center for just such an emergency. "No. I can't do anything with him. If I get near him he runs off with that queer smile and those cold, scary eyes. He doesn't seem to know me. Something's wrong, Sam."

Alex's condition had improved by the time Sam arrived at the horse show, and we managed to get him to swallow one of the pills. The Atarax made him sleepy, but we kept him on it until we reached home. Thankful that we had chosen to keep the state medical insurance and minimal DSS involvement, we contacted Ann. After some discussion, we decided the best course of action would be to send him to a shelter. It was not an easy decision, but Sam and I felt we had no choice. This creature who stared at us with such loathing was not our son. Ann completed the arrangements and took him to a place in Worcester.

At the end of one week, when I went to the shelter to bring Alex home, I sat in the office of the director, a rather pompous man, and listened to him deliver his prophecy of doom. "We haven't had much experience here with male victims of sexual abuse," he admitted as he folded his hands in front of him on the desk. "The prognosis is not good. Boys don't talk about it. Alex is not going to talk about it."

This hopelessly discouraging viewpoint was the last thing I needed to hear right now. If I believed what the director was saying, I would have to give up and consign Alex to the demons battling to possess him. "I don't agree with you," I said. "He will talk. I know he will."

The director shook his head sadly and looked at me as though he pitied my ignorance. "On two occasions," he continued, "it took our entire staff to restrain him."

That's why he's here, I said to myself. This was supposed to be a situation where he could safely let out his rage. Why didn't the director understand that in the aftermath of a flashback, the single most important therapeutic intervention was to get the child into an environment where it was permissible to release those first shock waves of the terrible anger accompanying integration? Alex had told me how being restrained had helped him. "It's not so scary to be that angry if they don't let me hurt myself or anyone," he explained.

I was quite sure there had been another flashback. And I

had a fairly good idea what it was. "When did you know?" I asked him during the drive home.

"At the show. After I won my class," he said.

The director's depressing prediction was still on my mind when we arrived at the house, and despite my conviction, I could hardly believe it when Alex ran toward the front door calling to me over his shoulder, "Come on, Mom. Come on! I have to talk about this. I want to get it over with so I can get on with my life. You're going to have to hold me."

I went into the living room and sat down on the couch, and Alex assumed his telling position. He lay down with his upper body against me and nestled his head in my shoulder. I held him close while he gathered the strength to talk. "I begged her not to leave me with him." He spoke in a low, level voice completely devoid of feeling.

"You mean Christine left you with Bert?"

"Yes."

"So what happened?"

"She left, and he would call in this man, a friend of his. I don't know who he was. The man held me down and watched while Bert put his . . ."

He was unable to say the word, and I swallowed hard and said it for him. "Penis?"

I could feel the affirmative movement of his head as he drew his knees up toward his stomach. My arms tightened spasmodically about him. I felt as if there were a thousand voices screaming inside of me, and I tried to quell the nausea rising in my throat.

"I thought he was ripping me to pieces, and I yelled and cried. When I went to the bathroom, there was blood in the toilet. I showed her the blood. She left me anyway. She didn't do anything."

He went on to describe the process of the flashback. "At first," he said, "there were pictures in my mind and there was a terrible fear that just took over. And another thing was I couldn't talk about the pictures. I could see them, but it was a whole week before I could find the words to tell what they were."

I could only imagine what it must have been like for Alex to be small and helpless and in the grip of such a catastrophic terror. And of course he couldn't talk about it when the pictures first came. What young child has the language to describe such unholy acts?

In a few days he tried to relate more of the details of the abuse by Christine. "I want to tell you about it," he said. But his eyes bulged with fear and he turned and ran from the room. He kept trying, and each effort was followed by a spell of out-of-control behavior. At one point, he left a note on his pillow. It said, "I'm leaving because I'm not fit for this family." I found him hiding in the hayloft.

It was five hours before he could stay in one place long enough to talk, and that was in the barn, in the tack room. He took me by the hand and led me there, and sitting himself down on a brassbound trunk flanked by several bridles hanging on the wall, he told me how she had made him suck her breasts. His head was bowed in his hands and his fingers were pressed against his forehead as if he were trying to squeeze his brains out onto the floor.

"What happened after that?" I asked.

"I can't say it," he said. "You have to help me. Mom, you have to help me!"

I hazarded a guess as to what Christine might have done. "Well, did she fondle you? Your penis?"

Alex lunged to his feet. His lips twisted and trembled and a shudder ran through him. A drawn-out yes was forced from his throat, and the rest of the words burst out in an explosion of pent-up agony. "She put her mouth on it! She put her mouth on it!"

But there was no expression of anger directly connected to the perpetrators. "Why not?" I asked him.

"If I let myself feel it," he said with a frightening calmness, "I would find them and kill them."

"Alex, how would you like to make-believe kill them? You could draw pictures, big pictures, and take a knife . . ."

Alex quickly entered into the spirit of killing by effigy, an idea as simple as it is ancient. It would not only give him an acceptable outlet for his anger, it would help to focus it on the people who had actually committed the crimes. I assembled a pile of colored markers and five-foot sheets of blank newspaper and laid them out on the living-room floor. "I'm going to draw Christine first," he announced. "I hate her the most." Biting his lower lip, he picked up a black marker. As his fingers flew across the paper, I could feel my flesh crawl. An inhuman monster was taking shape right before my eyes. The head consisted of a black and empty triangle with green snakes for hair. It was attached to a rudimentary body by a springlike coil. A black bull's-eye represented Christine's heart, and clawed hands sprouted daggerlike fingernails dripping red gobs of blood. The block lettering underneath labeled it "ALEX'S BLOOD."

When he finished with his conception of Christine he went to work on the drawing of Bert. I watched as the stark black outline of a man's profile developed: an empty eye socket, a protruding nose, a lipless mouth, and farther down, a very large and very erect penis. Opposite the profile, along the outer edge of the paper, he drew a vertical line.

"What's that?" I asked.

"It's going to be a telephone pole," he said.

"A telephone pole? What for?"

"You'll see," he answered.

A second line was drawn parallel to the first, and as the marker approached the jutting penis, it swerved in and around it and continued down to the bottom of the page.

A hole. Bert's penis was stuck into a hole in a telephone pole. It took but a second for me to understand the meaning of this action. Our eyes met over the drawing and we began to giggle, and then we broke into long peals of healing laughter. On our way to the counseling center for our therapy session that afternoon, we burst out laughing every time we saw a telephone pole.

Once we were in Bill's office, Alex showed him the drawings. Bill closely examined the one of Christine. "No eyes to see with. No ears to hear with," he observed grimly.

"I've read about certain cultures," I said, "particularly in the West Indies, where they really believe if they stick a pin in a doll representing someone they hate, the person will feel pain and sometimes actually die."

"So this can be pretty powerful stuff," said Bill. "Let's hope Christine and Bert will get a few twinges."

Alex's expression brightened noticeably at this prospect and we left the office. We made our way across the lawn to a wooded area where there was an old shed. Alex taped his image of Christine onto the rear wall, and I handed him a bone-handled hunting knife. Bill and I stepped back and watched him walk fifteen feet away from the ramshackle building. He turned and stared fixedly at the gruesome depiction of Christine. With his gaze riveted on the drawing, he began taking deep, short breaths, and each breath seemed to fill him with more and more hatred, a hatred that was sucked into his being until his eyes were burning with the wild fury of a blood-frenzied animal. The muscles of his throat grew taut and his jaw was set in rigid lines as he raised the arm holding the knife. For one brief moment he paused and the knife glinted silver in the sun. Coalescing all of his strength and power in one primal shriek, he lunged straight at the bull's-eye. He did it over and over and over until there was only a pile of shredded paper lying on the ground. And even this he stomped on.

Bill had another appointment and had to leave, but Alex and I stayed at the shed to finish off Bert. Alex fastened the second drawing to the wall. This time the first thing he plunged his knife into was the large, hated penis. His rage undiminished, he attacked the black outline with karate kicks as well as the knife. The building trembled and a few of the boards cracked and broke. When he had almost finished his savage assault, he gave me the knife and said, "Here, you have a part in this, too."

I grasped the carved handle, and I was completely unprepared for what happened next. I felt a strong tingling sensation, as though I'd received a shock of electricity. A strange pulsating energy flowed from the knife through my body, and as I drew back my arm to stab what was left of the mangled penis, Alex's rage became my rage; Alex's hate became my hate. Rushing forward, I cried out, "That was my baby you did that to. You bastard! That was my baby!"

XI

September 1987 to August 1988

Some Answers, More Questions

Alex entered the eighth grade that September and also resumed his dancing lessons at Miss Delia's. He had not, however, forgotten the purpose behind those lessons: football. His desire to play remained undiminished. The fact that the school officials believed our district was too small to have a football team did not deter him. He organized several of his friends and they went door to door asking residents to sign a petition in support of high school football.

The petition was presented to the school committee, but in spite of strong community support, the most they would agree to was a teaching program in the elementary grades. By the time these children reached high school there probably would be a team. Sadly, this would be too late for Alex and his friends.

As for his dancing, Alex had added ballroom lessons to his jazz and ballet. One Friday night, I stayed with several other mothers to watch Miss Delia's ballroom class from the sitting room of the studio. This room, bright with flowered chintz, gold-shaded carpet, and polished woods, was separated from the dance floor by a row of sliding glass doors. The doors had been left partially open and I could hear the lilting strains of a waltz. And I could hear Miss Delia. "One, two, three, one, two, three," she repeated as she stood in the center of the group and beat time with short, rhythmic motions of her right hand.

The plump, beaming mother of Alex's dancing partner

was seated next to me. "Don't they look good together," she said in a tone of maternal satisfaction.

My eyes sought out Alex and the petite, dark-haired girl with the white blouse and the sheer blue skirt that swirled about her legs. Poised and graceful, they circled the floor. "Yes," I agreed, wanting to hold in my heart the hope and the joy of the image and the sound of the music. "Yes, they do. They do look good together."

In the meantime, Ann had been to a seminar on post-traumatic stress syndrome. "Carole," she said, "I think that's what Alex has. They had a speaker, a Dr. Van der Kolk of Boston, and he claims children who have been badly abused can suffer from the same symptoms as Vietnam veterans."

Vietnam veterans! I remembered Sarah's puzzled comparison when I described Alex's trancelike state as he apparently saw and spoke to Bert. Could Ann be right? Did it really have a name, this crazy, weird behavior with its flashbacks and spells? Bill followed up on the information, and his research resulted in full agreement with Ann. Alex's symptoms were indeed consistent with post-traumatic stress syndrome. Somehow this made me feel better. It meant doctors were studying it and learning about it and writing about it. It meant there would be help. There would be answers.

She also told me Bill had filed reports of sexual abuse with her office and an investigator would be coming out to talk to Alex. Because of the statute of limitations, she explained, the department could only go into the abuse of the summer of 1981 when George was bringing Alex to visit Christine at the home of Howard and Patsy Henderson.

The investigator came in October. Alex greeted her with an air of somber determination, and I left them alone in the living room. I closed the doors behind me, but disjointed snatches of words were still audible:

"What position was she in?"

"I thought all kids did this with their mothers."

"And then what did she do?"

"What part of her body?"

"She blocked the door and windows and beat me. If I didn't want to do it, she beat me after she made me do it."

With a heavy, sickish feeling in the pit of my stomach, I retreated farther away to the kitchen and found some solace in a hot cup of herbal tea.

There was something else that happened that October. It was on the thirty-first of the month. Throughout the day Alex had been extremely agitated, and at nightfall, on Halloween, his actions became strange and frightening. He went into the bathroom and came out with his face painted with black and red streaks of mascara and lipstick. The shell of a protective hard hat used for horseback riding covered his head like a bowl. At first, I thought this was part of a costume he was getting together. "Alex," I said, thinking I would offer him a ride to town so he could go trick-or-treating, "do you want me to—"

"I'm Ricky!" he yelled at me. "My name is Ricky."

I noticed that his eyes were wild and unfocused, and he did not seem to know me. He ran out the front door and across the lawn to the woods on the other side of the stone wall. For the next hour, I glimpsed him darting in and out of the shadows. If I tried to get close to him, he would disappear behind the trees. I could not see him, but I could hear him talking as though he were having a conversation with someone. Someone who was not there. "Alex!" I called to him. "Stop it! Stop it this minute and come in the house!"

He came as far as the big oak on the lawn and raced around it in ever-widening circles while breathlessly repeating, "My name is Ricky. My name is Ricky."

Except to categorize this as one more symptom of post-traumatic stress syndrome, I had no idea what to think. It had been a year to the day since the mutilation of the frogs. It had been two years since the outrageous behavior following the attempted abduction. Halloween. Was any of this in any way connected to Halloween? And Ricky. Why was he saying his name was Ricky?

. . .

The Department of Social Services had validated the investigator's report and sent it on to the County District Attorney's Office. While we waited for the legal system to do its work, Bill and I tried to help Alex with some of the issues surrounding the sexual abuse. At last there was a book. Bill came up with a copy of *Treating the Young Male Victim of Sexual Assault* by Eugene Porter. Throughout this winter of Alex's thirteenth year, we would frequently refer to it in our quest for answers and insights. Although abuse by women was mentioned, the author dealt primarily with the difficulties confronting boys who had been abused by men. The greatest fear a boy has, Porter wrote, is that he has been "turned into a homosexual."

We were quite sure this was a problem for Alex, but as always, if he was to be helped, he first had to admit to it. In therapy, he folded his arms across his chest and stolidly refused to discuss the subject. Bill and I were forced to fall back on our technique of having him listen to our conversation. "It's very common," began Bill in a casual, relaxed manner, "for teenage boys to have doubts about their sexuality. And I think it's fair to say that most boys who have been sexually abused by men have some fears they are gay. These boys doubt their masculinity and often try to cover it up by acting tough and macho."

"Well," I said, "it wouldn't surprise me at all if Alex was secretly worried about this."

Alex suddenly blanched and his eyes stood out in dark contrast to the paleness of his skin. Jumping to his feet and knocking over his chair, he ran from the room—a sure sign we had come too close to a painful truth.

Over the next week I saw a sharp escalation in the macho conduct Bill had mentioned. It was as though there was a last-ditch defensive effort to bury any question about his sexual identity. Much of the acting out was associated with the informal touch football games Alex and his friends played after school on Tuesdays and Thursdays. When the principal called on Friday to report my son's dangerous behavior while riding home on the late bus, I took advantage of the opportunity.

"You really love football, don't you, Alex?" I asked.

Holding a deep breath that made his chest expand, he said, "Oh, yes!"

"It seems you love it more than most kids, in a different, more intense way. Do you agree?"

Alex barely considered the question before he willingly nodded his head. "Yes," he said.

"Why? Is it because those are real he-men out there? Do they represent the ultimate in masculinity?"

He regarded me somewhat warily, and his answer was slower to come. "Yeah, well, I guess so."

"So why does it mean so much to you? Why is it so important to you to play football and be like them?"

"I don't know."

"Yes, you do, Alex. Why? Tell me why."

Alex slid down onto the floor and hid under the table with his hands over his ears. He was sobbing piteously, and I felt so sorry for him. "Oh, Alex, do you think you're gay?"

"Yes, yes," he cried. "I'm afraid I am."

We brought this admission into Bill's office. He listened with one hand resting on his knee and the other reaching out, palm up, toward Alex. "You're not alone," he said. "It's not at all unusual for a boy to have these fears. But it takes a lot of courage to admit it. Alex, what Bert did to you could not make you gay." His voice rang with an honesty and sincerity that penetrated Alex's protective facade.

"How do I know?" he asked, looking from me to Bill. "How do I know I'm not?"

"From what Carole tells me, you feel a strong attraction for members of the opposite sex. Is this true?"

Alex squirmed around in his chair and blushed a deep red. "Well, I guess it is."

"There!" exclaimed Bill. "There's the proof! If you were gay, you wouldn't feel that way. You couldn't feel that way. You could not have a sexual attraction to a girl."

Alex didn't say anything, but I noticed his expression was brighter. He looked encouraged.

Sensing his advantage, Bill kept talking. "Sexual abuse does not have anything to do with a person's sexual preference. Sexual abuse does not have anything to do with sex. It has to do with power. And if you were gay it would feel perfectly normal to you and you would have been aware of it years ago. Since you find girls sexually attractive, I think it's safe to say you are definitely not homosexual."

Bill gave him much to think about that day, and Alex did not speak of it again until several weeks later when he said, "I'm not gay. I know in my head I'm not gay. The trouble is, Ma," he added plaintively, "inside—inside of me—I feel like I am." It would be a long time before Alex's intellectual assessment of his sexual preference coincided with his feelings.

Another issue Porter dealt with was the male victim's need for power. He quoted a report from another therapist who wrote that since the child was helpless to stop the abuse and was forced to submit to it, he develops a terror of being helpless or controlled. This terror is then generalized and the boy responds negatively to all orders and regulations. Porter went on to say, "The therapeutic goal is to redirect this thrust for power into some activity that can enhance self-esteem. . . ."

It was an exhilarating experience to read passages reaffirming the work we had done from the beginning with Alex, the work that had been the subject of so much controversy with Peter. The words fairly leaped from the page, because redirecting the thrust for power was exactly what we had accomplished in our efforts to give Alex legitimate controls through the horseback riding, karate, dancing, and the learning of other skills.

There were still episodes of controlling behavior, but they were associated with the traumatic period preceding the flashbacks. In therapy Bill accepted and normalized this need. "In the past," he said, "the adults in your life terribly abused you, so it's certainly understandable you would want to be in control. Anybody would. Children learn to trust other people through first trusting the mother. Your mother could not be trusted, so you never learned to trust."

"Your mother could not be trusted. . . ." Had Alex known to what extent this was true, he probably would have been in a state of perpetual terror and would have had no trust at all in me or Sam or Bill or any other human being. He would not have been able to function.

A subject related to control and causing a great deal of anxiety for Alex was his worry that he, himself, might become a perpetrator. "Some people," admitted Bill, "who have been abused as children do grow up to become abusers themselves. They try to control what happened in the past by reenacting it, by making others feel as helpless and powerless as they once were. They are compelled to do the same thing to others so they will feel powerful. You, Alex, are not one of those people. You have been able to do what they could not. You have had the courage to go back and understand how you were affected by what happened to you and you've been able to talk about it."

"I agree," I said. "And it says here in the book about male victims that not every kid who has been abused grows up to be an abuser, and it also says the best prevention is therapy. You've had some real good therapy, Alex. You've not only talked about it, you have felt the pain."

"An important point," added Bill. "I'll tell you, I've had people sit here and talk. They can say the words, but that's as far as it goes. It's all on the surface. They don't experience the feelings like you do. They have not felt their own pain, so they can't feel or empathize with the pain of another person. Christine and Bert had no empathy. They were entirely selfish people concerned only with their own needs. That's how they could do what they did. They were incapable of seeing your pain."

Bill and I were both wholeheartedly convinced Alex would never abuse a child. But we still didn't know what he had done before he came to us. And neither did Alex.

. . .

The next major event in Alex's life was his eighth-grade graduation dance. "My, don't you look handsome," I said admiringly as Alex proudly showed off the new clothes I'd bought him for the occasion. The outfit consisted of a light blue jacket and cream-colored pants with shirt and shoes to match. A pale blue tie, an off-white silk handkerchief, and a white carnation boutonniere completed his attire. "Doesn't he, Sam? Doesn't he look good?"

Not one to wax eloquent about such matters, Sam grudgingly agreed. "Yeah, he does," he said when Alex went to the bathroom to comb his hair for what seemed like the tenth time.

Sam delivered the kids to the dance, and just before eleven o'clock I went to the school to pick them up. After a short wait in the parking lot, I saw Alex and his date, a girl named Mary, emerge from the streamer-and-balloon-decorated gym. She was wearing a demure pink dress, and on her left wrist was the dainty corsage Alex had given her. They were holding hands and laughing and giggling, and as I drove toward Mary's home, I thought of how it made everything worthwhile to see Alex like this. Normal. A normal teenager. It gave me a real feeling of satisfaction.

That feeling did not last long.

When we reached the house, Alex escorted her to the door. Seven or eight minutes later he came hurrying toward me, not running but walking very fast. As he approached the car, I could see from his face that something was wrong. "What's the matter?" I asked. "You look like you've seen a ghost."

"I have," he said, huddling down in the seat and staring straight ahead. "She was there. I went to kiss Mary good night, and she was there, right there between us."

"Who? What are you talking about?"

"Christine. It was Christine. There was a blurriness and then I didn't see Mary. I saw Christine. The same thing has

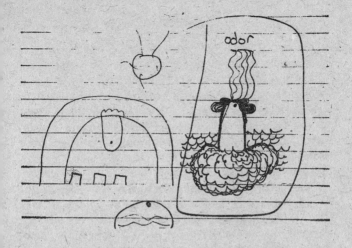

Predisclosed Drawing, June 1988

been happening in school if a girl gets too close. So I make up an excuse to get away."

An innocent good-night kiss, I thought. He couldn't even have a kiss. The past just kept reaching out to intrude upon and destroy the present.

A week after the dance, I discovered the drawings. I was cleaning out his room, and in a pile of discarded school papers there was a notebook. Leafing through it, I found long, undulating lines scrawled across each and every page. Except one. On that page Alex had made a detailed depiction of an ejaculating penis with semen flowing down the sides. Wavy lines emanating from the top were labeled with the word "odor." Although the identity of the object was unmistakable, my mind was incapable of grasping the significance of the picture.

On another part of the page there was an arch with an oblong shape protruding downward and several partly formed rectangles coming up from underneath. I turned it around and I studied it from different angles and I didn't understand that one either. I couldn't quite bring myself to throw the notebook away, so I brought it into the living room and placed it in the bottom drawer of my desk.

Putting the pictures and this business of seeing people who weren't there out of my mind, I concentrated on helping Alex get through his sex-abuse case. Much to Alex's delight, the DA's staff told us they would be placing Christine under arrest very soon. They were going after Bert, too, but that would take a little longer. Each day of the waiting began in eager anticipation. "Will today be Glory Day?" Alex would ask. "Mom, do you think today will be Glory Day?" Alex wanted to be in the courtroom to see the arraignment. He wanted to see how powerless Christine would be in the hands of the law. I made sure clothes were laid out so we could get ready at a moment's notice, and I hovered by the telephone waiting for the call.

It didn't come. There was nothing. We heard nothing. On the twenty-seventh of June, they did call. They couldn't arrest Christine until August, because they had decided to go to the grand jury first. This news was delivered in a casual, offhand manner, and my voice sounded hoarse and shaky as I expressed my outrage. "How can you do this?" I asked. "How can you tell a kid you're going to do something and then not do it? Do you have any idea what we go through? Do you know what this is going to do to Alex?"

"We will be ready in August. We will call you," was the professionally calm answer.

In spite of everything, we clung to that hope. It was all we had. And for Alex, knowing Christine and Bert could do such terrible things to him and walk free while he went through so much pain and suffering was eating away at him like some insidious disease. For Alex, punishment for the perpetrators was an integral part of his healing.

The remainder of that summer of waiting for this last promise of legal action was relatively uneventful. Until one day when a police sergeant showed up at our door, walked into our living room, and solemnly proceeded to read fourteen-year-old Alex his rights. "You have the right to remain silent. You have the right to . . ." For a moment, the words became an indistinguishable blur as disbelief deafened my ears to the dry, flat voice. After completing the formality, he asked Alex where he had gotten the four-wheeler.

"I found it," Alex answered steadfastly. "I found the four-wheeler in a field." His green eyes, leveled calmly on the officer, were without any emotion whatsoever, and his cool, self-possessed demeanor gave no hint of guilt.

"Don't lie to me, Alex. Don't lie to me, because I will find out the truth."

"I found the four-wheeler in a field. I found the four-wheeler in a field," repeated Alex, sounding like some kind of robot.

The sergeant stared at him for a moment, his frustration barely visible under the practiced mask of official control. "I know he stole it," he said to me. "And sooner or later, I'll prove it."

Alex must have heard the accusation, but his expression remained blank and inscrutable. Once again there was the feeling that I did not know this boy. I did not know who he was. And what had gone wrong? What had happened yesterday? In the morning, he had been so exuberant, so full of high spirits. Sam had taken him to work with him, and to lunch, and had bought him a box of baseball cards. When they returned home there was a sense of warmth between the two that gladdened my heart. Then without a word to anyone, Alex disappeared. This is what was always the most painful for Sam, the unaccountable switching, the normal, happy boy who could so quickly change into a cold and distant stranger.

Toward dusk, muddy and exhausted, he did come back but offered no explanation of where he had been or what he had been doing. Sam and I questioned him more closely, and he came up with a story about finding an expensive and practically new all-terrain vehicle, a four-wheeler, abandoned in a field. It had the keys in it, he said. He spent the afternoon driving it on a pipeline near the house of a friend, until the friend's father became suspicious and reported it to the police.

The days following the sergeant's visit marked a recurrence of stress-related behavior, the familiar pattern of affectionate hugs alternating with obnoxious acting out. There were also other symptoms. He was constantly eating. It was as though he always had to have something in his mouth. And he was having gory mutilation nightmares accompanied by cold sweats and feelings of immense loneliness. At the same time he was once more plagued by the black pictures fast-forwarding through his mind, pictures that would not hold still, pictures he could not see. From past experience, we knew that this signaled the advent of another flashback and that he should be in a safe place where he could be free to let out his anger without being in danger of hurting himself or anyone else.

Again with Ann's help, we brought Alex to the only available shelter. It was near Boston, and it was an excellent facility, but as the week progressed it became increasingly clear that rather than helping him to discharge his anger, the counselors were making every effort to keep it under control. They did not have the manpower, they said, to do otherwise. Hospitalization in a psychiatric ward seemed to be the only feasible alternative. There was, however, one major problem. Since Alex had not actually done anything to indicate he was a danger to himself or others, he was not committable and we had to convince him he should go to a hospital.

It was for this purpose he was transported to Bill's office for a meeting with Sam and me. When I walked in and saw him sitting in a corner between the desk and door, I was jolted by his appearance. His eyes were blank and expressionless, and a black stubble of beard seemed strangely incongruous on his young face. I wanted to hold him and comfort him, and I pressed my hand against his bare arm. His flesh was icy cold. It was like touching a corpse.

Sam was right behind me. He stood before Alex, and, filling the room with his vigor and confidence, he reiterated the issues we had worked on for so long. "You didn't do anything, Alex. Remember, you didn't do anything wrong. People did things to you. It wasn't your fault. You have every right to be angry and you need to be where you can get help with this. Alex, we want you home. We want you to get better and come home. Seven days. I promise you. If you will go to the hospital, it won't be more than seven days."

Alex's face was a frozen mask. Only his eyes moved, ever so slightly. "I will go to the hospital," he said.

All the rest of the day and into the evening, my stomach ached with a heavy anxiety that radiated outward in a creeping paralysis. Walking in circles, unable to accomplish anything, I kept thinking about the puzzling events of the last two weeks. What could it be? What could be coming into consciousness? That night, in half-remembered dreams, I chased bits and pieces of elusive images until I awoke to find myself sitting bolt upright in bed. There was no confusion. There were no doubts. Every nerve was pulsating with the certain knowledge I had the answer to my question.

The notebook! The notebook I had puzzled over last spring. I had to find it. Carefully slipping out of bed so as not to awaken Sam, I made my way to the desk and opened the bottom drawer. It was there, right where I'd left it. In the pool of white light from the lamp, I flipped through the pages, each with its eloquent wavy line. Drowning. Drowning in semen. The impressions were overpowering, and I caught my breath in dizzying gulps. Now the pictures made sense. The arched lines were obviously a mouth, the upward protrusions teeth, and the elongated object hanging from the top a penis. And the detailed depiction of ejaculation? Of course he would know exactly what it looked like. And smelled like.

I said nothing of this to Alex. He did not yet know about it, and for me to tell him would only add to his fear. My main concern was to get him into a place where he would be able to find out for himself.

Two days later, Alex and I were in the office of the secretary of the psychiatric unit of a hospital in another part of the state. An elderly lady who looked as if she should be presiding over an English tea table handed me some papers to sign. One of them contained a long list of rules. "Excuse me," I said as my eyes ran down the list, "there must be some misunderstanding. My son needs to be where he can safely let out his anger. That's the whole idea."

"Anger?" she said, raising her delicate eyebrows in shocked distaste. "I'm sorry, but control must be kept at all times. It says so right here. Rule number eleven."

"He isn't going to hurt anybody," I countered. "He might hit a wall with his fist and use some bad language or—"

"Oh, no!" she exclaimed. "I'm sorry. See rule number eighteen. No swearing, no abusive language allowed. You must also sign this sheet stating you will be responsible for any damage."

Feeling I had no choice, I left him there. And he did manage to keep control and obey the rules of the hospital, but when I brought him home he was worse than before he went in. The buried rage contaminated his every word, his every expression. It was like some noxious substance seeping from a foul, putrid cesspool. There would be no living with him until it was done. I waited until we were alone, and as he began making some particularly offensive remarks, I backed him into a corner of his room. "Don't touch me," he said in a low, menacing voice. "Don't touch me!"

I touched him.

"Get away from me," he warned.

I touched him again.

His eyes glittered with a ferocious glare. Breathing rapidly, he expelled air through his nostrils with a harsh, rasping sound.

"You'll what?" I said. "You'll do what?" I was not afraid, and I fastened my eyes to his, holding his gaze. He wanted to hit me. He raised up his arm to strike, and still I did not look away. With a deafening, explosive roar, he brought his arm down. At the last split second he diverted the blow to the wall and his fist smashed against the paneling with enough force to send the mirror crashing to the floor.

And then it was gone. It was over and he collapsed in a limp, sobbing heap onto the bed. I sat down next to him, my arm across his heaving shoulders. "Why don't you tell me about it?" I said softly.

He began to speak in a wrenching whisper. "I stole the four-wheeler. I broke into the garage down the street and stole it. I don't know why. Something just took over. It was like somebody else was doing it. Dad bought me baseball cards and was so nice to me and the black pictures started to come, and when I was in the hospital I could see them."

At least the hospitalization had accomplished something, I thought. It had helped Alex to feel safe enough to get in touch with what had happened to him.

"Bert was nice to me, too," he continued. He'd buy me things if I let him—he'd buy me things if I let him—put his penis in my mouth! He—he . . ."

"Ejaculated in your mouth?"

"Yes! Yes!" His voice rose to a shout that was throbbing with tears and pain. "Yes! He did it all the time. I was choking, dying. Dying. He had scissors. He said if I ever told anyone, he would cut my penis off!"

I saw in my mind the terrified, trembling little boy of four years ago crouching in a corner and crying out to Sam, "You're turning into a woman! You're turning into a woman!" simply because Sam was helping with the housework. I remembered how Alex had appeared to equate this with castration, and I was beginning to understand something of this fear.

Usually we had two or three months between Alex's spells. This gave us time to recover from the stress and the pain and was an important factor in our ability to cope. But the oral sex disclosures were hardly over when the pressures again began to build. These revelations had been particularly difficult for Sam, and I wished I didn't have to tell him of this latest round of obnoxious behavior. And another thing, I added: "He keeps talking about his younger half brother, how he used to have to baby-sit him all night and how scared he was."

"Georgie? George and Sandra's kid? He hasn't mentioned him since he ripped his page out of the book he had."

"Yes, I know. The Angry Book. He insisted there was no anger for Georgie. He loved him. He loved him more than anything in the world, he said." I thought of that now. How had Alex really felt, being pushed away by Sandra when the new baby was born, being beaten and abused by both George and Sandra, left alone at night with Georgie, frightened and hurting and hating?

Sam left the house, and with a sinking, sick sensation in the pit of my stomach, I went into Alex's room to find out what I already knew. It was far too risky to put off until next week's therapy session. Alex would run. He would put himself in danger and the police would be involved. This could not wait.

He had been reading for the last half hour, but I saw he had not turned the page. "Alex," I said, "you don't have any idea what's going on in the book. Why don't you tell me what the problem is?"

Alex thrust the book aside and buried his head under the pillows. "There's nothing to talk about," he said, and his muffled voice was filled with misery.

"I think there is, Alex." I paused to gather my strength. "If you did something to another kid, no one could blame you. Children do things to other children that have been done to them. They mimic adults. It's how they learn. You couldn't have been more than eight years old. After what happened to you, it would have been natural for you to do it to someone else, someone younger. It wasn't your fault. They shouldn't have left you alone with Georgie. Alex, you have a conscience now. You have empathy. It would never happen again. Did you do anything to Georgie?"

"No."

"Did you think about doing anything?"

A very faint "uh huh" came from under the pillows.

"Alex, we love you very much, and no matter what you did, this will not change. You did more than think about it, didn't you?"

"No, no. Leave me alone!"

"Did you touch him? Did you fondle his penis?"

"Bitch! You bitch! Leave me alone! Get out of my life!"

I knew then I was very close. It was right there, and until it was said, the pressure would build and build. "Alex," I argued, "you will put us through hell until you talk about it. We have never hurt you. We don't deserve this. What did you do to Georgie?"

There was no answer. Only a silence that was tense and strained. A silence to be ruptured with words that were like swords, words that cut and slashed.

"I raped him!" he said, and throwing the pillows aside with one wild fling of his arm, he sat up and looked at me. His entire face seemed swollen with suffering and his body shuddered as the anguished cry echoed in my ears. "I did. I did!"

XII

August 1988 to May 1989

Dr. Kingsbury

August went by with no word from the District Attorney's Office on Christine's pending arraignment. So did September and October. In November, I called the assistant DA, Paul Phillips. "Why haven't we heard anything?" I asked him. "You said you were going to pick her up in August. That's three months ago. Alex keeps wanting to know when it is going to happen."

"Alex wasn't living with Christine," Paul explained. "He was living with George. That means we have to find someone to testify she had access to him during the time that falls within the statute of limitations."

"But you've known from the beginning George had custody. Why did you wait till now to tell us you need a witness?" Since I got no reply, I went on to ask why he didn't talk to George. "He's the one who brought Alex to Christine. She was staying in Bainbridge with some people named Henderson."

"We don't know where George is. We can't locate him."

"Paul. He is in the area. His address is in the phone book."

"Oh. Well. He wouldn't make a good witness. I understand he just got out of jail. And the other lawyer would say he's trying to get back at Christine."

Alex's distress over this latest obstacle was somewhat alleviated when the detective on the case informed him she had called Christine into the police station for questioning. This was predictably met with protestations of innocence and

angry denials that either she or Bert had ever sexually abused
Alex. The detective also located the Henderson home and,
without telling Alex where it was, drove him around the
neighborhood. He had no trouble recognizing the house—the
House of Horrors, he called it—and, while sitting in the
parked police cruiser, he was able to describe a cement foundation for a screen house, a closed-in patio, a kitchen that
was separated from the dining area by a pass-through, and a
living room with a fireplace. He also said Christine's bedroom, where the abuse took place, was off the living room.
This information was checked out and it proved to be accurate.

That night, sitting across from me at the kitchen table,
Alex went into more detail about his weekend visits to the
Hendersons. "There were pictures of Howard Henderson's
two daughters on the fireplace mantel," he said. "They looked
like twins. They didn't live with him and Patsy. I think he
must have been married before. I played with their little boy.
His name was Bobby. He had one of those Playmate basketball hoops at the end of the driveway. Christine had a
boyfriend who would come over. He brought me this big orange stuffed animal. Sometimes he took me bowling or to
dart tournaments, and sometimes we went to Stoughton to get
my sister Donna. She was still with her adoptive parents and
they didn't know she came with us. We'd take her back after
two or three hours. One day when Donna was there at the
Hendersons, Christine had me in the bedroom with her. She
had just finished doing stuff to me and I was lying naked on
the bed. Christine was sitting on the edge of the bed putting
on her socks and underwear and Donna opened the door. She
said, 'Oh, I'm sorry,' and walked out."

"Did she know what was going on?"

Alex made a sound that was between a sneer and a laugh.
"She knew, Ma. She knew exactly what was going on. And
just being near there today, I was scared. I could tell it was the
right house. As soon as we drove by it. I could tell from the
way I felt."

"But you were with a policewoman. She was armed and in uniform. What reason was there to be afraid?"

"I don't care," he said. "It doesn't matter. I was scared." His voice had dropped so low I had to strain my ears to hear. "The patio. Ma. The patio. That's where the baby was. The baby slept on the patio in a little crib."

"Baby? What baby, Alex? What baby are you talking about?"

"Christine's baby. I mean I—I thought he was Christine's. I thought he was my brother."

That baby. I remembered now. When Alex came to us, he had insisted he had a baby brother. "I asked Ann about this and she said Christine did not have a baby. Could it possibly have belonged to Patsy Henderson?"

Alex's glance wavered, and he looked past me, beyond me, as though searching for the answers on the opposite wall. "I don't know," he said. "They both took care of him. They let me help. I held him. I gave him his bottle. I could make him smile. I thought he was my brother."

The detective asked the Hendersons whether Alex had been there with Christine, and they said yes, he had visited her that summer. But later on, for reasons we did not understand, they said he'd never been there at all.

And the baby? Maybe Ann had been mistaken. Since none of the children were with Christine, Ann might not have seen her on a regular basis. Christine could have given birth without her knowledge. Out of curiosity, I went to the town hall in Bainbridge and looked up the records. No child had been born to either Christine or Patsy in 1980 or 1981. The only other logical explanation was that the two women were taking care of the baby for someone else and seven-year-old Alex had simply jumped to the conclusion it belonged to Christine.

We heard nothing more on the legal case during the winter. And there were no more flashbacks until February. Until Sunday, February fifth, 1989. Alex and I were alone in the house when it began with the telltale agitation, the sarcastic defiance, the obnoxious manner. And then there was the dull thud of his fist pounding against the thick pine paneling in the kitchen. I tried to stop him. I tried to hold his arm and pull him away. But in his eyes was a chilling blankness, and I knew he was neither seeing nor hearing me. There was nothing I could do. I waited in the living room for the spell to run its course. I listened helplessly to the steady, relentless sound of flesh smashing into the hard, unyielding surface and to intermittent screams of hatred and dying and killing made all the more terrifying by their incoherence.

After it became quiet, I went to his room to peer through the open door. I saw he was on his bed, deep in an unnatural sleep, so I eased the door shut and walked into the kitchen. Something caught my eye on the paneling, near the telephone, under the calendar. I turned to look and a gasp of horror escaped my lips. A section of the wall was red with blood that had partially dried as it oozed downward. Snatching up a dishcloth from the sink, I wet it and I washed the wall, and the washing was mixed with tears and prayers. "Please, dear God, let this be over. Please, dear God, let there be an end. Please, God . . ."

Four hours passed before the pain awakened Alex. I took him to the hospital, to the emergency room, where X rays showed there were no broken bones and a doctor bandaged the raw and swollen hand. Codeine was prescribed for the pain, and later, resting as comfortably as possible on the living-room couch, he was able to talk of the newly emerged trauma. "It happened in early November, after my eighth birthday," he said. His voice was dry and flat. The violence of the feelings and emotions had already been spent and only the bare husks of words remained. "I was home for the weekend from the institution, and George took me to this place, some kind of a lodge where they all hung out to drink and play pool. I went outside and Christine was there and she said she was going to be nice to me and George was beating up on me a lot so I went with her. We walked for a long ways until we came to an apartment in a big, white house. I don't

think Christine lived there because she didn't seem to know
where the bathroom was. She made a phone call and fifteen
minutes later a woman came with a little girl about four years
old and two little boys who were maybe five or six. I recognized one of the boys. It was Howard and Patsy Henderson's
kid. It was Bobby.

"We watched television for a while and Christine told me
and the girl to go into the bedroom. She took our clothes off
and she took a pencil off the bureau and she held my hand
and made me push it inside of the little girl. The girl was
screaming, 'It hurts. It hurts!' but Christine yelled at her to
shut up because she had to do this. 'I have to do it! I have to
do it,' " he said, mimicking the compelling urgency. Alex
paused, and his expression was oddly contemplative. "I
think," he said, as though this were a common, everyday observation, "it was her first time."

I steeled myself against a sudden rush of grief and rage as
I realized that only in a world where children are consistently
the objects of sexual assault, only in a world where this is
more the norm than the exception, could such a remark be so
casually made.

"She made me lie on my back," he continued, "and she put
the girl on top of me and tried to put my penis in the girl with
her hands. It was like she was a teacher, like she was teaching me a lesson, explaining exactly how to do it. The girl
kept crying and she finally gave up and brought the two boys
in. They took off their clothes and Christine tried to have
them do it to the girl. Afterward, they started doing sex stuff
to Christine, sucking her breasts and all that. They really went
at it like they enjoyed it and seemed to know what to do."

He stopped talking and I could see the tension building up
in his body. I knew the worst was yet to come. "What happened next?" I asked reluctantly.

Alex exhaled explosively as though he had been holding
his breath. "She took the pencil and put it in my rectum and
went up and down. Like she was mashing potatoes!" he ex-

claimed with tortured indignation. "Like she was mashing potatoes!"

I didn't mention this last revelation to Sam. He had an especially difficult time handling disclosures that involved a mother's cruelty to her child. It was almost as if he himself felt threatened. But I did call Paul Phillips. I guess I was naive enough to think he would want to look into the incident. Perhaps Alex could identify that house as he had the other, and maybe an investigator could talk to the Henderson boy. I reached Paul at the County DA's Office and began to relate the contents of the flashback.

"I don't want to hear about it," he said, cutting me off abruptly. "Don't tell me. If I know about it, I will have to do something. The defense lawyer will say he did all those things and is trying to blame her for it."

There was no point in repeating this to Alex. Even if I'd wanted to, I wouldn't have known how. I put it out of my mind, and Alex nursed his injured hand so it would be healed before the last basketball game of the season. He was in ninth grade now and he had made the junior varsity team. Our school didn't have the greatest team in the world and Alex wasn't the best player, but Sam and I went to the games anyway. On this final night, the West River Indians were up against the Fairview Raiders. At the end of the first quarter, the Raiders were ahead by ten points. At halftime, their lead had increased to fifteen.

"Do you want something to eat?" asked Sam as the players left the floor. "Some kids are selling hot dogs and soda out in the hallway."

"Sure," I said shifting my weight on the hard bench. While I waited for Sam to return, friends and neighbors passed by, and we exchanged greetings and pleasantries. But my thoughts were on Alex. Would he get to play? He'd missed a week's practice sessions, and the coach didn't use every boy on the second string in every game.

Sam climbed back up the bleachers, handed me a hot dog and an orange soda, and took his seat. "It sure doesn't look good for us," was his superfluous comment.

As the Indians emerged from the locker room on the other side of the gym, I said, "I don't think they know that. Look at them, Sam. They're all smiles and high fives."

"The coach must have given them one hell of a pep talk."

Whatever it was, it worked. The Indians took the offense, and when the buzzer sounded the end of the third quarter the score was 32 to 37. We were only five points behind. Seven minutes into the fourth quarter, the score remained unchanged. The coach called a time out and two players, red-faced, chests heaving, took the bench. The numbers of the subs came over the loudspeaker. "That's Alex," said Sam. "Number eleven. He's going to play."

At five foot eight, Alex didn't have the height of many of the others, and sometimes he made mistakes because he tried too hard. But he was fast and he was agile. Within seconds he had the ball. He passed it downcourt. A teammate reached up, caught it, and made the shot. The Raiders got the ball on the rebound, tried for a layup, and missed. Our point guard grabbed it, drove toward the basket, and got fouled. The spectators fell silent as he stood on the foul line, his eyes riveted on the basket. Three bounces. Aim and thrust. He made the point. When this performance was successfully repeated, the fans on our side erupted into cheers and whistles. We were ahead by one.

Play resumed, and the boy Alex was guarding was trying to score. Alex jumped up and frantically waved his arms in front of him. It was to no avail. Swish. The ball went through the hoop. We were behind by one.

The crowd gave a collective groan. I glanced at the clock. Six seconds to go. We had the ball and our forward passed it half the length of the court. Alex caught it on the run, leaped into the air, and laid it up and in. We had won the game. It was only by a single point, but we had won.

The cheerleaders in their short-skirted red-and-gold outfits chanted Alex's name as the two teams lined up for the obligatory shaking of hands. Sam and I watched him as he walked down the line, his shoulders back, his chin up. "Walk like you are somebody," Miss Delia had said so many times. Alex was walking like he was somebody.

The winning basket and deluge of compliments from coaches, teachers, and friends had Alex feeling so good about himself that what happened next was not unexpected. I was not really surprised when this boost to his self-esteem gave him the strength and courage to unlock another piece of his past. It began with a phone call. "You've got to come to the school and get me," he said.

"Are you sick?" I asked in alarm.

His whispered reply held a frantic urgency. "I'm bleeding."

There was a sinking sensation in the pit of my stomach. Not again, I thought as I grabbed my jacket and car keys. Not again! The rectal bleeding, usually accompanied by abdominal pain, had been occurring intermittently over the past four years but lately it was increasingly frequent. This was the second time in a month I'd had to go to the school and pick him up. Bill seemed to think it had something to do with the flashbacks, and in fact many of the episodes did coincide with flashbacks. How could that be? I wondered. What did one have to do with the other? I made a quick note to set up an appointment at Children's Hospital in Boston. The doctors there would certainly be able to discover the cause.

"I've got to talk to you," Alex told me when he got into the car. "As soon as we get home." A few minutes later he was slumped dejectedly in the antique rocker before the fireplace, and I mentally compared the 140-pound, fourteen-year-old youth before me with the small boy I had rocked for so many hours in that very same chair. "Ma, something . . ." He stopped and shook his head and looked at me beseechingly.

"Alex, what is it? What's wrong?"

"It was weird," he said, and his forehead was wrinkled in

a puzzled frown and he gave another little shake of his head. "It was so weird. I—I was in algebra class, but I didn't know where I was. I didn't recognize the teacher or any of my friends. When the teacher said to write your name on the paper, I couldn't. I couldn't. I didn't know my name. I didn't know who I was. This has been happening a lot lately. Kids call out to me and say my name and I don't answer because I feel like I'm somebody else. I don't feel like myself."

"You feel like somebody else?" I said, attempting to keep calm while my mind was racing in circles trying to make some kind of sense out of what he was saying, trying to figure out where to go for help. Aloud I said, "That must be a very scary experience."

"Yes," he said. "I'm scared to death. Sometimes the clocks just jump ahead and I don't know what happened to the time. And there are these pictures. They come on the blackboard, and when I see them, I hear screaming. Another thing is I think somebody's playing tricks on me. I keep finding stuff in my locker. There was a set of keys from the office and odd earrings and other kids' books. Someone must have put them there. Someone must know the combination to my lock."

I thought of Dr. Van der Kolk, the world-renowned expert on post-traumatic stress syndrome I'd heard so much about from Ann. I called him, and I could hardly believe it as he kept saying in his heavily accented voice, "Oh, yes, of course," while he listened to my litany of strange and bizarre behavior. I could hardly believe someone out there knew what I was talking about. "I want you to contact my child psychologist, Dr. Nina Fish-Murray," he continued. "She does much work with cases like this."

I got hold of Dr. Fish-Murray and recounted as much as possible of Alex's story, including a description of the last flashback and the self-inflicted injury. "You're doing a fantastic job," she said. "You are doing exactly the right things. The dancing lessons, everything you are doing, I highly recommend."

"But there's more coming." My voice trembled. "The

nightmares are back. And the fast-forwarding pictures. I can't take any more."

"You don't have to," Dr. Fish-Murray responded gently. "I know someone who can help you. There is another way. His name is Dr. Steven Kingsbury. He is very, very good. He uses hypnotism."

Hypnotism! Even the word conjured up fear and trepidation. I had visions of secretive explorations into the dark, netherworld of the subconscious mind. Then I saw Alex smashing his fist into that wall. I saw the dripping blood. "How can I reach him?" I asked. "How can I get hold of him?"

Dr. Fish-Murray gave me both the office and home phone numbers for Dr. Kingsbury. Almost as an afterthought she added, "I wonder if he could be a multiple."

"A what?"

"Multiple. Multiple personality. It's not uncommon for children who have suffered like this to become multiple, you know."

No, I didn't know. And if the mention of hypnotism was frightening, the concept of multiple personalities was a hundred times worse. My first reaction was to recoil from the whole idea. But what about those inexplicable incidents that had occurred over the past several years? What about that June twenty-ninth when Alex first knew of the sexual abuse by Christine? The whimpering voice: "I'm four. I'm four years old." Was it a flashback or was it something more? What about last Halloween, when he had kept saying his name was Ricky? Who was Ricky? I thought of the mutilated frogs and the stolen four-wheeler. "It was like watching someone else." That was what he had said. Like watching someone else. I thought of the times when he did not seem to remember his school lessons or what he had said or done. One incident in particular. The hospital. After Christine's visit. Had he really been too embarrassed to admit to his behavior? Or was there another explanation? What about the hate-filled entity who did not seem to be our son, our Alex?

And who had drawn those two very different pictures of the barns? Now he was telling me he didn't know his name. He didn't know who he was and he felt like somebody else. Who? Who was he? Who was this somebody else?

But the dire necessity of the immediate situation took precedence over any conjectures concerning multiple personalities. On Dr. Fish-Murray's advice, we kept Alex on Valium to help him endure the agony and to delay the flashback until we could get him to Dr. Kingsbury.

And Valium or no Valium, it was right there. The symptoms had returned in full force: the sleepless nights haunted by bloody visions, the sound of screaming pictures on the school blackboard, the hours and days either lost completely or speeded up so two weeks seemed to have passed.

The psychiatrist Dr. Fish-Murray recommended had accepted a teaching position at Harvard Medical School. For now, however, he was still associated with a private hospital in Nashua, New Hampshire. On the thirteenth of April, Bill drove us up there to meet with him. During the ride, I looked out of the car window at the barely greening landscape, too tense and apprehensive to find comfort in the signs of spring. What would happen? What would this venture into the unknown be like? How did hypnotism work? I tried to allay my fears by focusing on the high expectations we had of this doctor. He would surely be able to help Alex find out what was going on.

Dr. Steven Kingsbury. I had the feeling I was before a historic figure. His was a presence that transcended the bearded and bespectacled visage, and even the numerous degrees hanging on the wall over his desk. He was a pioneer in his field, and there was about him an aura of destiny and mission. But to us, to Alex and Bill and me, he was hope. He was a way out of this morass of mystifying events.

Having given us some background information on hypnotism, he explained that when terrible things are done to a child, things that cannot be tolerated by the conscious mind, some children are able to put themselves into a hypnotic state and these horrible experiences are relegated to the unconscious. "They become islands," he said, "islands outside of the conscious mind. Because they got there through hypnosis, it is through hypnosis these experiences are retrieved. When Alex is having a flashback, he is in a hypnotic state."

I listened with awe and leaned forward to hear more. It was all so new to me and so fascinating. But the doctor had turned his attention to Alex. "Are you nervous about this?" he asked.

Alex squirmed self-consciously in his chair, and an expression of apprehension flitted across his features. "A little," he said.

"Well, why shouldn't you be? Here they've dragged you to some stranger who for all you know might be mumbling voodoo."

"Oh, it's not that," replied Alex. "I'm nervous because I don't think it's going to work. I don't think I can be hypnotized."

Dr. Kingsbury nodded knowingly, and his brown eyes twinkled behind his rather thick glasses as he addressed both the spoken and unspoken fears. "Every time you put yourself in a dissociative state such as a flashback or not knowing where you are, you are hypnotizing yourself. I am not going to do anything to you. You will do it to yourself, and you are in control. I am just the guide. I will help you, but you do it yourself. Now, if you are willing, I'm going to help you enter a light hypnotic state."

"Okay," consented Alex, still tense but somewhat more trusting.

"Just make yourself comfortable. That's right. Let your hand support your head." The doctor spoke in an easy, conversational tone as he encouraged Alex to relax. "Let your eyes close. You are with people who love and care about you. Now imagine—you are floating—way over—the water—the ocean—looking down—see the water—see the pattern—of the waves—notice the shades—of the coloring." The doctor's attention was focused on Alex, and his voice, vibrant and soothing, paused after every three to five syllables. Gradually it became lower and lower. "Find a place—a safe place—where you will be safe—very safe— free from harm—very safe. When you awake—you can share—it with us—if you wish—only if you wish." He took Alex to a beautiful beach where he could feel the warmth of the sun on his back. And he took him to white, multishaped clouds that drifted high over the earth. After six or seven minutes his voice returned to normal tones and he said, "You can will yourself awake. When you are ready. When you are ready."

Alex had stirred slightly but still seemed to be in a restful sleep. "He'll wake up in a moment," said Dr. Kingsbury in re-sponse to my inquiring glance. "Do you mind if I smoke?"

Bill and I both responded that we did not, and the doctor took a cigarette and lit it without taking his eyes from Alex. "My one vice," he said unapologetically.

Alex's eyelids fluttered. He blinked and raised his head and appeared to be confused, as though he didn't know where he was. Turning his head to look at us, he said incredulously, "I was hypnotized. I was actually hypnotized." And with a note of sadness, "I was above the earth. That was my safe place, floating on a cloud above the earth."

"I don't blame you," said Dr. Kingsbury. "This world has not been very kind to you. Now, let's try it again. I under-stand you've been finding strange objects in your locker."

"Yes," answered Alex, knitting his brow in concern. "Es-pecially the keys from the office. I don't know how they got there. Someone must have put them in my locker."

"Let's see if we can find out," said the doctor as he extin-guished his cigarette. "Relax again. That's right."

Alex stretched his legs out and leaned his head back and closed his eyes, and this time the doctor's calm, steadying voice led him into a castle. "This is—a magic castle. It is— a place—of peacefulness—and of great safety. You're walk-ing—down the stairs—stone stairs—notice the texture—of the rocks. You're going down—into a room. It's very— comfortably furnished. There's a chair—a comfortable chair—and a television—a very special television. You make yourself—comfortable—and you turn on—the television—and you will see—how the keys—got into the locker. If you like you may share—this information—with us—but only—if you like."

Dr. Kingsbury intensely scrutinized the boy as he lit another cigarette. Puffing meditatively, his gaze never wavered from Alex. Noticing the almost imperceptible movement of a finger, the doctor said, "Now you will begin to wake up. That's it. You will awaken."

Alex lifted his head. As he opened his eyes, he gave a gasp and doubled over. Burying his face in his hands, he moaned, "Oh my God! I took the keys. I did it. I took the keys. I had no control. I could see myself on the television, going into the office and taking the keys."

"How do you feel about it?" queried the doctor. "Are you feeling bad because you're ashamed or because you had no control?"

"Both," he answered.

I was still trying to recover from my astonishment that Alex could have taken the keys and the other objects without knowing he had done so when I heard Dr. Kingsbury say, "Alex has worked hard. He's done enough for today."

Bill and I looked at each other with shock and disappointment. Nothing has been accomplished, I said to myself. Nothing has been done. We are going to return home to face the same hell when the flashback comes.

Dr. Kingsbury was regarding us with a slightly smug air of serene confidence, and I thought I detected a fleeting satisfaction in our discomfiture before he began to explain. "You want Alex to remember whatever is causing the problem."

"Yes, of course," I said. "Isn't that what we came for?"

"It is important," he went on, "but my goals are different from yours. I want to teach Alex he can control his dissociative states. I want to teach him he is safe and he does not need to be threatened by them. And that is the most important thing. To know he is safe. That," the doctor concluded, "is what I want to teach him."

"No!" exclaimed Sam two days after our session with Dr. Kingsbury. "No way." He gave a short, disparaging laugh as he stirred the sugar in his coffee with such agitation it spilled over onto the table. "You're saying Alex came up and told this story and there was no acting out, no obnoxious behavior, no nothing. You can believe it if you want to, but I think he's making it up to get you to feel sorry for him."

"I didn't say I believed him," I answered defensively, and in the face of Sam's denial and my own confusion, I didn't know what to think. "I was only telling you what happened. Alex was using a screwdriver to remove a link from a new bicycle chain and he came in and very calmly told me he had just had a flashback. He said Christine had taken a screwdriver and put it into two girls from the front, and the details weren't clear yet."

"I heard it once!" shouted Sam. "I don't need to hear it again." And turning on his heel, he strode angrily from the kitchen.

I was left alone with my own chaotic thoughts and doubts. Maybe Sam was right. It did not, after all, seem possible Alex could disclose something so awful and still remain so tranquil and composed. Questions came into my mind, disturbing questions. Why couldn't Sam bear to hear this about the girls? Why was he looking for excuses not to believe? And why didn't the assistant district attorney, Paul Phillips, want to hear about the pencil rapes? Was it because the people who did these things, people like Christine, bore enough of a semblance of normality to enable them to function in our society? Was it because they worked and they shopped and they walked among us and there was no way to tell who they were? Was there something in the human psyche that needed to believe the perpetrators of such atrocities against children had to be obviously insane and candidates for the snake pit? Were we compelled to blind ourselves to the truth in order to prevent the very foundations of our secure little worlds from being shaken asunder?

Alex walked into the kitchen and stood before me. His face was red and wet with tears, and I knew he had overheard at least part of what Sam and I had said. His voice held the agony of his frustration as he faced me accusingly. "You don't understand! You don't understand what Dr. Kingsbury did! He's a miracle worker. He went inside my mind and it's like I was reborn, like I had just come. I feel like the bad energy is gone, the energy I used to repress things. It is all gone! When the flashback came I kept my self. I did not lose my self! I had control over it."

Control! That's what Dr. Kingsbury was trying to explain to us. It was true. Alex did have control over this flashback. He had this control because he felt safe, safe enough to face whatever had happened. "That is the most important thing. To know he is safe." What had been just so many words became a living, pulsating truth.

It took ten days for the black, fast-forwarding pictures of this flashback to clear. On Monday, the twenty-fourth of April, Alex called me from school. "Ma," he said, "I don't feel right."

"Do you want me to pick you up?"

"No, no. I just needed to hear your voice. I know what it was. The girls were my sisters. It will probably take a few days before I can talk about it."

Alex was very quiet that night but otherwise he appeared to be reasonably normal. The next day, however, my concern mounted when he did not return home from school, and by five o'clock I was out searching for him. As I drove through the center of town, I spotted him and pulled over to the side of the road. Getting out of the car and going over to him, I saw his eyes, glassy and unfocused and dark in the ghastly white pallor of his face. "Oh, Ma!" he cried out. "It kept com-

ing! It kept coming all day. The details. One after another.
The rest of the details. It kept coming. It was the worst day of
my life. I had to keep running to the bathroom. I was bleeding again. And I was sick to my stomach and throwing up.
You will, too, when I tell you about it. I made it, though," he
added proudly. "I made it through the day. I stayed in
school."

Later in the evening, Alex was able to tell how Bert and
Christine had taken turns forcing a screwdriver into the girls'
vaginas. "There was so much screaming," he said. "And there
was blood all over the place. While one was doing it, the
other took pictures with an instant camera. I saw them. They
were horrible. There was one of Bert doing it to me with his
penis. I was five, Ma. I was five years old."

It didn't hit me right away. I felt as though my entire body
had been shot full of Novocain. Numb. Until I thought of the
pictures, until I thought of the child looking at the pictures
that indelibly fixed the horror. Then came the queasiness and
the nausea and the bitter gall in my throat. Alex had said that
when he told me about it I would be sick. He had been right.

After this, there was another of those blessed periods of
peace and calm and healing. The only unusual occurrence
was the discovery of more of those predisclosure drawings.
Again they were in a notebook. The figures at the top of the
page bore a resemblance to tongues. Under these were several
triangular forms and a detailed depiction of a vagina. It didn't
take me long to guess what they represented. But on the bottom of the page, there was a fourth drawing, and what that
meant, I hadn't the slightest idea. It was a fish. An exquisitely
drawn finned and scaly fish. A fish with human eyes.

Since there were no symptoms of any impending problem, I
decided to take Alex to the first major horse show of the
year. I thought of how far he had come with his riding as I
stood at ringside waiting for his Junior Exhibitor English
Pleasure class to begin. This was an evening class and the
ring was illuminated by large floodlights. Around the lights,

Predisclosed drawing, May 1989

there were clouds of moths swirling in frenzied circles. In the center of the ring a Victorian gazebo, banked with shrubbery and flowers, served as the judges' stand. Next to the gazebo, watching for the judge to make her appearance, was the ringmaster. He was past middle age, a stocky man who sported thick gray sideburns. His outfit, dictated by tradition, was most imposing. It consisted of a bright red hunt coat with brass buttons down the front, white breeches, and black patent-leather boots. On his head he wore a tall top hat with the rare confidence of a man accustomed to wearing top hats.

The judge, a fairly young woman in a pale blue evening gown, swept across the arena to take her place next to the ringmaster. Her earrings and necklace glittered with the reflected light, and on her left shoulder she wore a corsage of tiny pink roses. Picking up her clipboard and pencil and nodding to the ringmaster, she looked toward the in-gate. There was a fanfare of music and the twelve junior exhibitors, boys and girls under the age of eighteen, trotted their horses into the ring.

"Class is complete," said the announcer. "Walk please. All walk." I watched the judge study the class. I knew she was looking for a relaxed, flat-footed walk. Several of the horses in the ring were tense and jigging. They would not settle into the walk. The judge busily made notations on her pad.

The riders were requested to trot. I kept my eyes on Alex. He was posting so effortlessly he almost seemed to float above the saddle. Blaze was attentive and responsive. His ears were forward, his neck was arched, and he was moving with cadence and balance. I felt a little thrill of anticipation. If nothing went wrong, they just might win this class.

The riders were asked to walk again, and then the voice over the loudspeaker said, "Canter, please. Show your horses at the canter." The organist played a lilting melody, and the ring was alive with controlled motion. At this point, I mentally compared Alex and Blaze to the other entries. It was with some dismay that I saw two horses who were doing as well. One was a striking chestnut gelding with a light mane and tail and the other was a gleaming black mare.

The call came to reverse, and the horses went through their paces in the opposite direction. At the canter, the gelding led with his outside front leg rather than the correct inside leg. That would be enough to put him out of first place. But there was still the black mare.

"Line up in front of the ringmaster. Please line up." The riders guided their mounts into the center of the ring. The judge walked down the line, still jotting notes on her pad, and asked each competitor to back up his or her horse. Both Blaze and the mare were supple and obedient at the rein-back. Either could win. I could only wait for the result.

When it came, it was Alex. I let out a whoop and gave a jump in the air, and along with the rest of the crowd I enthusiastically clapped my hands. Barely able to contain myself, I watched the photographer come out to take pictures in front of the gazebo. The shimmering blue ribbon was fluttering from Blaze's bridle and the ringmaster was standing at the horse's head. In his hands he held the trophy, a polished pewter bowl. Alex turned his head toward the camera. His face was wreathed in smiles and his eyes were dancing with joy.

Back at the barn, he proudly handed me his prizes, untacked his horse, and put him in the stall. "Good boy," he said, and Blaze pricked his ears and nickered softly. Alex laughed and leaned over to kiss him affectionately on his moist nose.

I saw the glow of victory give way to a look of utter revulsion, and he dropped to the ground as suddenly as though he had been shot. Flinging ribbon and trophy aside, I helped him into a nearby chair. A shudder went through me as I touched his skin. It was icy cold, exactly as it had been last August when the things Bert had done to him, the acts of oral sex, were coming into consciousness. A slow trickle of blood coming from one nostril was in sharp contrast to the deathly paleness. "Ma," he groaned, clutching at his stomach. "I feel so sick. I have to go to the bathroom."

Alex spent most of the next two hours coping with bouts of vomiting and diarrhea, but he did not lose control. Wondering what had happened, I began to put the pieces together. I thought of those predisclosure drawings, the tongues and the intimately detailed vagina. And there was the triggering factor, the kissing of the horse's nose. Apparently, my guess about the drawings had been correct, and within a few days this was confirmed by Alex.

Much later, I happened to learn how the combination of semen and other bodily fluids smells exactly like fish. It wasn't until then that I knew the meaning of the fourth drawing, the one that had been so puzzling. The fish with the human eyes.

XIII

The Twin

"We could not find anything wrong. We don't know what caused the bleeding." There was just the merest hint of puzzlement and frustration in the doctor's voice. And even that seemed out of place in this clinical, antiseptic atmosphere, in this Boston hospital that was among the best in the world, a citadel of medical knowledge where one expected to find solutions to problems and answers to questions.

I was completely unprepared for this result, but there was also a feeling of relief. Alex was okay. He hadn't been physically damaged.

The doctor had thought it best to anesthetize Alex for the procedure, so I sat down to wait for him to come out of the recovery room. I leaned back and closed my eyes and my thoughts touched on the events of the preceding months: the emotionally draining flashbacks, the visit with Dr. Kingsbury, the ongoing battle with the legal system. In February, I had asked Paul Phillips, the assistant DA, to tell us in writing why he was not going forward in his efforts to indict Christine for sexually abusing Alex. When no response was forthcoming, Ann pushed for a meeting of all concerned parties so Paul could tell Alex how the investigation had been resolved and give him the reasons. Since she was fairly certain there would be no indictment, she wanted Sam and Bill present at this meeting. She hoped they might help Alex with his anger.

And that anger? It burgeoned and billowed inside of him, amplifying into a combustible rage, volcanic in proportion and focusing entirely on Christine. "I will kill her," he wrote in a letter to his grandmother, whom he had seen briefly in an unsuccessful attempt to enlist her support in building a case against Christine. "I mean it. I will kill her even if I have to go to jail." A sketch of a sharp and bloody dagger was captioned: "I will stab her right in the middle of her heart." I confiscated the letter and did not allow him to mail it. I was afraid it might get him into trouble.

On the day after Alex was discharged from the hospital, he had another one of those strangely agitated spells that ended with his taking off on a moped Eddie had left in the barn. We contacted the police, and by nightfall a state trooper called to report they had found him. "I asked him where he was going," the trooper said, "and he told me he was on his way to Bainbridge to kill his parents. He was very matter-of-fact about it, like he was going for an ice-cream cone or something. He sounded more like a little kid than a fifteen-year-old."

Our son was released into our custody, and back home, sitting him down at the table in the kitchen, we tried to talk to him about what he had done. "Alex," said Sam, "why did you take Ed's moped?"

"I didn't."

Sam half rose from his seat and leaned toward the boy. "What do you mean, you didn't? You were caught red-handed. How can you say you didn't?"

"Okay, I did. I just wanted to go for a ride."

"I spoke to the trooper myself," I said. "You told him you were going to Bainbridge to kill George and Christine."

"No, he's got it all wrong. I didn't say that."

Sam let his weight drop onto the bench in a resigned slump. "Oh, so now the police are just making stuff up."

The sequence of denials and excuses that continually retreated and changed in the face of concrete evidence went on for another half hour, and I suspected he was trying to fill in the blank spaces of more lost time.

The police did not take Alex's threats seriously. But Ann

Dear Grandma

I am telling you the truth, if you dont believe it or want to believe it I can't change that, But I wouldn't Lie to you and you Know that. When she tells you she doesn't know what I am talking about She's pulling your leg. When the case comes and if somehow (highly doubtful) I dont win. I will kill her. I mean it I will kill her even if I have to go to ▦▦▦.

P.S. I will stab her right in the middle of the heart.

Letter to Grandmother, May 1989

did. She said she was obliged to at least give warning of
Alex's intent. We heard later that this information was terrifying to Christine. She refused to go outside without first
having someone check behind every tree and bush. She refused to go into the cellar alone, and she was actually looking under the bed and behind the shower curtain. The idea of
a timorous Christine peeking around corners and living in
fear may have been a small revenge, but in one of our therapy sessions it was enough to give Bill and Alex and me
some cause for laughter.

As for the meeting Ann wanted, her requests were repeatedly disregarded. Only when we had our state representative,
Marie Parente, and a lawyer from a state agency that advocates for the rights of children call the County District Attorney's Office were we notified that they were going to have
another assistant district attorney, a woman named Janet Travers, meet with Alex. On one condition. "I want to question
him alone," she insisted. "I want to question him about the
sex abuse to see how he will hold up in court."

The prospect of talking of this once more caused him to be
sick for three days prior to the meeting. "It's worth it, Ma,"
he told me. "If the new district attorney wants to find out
how I'm going to hold up in court, it's got to mean I have a
good chance of getting there."

Ms. Travers never mentioned the sex abuse at the meeting.
She wanted to get acquainted first, she said. A second meeting was set up. Again he was sick. Again Ms. Travers did not
ask a single question about the sex abuse. She spoke about
court procedure. She spoke about how hard it would be for
him if he lost. She spoke about her daughter. On top of all this
she was unable to make eye contact with Alex. "She was so
nervous," he said. "She couldn't look at me, Ma. She couldn't
look at me. It made me feel like there was something wrong
with me."

And then it was July and it was hot and the blinds in Bill's
office were closed against the sun. "I saw this boy today,"

said Alex at the beginning of the session. "I'm sure he's my brother."

"If you mean some kid from one of George's many relationships," I commented disdainfully, "I doubt if he'd be around here. It must be a coincidence."

"No, no!" objected Alex, annoyed at me for not taking him seriously. "I saw him, I tell you. I saw him. He looked exactly like me. He looked like my twin. He has to be my brother!"

Neither Bill nor I considered the matter to be of any particular consequence. I put it out of my mind until three weeks later when Alex came home and, crying piteously, threw himself on his bed. What now? I wondered. What had happened now?

I went into his room and tried to comfort him. When the racking sobs subsided enough so that he was able to speak, I knew I had never before heard such wretchedness and crushingly hopeless despair in his voice. "Mom, Ma—I—oh, God—" He choked back another rush of tears and, turning over with laborious slowness, raised himself on his elbows. "You know that time in Bill's office—I told you I saw this kid who looks like me, like a twin. I've been seeing him quite a bit. I saw him today, in the park, at the ballfield. I was at the edge of the baseball diamond watching a game. This kid, the Twin, was right next to me, and I started talking to him. My friend Ryan Donnelly was standing about ten feet away and he said, 'Hey, Alex! What's going on? Who you talking to? There's nobody there.' Oh, Ma, I'm so embarrassed I want to die! He's so . . ." His words trailed off bleakly as he gave me a long, appraising look. "I can see him just like I can see you right now. He's as real as that. But today after Ryan said what he did, I knew I was the only one who could see him. Nobody else can see him, Ma. Only me. Nobody else."

A tingling sensation crawled over my skin, up my arms, and along my spine. A sudden, frigid cold immobilized me. When I was able to move I took a step backward in an instinctive withdrawal. When I was able to think, I fastened my eyes on the nubby brown tweed material of the drapes. And the rounded maple bedposts. And the wall covered with pictures of horses. Real. They were real. I could see them. And I could touch them.

"Is—is he—here now?" I stammered, and my eyes darted nervously about the room. "Do you see him now?"

"No," replied Alex with an unexpected nonchalance. "He only shows up when I'm with my friends. I'm crazy, Ma. Let's face it. People who go around seeing someone who isn't there and talking to someone who isn't there have got to be crazy."

The finality and acceptance in his voice reached through my curtain of fear, and I went to him and held his hand in mine. "No, Alex, you are not crazy," I said. "Whatever is going on is not because you are crazy." At least that would be an explanation: the hallucinations of a deranged lunatic, or a drug addict, or an alcoholic suffering from delirium tremens. If the Twin was none of these, who was he? Where had he come from? And why had he come?

"I wonder if he could be a multiple." That was what Dr. Fish-Murray had said way back last winter, and I had not thought about it since. I was not ready. I could not handle it. If I ignored it, maybe it would go away. But I had known she was right, and now there was only one thing to do. I had to get Alex to Dr. Kingsbury.

He was now teaching at Harvard and was also associated with the Massachusetts Mental Health Center in Boston. On September fifteenth, Alex and I went in there to meet with him in the high-ceilinged, book-crowded room that was his office. Seated at his desk and attired in a rather rumpled brown suit and pale yellow shirt, Dr. Kingsbury swiveled his chair around to face us. His right hand absentmindedly stroked his neatly trimmed beard as he peered at Alex through the thick glasses.

"The first thing I want you to know is you are not crazy!" he said, reiterating my initial observation with an emphatic confidence. I recalled the little boy of five years ago who was so motivated to give up his tantrums because he didn't want people to think he was insane, and I realized this was what he needed to hear. "In fact," continued Dr. Kingsbury, "for you to create a personality to handle intolerable trauma was the sanest and most intelligent thing you could have done."

In response to the doctor's questions, Alex described the Twin as nine or ten inches shorter than he was and said he was seeing him almost every day. "He always comes when I'm with my friends," said Alex, frowning slightly. "Never when I'm alone."

"How do you think he feels?" the doctor asked. "Without thinking about it, how does he feel?"

"Angry."

"I would like to try to talk to the Twin. Is that all right with you?"

Alex stiffened involuntarily and for a moment appeared to brace himself against his chair. "Well, okay, as long as I'm out and don't know about it," he said with some nervousness.

Dr. Kingsbury began by speaking of where he had gone before under hypnosis: shining seas and warm, sunny beaches and floating clouds. And slowly and gradually the resonant voice led my son into the protection of that fortress with its moat and its drawbridge and its soaring towers. He led him into the safety and tranquillity of the magic castle. "You're walking down stairs—step by—step—down a long—deep staircase—solid walls—on each side—solid stairs—step by step—deeper and deeper. You have come—to a landing— and you see—a door. You know that—if you open—the door—you will find—a quiet, peaceful place—where you can rest. You can explore—the quiet—and the peace—and the safety. This is a—special place—a healing place. It is far away—from all aspects—of the world—except my voice. The only thing—you can hear—is my voice. That's right. You are going—lower and lower. You are going—deeper and deeper. You are finding—greater and greater peace. You have great—skills and strengths. You have a twin—who also—has great skills and strengths. I would like to meet you. I want you to use Alex's body."

I was sitting back out of Alex's line of vision, but by leaning forward I could see the changes come over him. I could see his features harden and become set in taut lines. His brows were drawn together in a frown and he took in quick, short breaths of air.

"That's right," continued the doctor, his eyes riveted on the boy's countenance, "you can take over now. I want to know your needs, too. Do you need privacy? Do you need to share? Do you need revenge? I'd like to meet you. You can choose when Alex can hear you or not hear you. You want us to know you. By showing yourself, you want to be discovered. You have pain and you have anger. You did much. You deserve credit. Do you want to meet me?"

"Yes," replied the Twin, sitting straighter in his chair and looking around as though he had never seen the room or the doctor before. And, of course, he hadn't.

With intense sincerity, the doctor said, "I want to help you. How may I help you?"

The Twin's voice, slightly higher and thinner than Alex's, seemed to come from a far place, and I heard the fear and anguish in that desperately imploring cry. "Save me," he called out. "Save me!"

"From what?" asked the doctor. "What is it you want me to save you from?"

"Destruction," answered the Twin.

After eliciting the information that the Twin had first come to Alex when he was six years old and was now eight, Dr. Kingsbury proceeded to his next question. "What did you do for Alex?"

"I saved him. I took over. I took the pain."

"So you are a protector. You are a capable saver, and you started to show yourself because you thought Alex was going to leave you. I want to get to know you better so Alex can appreciate you and never leave you. If he did, he would be incomplete. It would also hurt Alex if you left him. My goal is not to destroy you. I do not want to destroy you. I want to help save you. How did you help Alex?"

"I helped him escape," replied the Twin in the tone of a child sharing a confidence.

"You solved problems under pressure?" asked the doctor in an attempt to elaborate on this statement. "You took over when Alex was scared?"

"Yes."

"And you wait to come out until he is with other people?"

"Yes," said the Twin. "I need other people."

Cognizant of the integrity of the personality and any desire for confidentiality, Dr. Kingsbury asked the Twin if he wanted Alex to be aware of his fears and of his needs.

"I do," he said.

After the doctor had the Twin practice his coming and going so he could be more in control of it, he said, "My job is to make sure you are appreciated and understood. You don't need people to talk to Alex. You can talk to him if he is alone. I have to end for now. Is it all right for me to meet with you again?"

"Yes," said the Twin, and there was a faint note of hopefulness in the quick, clear response. This brief encounter between Dr. Kingsbury and the eight-year-old personality had established the beginnings of trust.

His eyes still alertly concentrated on the Twin, the doctor slid a cigarette from a pack and lit it. The thin smoke curled upward as he took a short puff. "I want to ask you to go to sleep and give Alex back control of his body. Alex, hold on to the peace and quiet. I want you to awaken and know that you have accomplished good further work."

Alex had no memory of what had transpired, and later, when we were at home in the living room, he expressed some curiosity about what had happened. I told him about it and his disbelief erupted into anger against me and against the doctor. "You're crazy," he shouted. "Dr. Kingsbury is crazy. You're all crazy!"

As he was able to listen, I told him of what I had seen and heard. "The Twin is a protector, Alex. You saved yourself by inventing him. He's a part of you and he's afraid you don't need him anymore and he will be destroyed. He needs to talk to you, to communicate. He wants you to know what he did for you so you can appreciate him."

The Twin's activities during the following two weeks did little to foster the desired understanding and communication. Alex was now in his sophomore year, and there was hardly a day that he did not come home from school without a tirade of bitter accusations against the Twin. "I hate him!" he cried. "He follows me around. He sits next to me in class. How am I supposed to pay attention to the teacher with him right there? You want to know what he did this morning, Ma? He walked alongside me down the corridor and he was totally naked. I was so embarrassed I almost died. I didn't remember the other kids couldn't see him."

Worse than that, I began receiving calls from Alex's tenth-grade teachers. There were reports of defiant acting out and of objects being thrown at the teacher's desk. Mrs. Choate, the history teacher, was at her wit's end over this. She said she was completely drained of energy when Alex was in her class. "I didn't do it, Ma," he said tearfully. "Mrs. Choate took me out in the hall and gave me a lecture. I didn't have the slightest idea what she was talking about."

And there were the pushing episodes. Teenage pranks, I thought. Or Alex was misbehaving and didn't want to own up to it. He told me that as he was going into the cafeteria, he felt a strong push that sent him lurching forward. "I turned around right away, Ma. No one was close enough to touch me. No one." And on two occasions, while he was sitting in class, his chair suddenly toppled over backward. "I didn't do it," he said. "What will my friends think? I don't act like that! I didn't do anything."

I believed him. His distress over what his friends would think seemed genuine. But if Alex wasn't responsible for the disorderly conduct, who was?

When the idea first came, it was like touching a red-hot stove, and I pulled back and away from it. How could someone who wasn't there have so much strength? I asked Alex once again to describe what had happened. "Ma," he said in exasperation, "all three times I was minding my own business and I felt this force. It was like a strong gust of wind and it pushed me over."

If Alex was telling the truth at all, the only one who could be responsible for this poltergeist-like activity was the Twin. As incredible as this was, Dr. Kingsbury was not surprised. There was not as yet any valid scientific explanation for this phenomenon, but still he was not surprised. And at our next session, the Twin, again using Alex's body, came right out and told the doctor that he had indeed pushed Alex. "I was trying to talk to him," he said. "I was angry. He didn't pay attention to me."

The doctor concentrated on the task of facilitating communication between the Twin and Alex. "If I ask you to write to him," he said to the Twin, "can you say hello?"

The Twin took a pad and a pen and very neatly wrote "HELOW" with his left hand. Alex was right-handed and afterward he was unable to replicate this exercise.

Gently but firmly, Dr. Kingsbury continued to urge them to come closer together. "Come to the door of the room in the castle. Alex, come to the door so you can meet the Twin. You are safe. You can go back anytime you wish. And you, Twin, let me know when you sense Alex is there. Alex, I want you to be there. You want to be there. You need to meet this part of yourself. Twin, talk to Alex in your mind. Tell him what you have to tell him. By communicating you can grow together. There is no need for you to be destroyed. Or for him to be destroyed. You can grow together."

Dr. Kingsbury videotaped this session, and I borrowed the tape in the hope that I could get my husband to watch it. It would have helped so much if Sam had a better understanding of the situation. But he refused to look at it.

Although Alex did try to communicate with the alter,

some part of him resisted hearing what the Twin had to say. In school, increasing amounts of time were being lost, and in a desperate attempt to keep up, he resorted to bringing a tape recorder to classes. This measure did not help during exams, when he would black out after hearing a ringing sound in his ears. The results of the tests that he had no memory of taking ranged from excellent to failing, and he never knew which to expect.

On the morning of the fifteenth of October, Alex called me from school. He was bleeding again, he said, but thought he could make it through the day. An hour later I received another call. It was from the guidance counselor. I was told there was an emergency and that I should come immediately. When I got there, panic-stricken officials met me at the entrance and, with quiet urgency, ushered me down a long, empty corridor. I couldn't imagine what had gone wrong, and no one would tell me. The principal opened a door on the right. It was the algebra classroom. I hurried inside and saw that Alex was the only student in the room. He was at the first seat in the third row. The left side of his face rested on his desk, and his arms, bare under the short sleeves of his shirt, hung limply at his sides. His books lay at his feet.

"Oh, my God," I said as I saw the dark color of his skin. It was almost purple. "What happened?"

The school nurse hovered over his inert form. Her fingers were on his wrist. "He just went into a trance. The teacher couldn't arouse him. We got the rest of the kids out of here. There. There's a pulse now. It's slow but it's better. I couldn't get any pulse at first. And his color is improving. Do you want us to call an ambulance?"

As I quickly considered this option, Alex began to stir.

"Oh, good!" the nurse exclaimed. "He's coming out of it."

I went to him and knelt down beside him. He lifted his head, tensed his body, and quickly glanced around as though searching for an avenue of escape. "Alex, are you okay?" I asked.

"I don't know you," he said, spitting out the words in angry contempt.

I looked again at his face, the hardened features and the taut lines. This was not Alex I was seeing. This was not Alex I was talking to. This was the Twin.

The Twin did come to know me. He never said how or what he felt about me, but I knew how I felt about him. Every time I recalled that plaintive, heartrending plea to be saved, I wanted to help him and comfort him. On the other hand, my primary concern was for Alex, and I was afraid the Twin might harm him in some way. Although my son had recovered from the trance with no ill effects, I kept thinking of how the school nurse had said she couldn't find a pulse. The implications of this were very frightening to me. Suppose the personality had the power to actually stop Alex's breathing? Or suppose he were to put Alex into a trance while Alex was in a dangerous situation such as walking through heavy traffic or swimming or engaged in any of a number of other activities? If the Twin could push Alex around, what else might he be capable of doing?

When I had first become aware of the Twin's existence, I often felt as if I were living in some mysterious twilight zone. Then, toward the latter part of October, I was amazed to find I was actually getting used to him. Alex was lying on the couch in the living room. He was telling me about something that had gone on in English class. Stopping in midsentence, he looked up and fastened his eyes on a spot across the room. "He's here, Ma," he said.

"Where?"

"Right over there. On the cedar chest by the window."

I stared at the cedar chest. "What's he doing?"

"Nothing," replied Alex rather nonchalantly. "Just watching me."

There were no chills or prickles running down my spine. There was no uneasiness, no apprehension. It was almost normal. There was something else, however, that wasn't nor-

mal. Afterward, after the Twin had gone, I felt strangely list-
less and tired. I remembered what Mrs. Choate, the history
teacher, had told me about feeling drained of energy when
Alex was in her class. And the Twin had said he needed other
people to come out. He might not need them to talk to Alex
in his mind, but could it be possible that for the Twin to show
himself or to exert a physical force, he had to use the energy
of these other people?

The next trance occurred during a birthday party at a
friend's house. "He won't leave me alone," Alex complained
on the way home. "I was having a great time, and all of a sudden I was flat on my back. I couldn't move or say anything
but I knew what was going on. I had my eyes wide open and
the kids were trying to make me blink. When I didn't, they
thought it was some kind of trick."

"I think it's going to keep happening," I said. "He's going
to keep right on doing this until you're ready to listen to him."

Within forty-eight hours, Alex was ready to listen. He was
able to hear how the Twin had saved him and to know the
pain he had taken for him. It was on a day in early November. I was in the kitchen stirring a pot of spaghetti sauce that
was simmering on the stove and Sam was nearby on the telephone when screams for help came from Alex's room. Dropping the sauce-laden spoon on the counter, I hurried to his
side. "Alex, what's wrong?"

"Ma," he cried as he clutched at his groin and ran around
the room in frantic circles. "Ma, the candle. It hurts. It hurts
so bad. The candle!"

Sam had followed close behind me and was standing in
the doorway. An expression of concern mingled with confusion spread across his features. "Jesus, Carole, what is it?
Should we get him to a doctor?"

Before I could answer, Alex fell onto his bed. Curling up
into a protecting fetal position, he lay quiet. As quickly as it
had come, the pain was gone. I sat next to him on the edge of
the bed. He leaned his head against my shoulder and held
tightly to my hand while he told me what Christine and her

brother Harold had done to him. A chill struck my heart at the mention of Uncle Harold. I hadn't thought of him in years, not since Sam and I had looked at his picture. I thought of that picture. I thought of that zombie-like face and those blank, empty, staring eyes. "I fought him," said Alex solemnly. "I wouldn't let him do what he wanted to do to me again. I wouldn't let him." He paused here and swallowed hard. "Uncle Harold held me down and my punishment was— Christine—she took a candle—and she held the flame under—under my penis, and she burned me! She said she would do it again if I didn't do what they wanted. So I had to."

Ever since the disclosures that had followed the first visit to Dr. Kingsbury, Sam had wrapped himself in angry denial. Whenever I tried to talk to him about the Twin or the recent sequence of strange events, he turned away in acute discomfort. Well, maybe he couldn't believe in the existence of the Twin, but, having seen Alex's suffering with his own eyes, there was no way he could escape the reality of the boy's pain. Along with my husband's acceptance that something so terrible had happened to Alex, there was outrage. He expressed it loudly and unequivocally. "Those sons of bitches! Those goddam bastardly sons of bitches! Carole, how about marks or scars? Why don't you take him to a doctor and find out? And call the district attorney about this."

"Call the district attorney?" I repeated incredulously. "It won't do any good. They aren't going to do anything. As near as I can figure out, someone in the DA's Office made a mistake. Something went wrong back in June of '88 when the victims' advocate told us they were going to arrest Christine. Maybe he wasn't supposed to tell us that, or maybe they decided not to go through with it. I don't know. Rather than give us the truth straight out, they've gone to great lengths to string us along and give Alex false hope. The legal system is abusing him every bit as much as the original perpetrators. I think they're afraid to come right out and tell him Christine is never going to be brought to justice. I think they're afraid he'll take the law in his own hands. He's already tried it. Suppose the police hadn't caught him before he got to Bainbridge? And what was it he was going on about yesterday?"

"The hit man?" Sam suppressed a smile. "Hiring a hit man to get Christine? That was just talk."

"I wouldn't be too sure about that. How do you know what he might do to them when he has these spells?"

"Carole," insisted Sam, "I really think you should have this checked out by a doctor and tell the DA about it. If it's proof . . . ?"

I did take Alex to his pediatrician and he said there were marks. They had stretched with growth and faded with time, but there were oblique red marks. I also called Ms. Travers and told her how Uncle Harold had held Alex down while Christine put a lit candle to his penis. My hand gripped the phone as I heard a laugh on the other end of the line. "Oh," she said with a high, nervous giggle, "I don't think we have a legal category for that. Let's see. Perhaps we could call it indecent assault."

"Indecent assault?" I said, my voice shaking.

"Yes," she replied coolly. "After all, it didn't involve penetration. The law says there has to be penetration for it to be sex abuse."

I informed Ms. Travers in no uncertain terms what I thought of the narrowness of this law, but in the end it didn't matter. There was no way to prove what had caused the marks, and the statute of limitations had run out. A month later, DSS received a report from the police that Uncle Harold had allegedly sexually molested a two-year-old girl and it still didn't matter.

Now that Alex understood how the Twin had helped him, he was in frequent communication with the personality. The doctor had taught him that he could do this at home on his own. The conversations between the boy and his alter were a private matter. He never did tell me anything of what was said until one afternoon shortly before Thanksgiving. "What's wrong?" I asked, wondering why he was so quiet and preoccupied. "What's the matter?"

Alex was sitting at the trestle table. He looked up at me, his eyes soft and sad. "I said goodbye to him, Mom. Last night. I went into the castle and I said goodbye to him."

I reached for his hand and held it in mine. "He's not completely gone. He's with you. He will always be with you. He's a part of you."

A pensive expression came over Alex's features, and he smiled a small secretive smile. "I know," he said. "When I finally talked to him, he was—he was like a friend. I miss him but I'm glad it's over."

I didn't have the heart to tell him it wasn't over. Dr. Kingsbury had told me that it would be extremely rare for there to be only one personality and in all probability there were more, many more.

And it was not long before the next child came forth. That very weekend Alex had a severe attack of abdominal pain and I rushed him to the hospital emergency room. He was moaning and holding his arms tightly against his stomach, and the doctor was certain it was appendicitis. Then the tests came back, and he didn't know what to think. It wasn't that and it wasn't anything else. In two hours the pain began to ease and Alex looked up at me from his bed. "It's another one," he said wearily. "He's five. I know what happened. It was just before George took me from Christine. She wanted to make sure I didn't tell, so she beat me. It was a terrible beating. She hit me with everything she could lay her hands on. Pots, pans, brooms, everything."

"Alex, that was ten years ago. How can this be? How can you be in pain from something that took place ten years ago?"

"I don't know, Ma. I'm fine now. Can we please go home?"

Even though I had heard the Twin say he had taken the pain and I had seen Alex feel the burning from the flame of the candle, the idea that a person could be injured in 1979 and never feel the pain from that injury until 1989 was something

I could not readily assimilate. It was too far beyond my everyday experience. But here in the hospital, holding Alex's hand for these last agonizing hours, I came face to face with the fact that for the personalities to merely tell him what had happened was not enough. It was necessary for him to actually feel what they had felt. In the cases of the more violent rapes, there must have been rectal bleeding. If the personalities had held the pain for him until he was able to handle it, did they also hold the bleeding? Was that why the bleeding had often accompanied the dissociative states involving sodomy? Was that why the doctors at Children's Hospital could find no physical cause?

At school there was another trance. The nameless five-year-old had something else to tell him, Alex said, and I admired his courage as he prepared to face yet another horror. With this goal in mind, we went in to see Dr. Kingsbury. Bill came with us, and before the session was over, I would be glad he was there. The doctor had no sooner guided Alex into the safety of the room in the castle than a change came over his features. His eyes and lips were pressed so tightly together that his entire face appeared to contract into an expression of unbearable pain.

"Who are you?" asked Dr. Kingsbury. "Who are you?"

He tried to speak but could not, and he began banging his head against the wall behind his chair. Bill quickly moved to cushion the blows with his folded jacket, and as he did so, the boy suddenly fell forward. The upper part of his body was bent over his knees and his arms hung straight down with his hands touching the tops of his sneakers. I heard a low moan that was followed by the tremulous, fearful whimpering of a small child. This whimpering gave way to a sound coming from deep within Alex's throat. It went on and on, long and sustained and unwavering, a high-pitched sound, a sound that pierced our souls and forced us to share an unforgettable agony. And to know that none who heard it could ever again be the same.

After what seemed an eternity, the sound ceased and, still doubled over, Alex began making strangely rhythmic, groaning cries that came at intervals of two or three seconds. With each cry his entire body jerked forward as though some external force were being applied. Enveloped by a numbing shock, I desperately tried to deny what I was seeing and hearing, and when I could deny it no longer, the room began to whirl and darken until there was only Dr. Kingsbury's voice leading Alex through the pain, keeping him in the safety. "You have lived through this," he reminded him. "You have survived this. You are safe. Hang on to the safety. You are safe. It will be over. It will be over."

As the mists before my eyes cleared, I could see the doctor leaning toward Alex with his hands slightly outstretched to catch him if he fell. Beads of perspiration had gathered on his forehead, and his every nerve seemed concentrated on the awful task of staying with the boy, deep in the pain, talking him through it, diminishing and alleviating past terror with the sure and certain knowledge of present strength and security and power. As before, there was a sense of a birthing process. This time it was curiously simultaneous. It seemed that while the monstrous horror was being delivered, another part of Alex was being reborn.

At last the spasmodic movements ceased and it was ended. Giving comforting assurances that he was indeed safe, the doctor asked Alex to come back, to take over his body. He did as he was directed and, with his hands covering his face, lifted his head and sat upright. "I'll kill the son of a bitch," he said with dire fervor as he pulled his fingers slowly downward over red and swollen features. "I'll kill the son of a bitch!"

Disheveled and exhausted by the ordeal, Dr. Kingsbury asked Alex if he cared to share what had happened. "What did the bastard do to you?" he added bitterly.

"Yes," replied Alex. "I'll tell you what he did. I was five years old and Christine left me with Uncle Harold. He taped my mouth and tied me to the bed. He boiled water in a teakettle. And he poured the boiling water on me. And then he raped me."

Later Alex would tell me that the sustained, high-pitched sound was what he had heard while he lay tied to the bed with his mouth taped. It was the sound of the shrill whistling of the teakettle.

XIV

October 1989 to April 1990

Ricky

At first, I didn't pay much attention to what appeared to be idle doodling. I didn't pay much attention to how Alex's fingers busily filled any available space on margins and notepads with five-pointed, circled stars while he was supposed to be doing his homework. It was nothing, I told myself, only absentminded scribbling. But persistent, nagging doubts kept intruding into my acceptance of this facile explanation, and I took a closer look at the strange symbols.

I had seen one of these before. A long time ago. Salem. That was it. In Salem. The Witch Museum. I recalled the frighteningly darkened interior with only the center of the floor brightly illuminated. And in that center, there was an intricate design of inlaid tiles forming a star enclosed by a circle. A pentagram. The sign of Satan. Alex was filling page after page with pentagrams.

I began seeing the pentagrams shortly before Halloween of 1989. In mid-November they were joined by pictures of devils that had squat, misshapen bodies, horns, and leering grins. One of the sketches, separate and apart from the others, was labeled with the odd name of Goldstem.

Feeling somewhat embarrassed and concerned he might think I was making something out of nothing, I called Dr. Kingsbury and hesitantly mentioned the drawings. To my astonishment, he received the information with attentive consideration and gravity. His tone was serious and his words

Predisclosed Drawing, October 1989

crystallized my unformed fears. "Many victims of cult abuse develop multiple personalities," he said.

My mind could not begin to deal even partially with the significance of this. I had some vague idea that these cults did terrible things like killing cats and dogs, but I was blessedly ignorant of more detailed knowledge. In any case, the process of entry could not be forced or rushed and the most essential emphasis had to be on safety. Dr. Kingsbury continued to teach Alex how to be in control of his dissociative states and to use them to his own advantage. He taught him he could, at home and on his own, seek out the safety of the castle. There was nothing else to do but wait, and in the meantime I focused my energy on working with the school system to help Alex get the education he needed.

After he had experienced the last trance episode in class, Bill and I felt our only choice was to explain the cause of the disturbing phenomenon. To this end, we met with school personnel and Bill briefly described some of the trauma that Alex, as a young child, had been unable to endure. He told how this child had creatively saved his sanity by inventing personalities to hold on to those events until he was old enough and strong enough to deal with them. He also carefully pointed out how the personalities were not like those in the popularized accounts of Sybil or Eve. Since the boy was so young, they were not yet fully developed. They did not take over his body for extended periods of time.

For my part, I related the story of Alex's regressions and subsequent reparenting and reviewed the various developmental stages he had been allowed to live through in a normal and corrective way. Although most members of the staff responded with support and compassion, I couldn't believe what I was hearing from a few of the others. "He gave me a black look two weeks ago," said the Spanish teacher. "Does that mean he was going to attack me?"

Making every effort to keep calm, I said, "Alex has never harmed anyone, and his conduct marks these past years have ranged from good to excellent. The only people he might possibly ever hurt would be the perpetrators. As far as that goes," I added, thinking of how I had felt following the more horrific disclosures, "I couldn't guarantee they would be safe from me either. According to Dr. Kingsbury, Alex is simply integrating past trauma and is not a danger to anyone."

I looked around the room and remembered my own anxiety and apprehension when I had discovered Alex was multiple. But I had listened and read and learned. I looked at the closed faces of some of these educators and I knew they did not want to listen. Fear had deafened their ears. Fear would keep their minds blocked by ignorance.

The humiliation of going into trances in front of his classmates had been too much for Alex. He refused to go to school until his friends began to call and tell him they missed him and wanted him to come back. Upon his arrival at the school, however, the principal sent him home. He tried again. And again he was sent home, "for the safety of the entire school community," said the principal in a letter.

"Why, Ma?" asked Alex. "Why are they doing this? I haven't done anything." Bewildered and devastated, he cried and cried and could not be comforted.

The Massachusetts Department of Education concurred. Alex had not done anything. The principal was in violation of the law and was ordered to permit Alex to return. It was a hollow victory. The school would not allow him to attend his classes, and he was told he had to stay in the room used for special education until he made up all of the work he had missed during the ten-day absence. While he was doing this, he got behind on the present assignments. It was a no-win situation.

The sketching of the pentagrams continued throughout the December of Alex's sixteenth year. I had not yet brought this to his attention, nor had I mentioned anything to him about cults, but one day I picked up the pad of paper that lay next to his books. Pointing to the figures covering the top page, I handed it to him and said, "What are these?"

He looked from the paper to me with blank, innocent eyes. "I don't know," he said. "I didn't do it. Ma, do I draw like that?" he added contemptuously.

I glanced at the page again. Alex did have some artistic talent, and his work was always done with the precision and neatness of a draftsman. These had the appearance of having been drawn by a young child. They were wild and erratic with uneven, wavering lines. Even though I had actually seen Alex making some of the pentagrams, I knew the answer to his question was clearly no. I was struck with the realization that someone else, another alter, another child, had been using Alex's body for this purpose.

It wasn't until after Christmas that Alex was able to listen to this child, not all at once, but in bits and pieces of slowly dawning horror of black-robed, hooded figures carrying candles and marching in unholy procession to strange and eerie music. And it was later than that when he could relate the information in any kind of coherent and chronological fashion. "It happened at Halloween," he began. "I was five. I had just gone to live with George and Sandra, but Christine told them she wanted to take me trick-or-treating, so they let me go with her. I was in her apartment. It was on a main street in Bainbridge, up over a store. Someone—I know it was a man but I don't know who—came up from behind me and put a blindfold over my eyes. He carried me downstairs and put me in a car."

Alex was sitting in the old Boston rocker by the fireplace. His head was resting against the top of the chair and he had a faraway look on his face. I felt a tremendous amount of apprehension as I sat close by, waiting for him to continue. I was afraid of what I was going to hear. He reached out, not moving his head, groping for my hand, holding it in his before he could speak again.

"No one said anything, so I don't know who was in the

car. The radio was on. They kept me on the floor. They drove
for about twenty minutes. When they stopped and took me
out of the car, there was pavement under my feet, like a parking lot. They led me up a flight of stairs and into a place
where I could hear chanting and scary music. There were
other kids there, too. I could hear them crying. I was pushed
down on the floor, and they made me crawl through slimy
things they said were worms. There was something smooth
underneath."

Alex paused here, shifted his position, and gripped my
hand tightly. "I was so afraid, Mom. I was so afraid. I thought
it really was worms," and with a touch of pride, "but now I
know it wasn't. It had to be cooked spaghetti. Spaghetti on
top of plastic. That's what the smooth stuff had to be."

"Spaghetti?" I said in some amazement.

He looked at me and gave me a slight smile. "Spaghetti,
Ma," he confirmed. "When they took the blindfold off, I was
in a big room. The windows were covered with some kind of
black material, and there were posts going from the floor to
the ceiling. At one end there was a fireplace and an altar
made of bricks piled on top of each other. Some people were
sitting at a round table in the middle of the room. They were
wearing black robes with hoods. The hoods fell forward over
their faces so I couldn't see who they were, but I think they
were men. There were a lot of other people dressed the same
way—black robes and hoods. Two of them stood by the
door. They never moved, just stood like statues. One of the
men at the table must have been the leader. He kept talking
through some kind of microphone. It changed his voice. I
guess he didn't want anybody to know who he was. He used
the words 'thee' and 'thou' when he talked, and he went on
about how great and powerful Satan was and how Satan
could give power to those who did things for him and why no
one could ever, ever tell about the meetings."

"Was Christine there? Did you see her?"

"I couldn't tell. The only light was from candles. I think

she must have been. And Harold, too. He had been visiting that night."

The uncle again.

"They took our clothes off—me and the other kids—so we were bare to the waist, and they tied us to these pieces of wood that were like upside-down crosses. They tied the crosses to the posts I told you about and someone came up to me—he had this cup with blood in it—and said, 'Are thou one of us? Does thou believe in Satan? Drink in the name of Satan.' He tried to make me drink the blood and I wouldn't. I spit it out and they beat me."

Here Alex paused and closed his eyes. His left hand curled around the curved end of the arm of the chair and he rocked slowly back and forth. Then the rocking stopped and he leaned forward, toward me. His face held so much suffering. I wanted to turn away.

"They marched around the room while the eerie music kept playing. They were carrying candles and chanting. The chanting got louder and louder. I guess it was about midnight when someone brought the babies in. Two of them. Little babies, Ma. Crying. Tied to crosses. Upside-down crosses. They put the first baby on the altar. They poured gasoline around it and lit it. I tried to close my eyes so I wouldn't have to see, but someone behind me put their hands on my eyelids and forced them open. They made me pour the gasoline around the second baby. They made me light it. They said they would do it to me if I didn't, and I believed them."

My heart was bursting with a compassion that I had no words to tell. I blinked away the threatening tears. "How do you know these things, Alex?"

He slipped his hand from mine and held his arms against his chest. To admit to more personalities, to give them the reality of names, was an additional trauma. It made him feel set apart and different. It made him know that he was not what he most wanted to be: a normal teenager. "Ricky," he said with a startling suddenness. "Ricky. In the castle. I didn't know about it until he showed me. Ricky went to the meeting. He took over for me. Ricky did the sacrifice."

Ricky. Ricky of the mascara-streaked face. Ricky running wildly about on Halloween. So that's who he was and that's why he had acted the way he had. And that's why Alex had run away the day of the West River Horse Show when Christine had said she wanted to take him trick-or-treating. Some of the pieces were beginning to come together.

Ricky, Alex disclosed, was five years old when he first came but was now eight. This child continued to communicate with Alex. He was not yet finished. He had more dread sights to reveal before he could become integrated. Within a matter of weeks, Alex was able to tell of the sacrifices made during his eighth summer. He said the meetings were always held on nights when the moon was full, and even as he spoke, I wondered if this was the answer to another question. Could this explain why Alex had always become so intensely agitated at the time of the full moon? Especially during the summer? He went on to say that Christine and Uncle Harold no longer bothered to hide their identities, and he described how they led him through rows of apple trees to a secret place. The light from the moon partially illuminated the surroundings, but every so often the uncle would check the base of a tree trunk to find a black arrow pointing out the direction. Alex remembered hearing a sound, like the moaning of wind through the branches. Only there was no wind. When they came to a field at the edge of the apple orchard, he realized what he had heard was a humming chant that came from a group of men, women, and children. They were standing in a formation consisting of a circle within a circle, and the chanting was to summon the presence of Satan. Out of all these people, Alex was the only one who wore a red robe. It was made of satin and embroidered with satanic symbols.

"How did you get this robe?" I asked.

"I don't know how I got it," he said. "I don't know who gave it to me."

He told of how the leader, a new one who seemed to be constantly spitting, marked the bare backs of chosen men with a strange insignia. Two or three children were marked in the same way. These children, bound and gagged, were laid out on a crude wooden table serving as an altar. The signed men stood over them and in their hands they held knives with scythe-shaped blades.

And he told of how the chanting got louder and higher and faster as the leader convinced the gathering that this was right. "Thee must know this must be done. Thee must know these sacrifices are the will of Satan, the all-powerful Satan."

Did it happen? Did those children really die? With no names. With no prayers. There in the moonlight. In the field, near the apple orchards. And at Halloween? Were babies really sacrificed at Halloween?

I didn't know. I was not there. I did not want to believe it, and I searched for other explanations. A book, or perhaps a movie, might account for his detailed information on cult practices. But what about Ricky and the pentagrams and the bizarre behavior we had seen over the years on Halloween and at the time of the full moon? The results of an elaborate scheme involving planted memories? How? No one had been able to get Alex into therapy until he met Bill Conti, and he had never been alone with either Bill or Dr. Kingsbury. Even if he had, they would never, ever do such a thing.

I did obtain information that lent some validity to Alex's story. In another attempt to get revenge on the perpetrators, one of the alters went to George's apartment and tried to get his hands on a gun. I couldn't believe it when this man actually called me. He sounded scared to death as he described my son's dangerous actions and told me how he'd had Alex picked up by the police. I wanted to tell him I was glad he was afraid, and when he had the nerve to go on with how he'd always been there for the boy, I thought I would choke. I angrily accused him of the beatings and abuses, and he denied it all with a casual nonchalance that was infuriating. "And what about the cult?" I asked. "Did you know Christine had him in a cult?"

He said he didn't but he did know that her brother Harold was a worshiper of Satan. He had seen him with his own eyes throwing darts at a large picture of Jesus while yelling, "Satan is the only true god!"

Although the alleged cult meetings had occurred years earlier, it seemed to me we should take steps to notify law enforcement. A police department in the town of Northboro had a satanic task force, and I took Alex in to be interviewed by these officers. After listening and asking many specific questions, they indicated they thought he was telling the truth.

Cult involvement of Christine and her brother could also explain how they could do such terrible things to Alex without being certifiable lunatics. As members of a satanic cult that most likely encouraged and promoted every conceivable perversion with a religious fanaticism, they could easily justify anything they did. Evil was good. Good was evil. And if they had to sexually abuse children and shed the blood of babies to earn Satan's grace, it was the right thing to do.

Dr. Kingsbury pointed out how the deaths could have been staged with lifelike dolls, theatrical props, and sleight of hand. It was possible. I had to admit it was possible. The result would have been the same. A child might be easily tricked. But my son refused to be convinced. And when all was said and done, that was what counted, that was what mattered. For whatever reason, if he himself believed this had happened, we had to deal with his perceptions and his reality.

For Alex, it was not over with the telling. I watched helplessly as the smothering fear came around him and about him. He heard it in the cold winter wind. He saw it lurking in the skeletal January branches of the oak tree near his window. He felt it in the very walls of his room that threatened to close in and press the life from him like some gigantic torture machine of the Inquisition. One morning he came to me and showed me a poem he had written. "This is what it is like," he said.

> As the night falls,
> I am afraid,
> Someone, somewhere, somehow
> They will get me.
>
> As the dusk comes,
> The darkness
> Leaves a hollow, Black Hole
> Inside of me.
>
> As I try to sleep,
> Frigid dreams
> Come upon me.
> And I am lost
> In a field of Nowhere.

With this fear there was a voice. "We will kill you," it proclaimed with undeniable certainty. "We will find you and we will kill you. You must die! You have told. You have betrayed the secrets of the cult. You have betrayed Satan. Die. You must die. We will find you. We will kill you."

Day after day, night after night, the voice filled his head, sometimes mocking, sometimes screeching a variation of its deadly message. "Why don't you do it yourself? You know you deserve to die. Just walk in front of that car. It's easy. You must die. You have betrayed us."

With Dr. Kingsbury's help, Alex was able to go into the magic castle to his inner place of peace and security so he could explore the source of the voice. "You have the power," began the doctor. "You have learned—you can keep yourself safe. When you were young—there were things—you did not understand. A three-year-old does not understand.

Now—with your age—and understanding, Alex, you can
listen—or choose not to listen. Follow my words—to the
memories—of chants and ritual. Part of you—will know you
are safe—so part of you—can understand things said to a
mind—that was overwhelmed and confused. That is no
longer true. And you can help—the part of you—that doesn't
understand. You can remember—things safely. Some of
these messages—can be played back—again and again. You
have been hearing—the tape—the programming. Follow my
words—to the memories. Die! Death! Destroy! Part of you
knows—how you've grown—past those words. Part of
you—experiences those words. You can remember—and be
alive—and how comforting—that is to know. Feel your
strength—and safety."

As Dr. Kingsbury paused for a moment, I looked at Alex.
His composed features radiated the peace and tranquillity he
found within the castle. "Isn't it strange," went on the doctor,
"how part of you—can be afraid—and the other part—so
peaceful. Now you are free. You are not a robot. You have
grown past—the awful games—such people play. Remember! And grow! And be strong! And remember the words of
the Holocaust—with all the torture. Never forget. They survived—and were human. You have survived—your own
Holocaust. Never forget. Look up—and be proud."

So it was that Alex was able to fortify himself against the
terror and face the leader of the cult. He saw him, monstrous
in his hooded facelessness, and he heard him repeating over
and over, "You must never tell. You must never tell. If you
ever tell, we will find you and kill you. And if we don't find
you, you must kill yourself. You must never tell. Never be-
tray or you must die!"

"Alex was programmed," the doctor told us afterward. "It
is not difficult to brainwash a frightened young child. Of
course, once the programming is recalled, it no longer works.
It has no effect." And that is exactly what happened. As Alex
knew what the leader had said, the words lost their power.
The voice was silenced.

. . .

Alex's situation at school was becoming more and more desperate. They had finally realized it was impossible for him to make up the mountain of work and began putting him back into his classes. But it was too late. After having been out of some of these classes for ten weeks, he felt isolated and stupid when he didn't know the material. "You could do it if you wanted to," the principal told him. "Just between you and me, you've got to stop playing games and get on with your life. Your problem is you're too lazy."

This accusation left Alex more hopelessly depressed than ever. "I am trying, Mom, I am," he cried. His attempts to study, however, were futile. He was agitated and unable to concentrate, and the ongoing integration of cult-related trauma was taking its toll. In early January, the school provided him with a tutor. This did help him keep up with his lessons, but during the first week of March, the tutor found a full-time job and left. And that was the end of school for Alex. Discouraged and feeling rejected, he gave up and stayed home.

For two full months, during March and April, I literally begged the Special Education Department for another tutor to come to our home. My pleas were ignored. There was no tutor. There were no educational services whatsoever. My repeated requests for a copy of Alex's Individualized Educational Plan from his core evaluation were also ignored. The rules regarding these matters say the first step in obtaining the services parents deem necessary for their child's education is to reject all or part of this plan. Without the IEP, I could go no further. I was forced to file a formal complaint with the Department of Education.

While going through some of Alex's old report cards, I came across copies of the comprehensive tests of basic skills that were given each year. The seventh-grade results were quite high, but the more recent scores showed Alex was testing far below average. Apparently very little learning had taken place during the integration of trauma. It was becoming increasingly clear that he needed a special school to provide a day program of very small classes, emotional support, and esteem-building experiences.

The special ed people did not agree. When I did receive my copy of the IEP, it said that with tutoring, Alex would be able to complete his courses and be promoted. Since they were not providing him with a tutor and it was now mid-April, this was a ridiculous goal. Sam and I promptly rejected the entire plan. We hired a lawyer and set up an appointment for a hearing where a Department of Education officer would make a decision the district would have to obey. On the day before the hearing was scheduled, the school system had a change of heart. Beginning in September, Alex would be allowed to repeat the tenth grade at a special school.

Along with the school problems, there was something else going on. Alex began behaving strangely around mirrors. It was customary for him, as for most teenagers, to spend a great deal of time looking at himself in the mirror to make sure his hair was combed just right or to search diligently for the first sign of zits. Now he was sidling up to a mirror as though to take it unawares, peeking into one corner of the glass and suddenly jumping backward. Then he began avoiding mirrors altogether. This behavior made no sense at all. Until it was over. Until he told us about what had happened in the church.

"Christine took me to a church," he said, "and she put me in a big box. There was someone on the other side. I could hear a man's voice but I couldn't see him."

"That must have been what they call a confessional," I explained. "It must have been a Catholic church."

"Well, anyway, the man on the other side was saying, 'You are one of us. You should be proud. Very proud. You are one of us now. You belong to Satan. You are a child of Satan. But you must never tell. You must never tell. If you do, if you ever tell anyone anything about us or about our secrets, Satan will punish you. Satan will take your soul.' And stuff like that. And he kept on saying it, and later, Christine kept on saying, 'If you tell, the devil will take your soul, and when he does you will know. You will know because you will lose your image. You will not be able to see yourself in the mirror.' "

For the past two weeks, Alex had not been able to see himself in the mirror.

XV

May to July 1990

He Who Handled Drugs

That spring of 1990 marked one of those long periods of stability, and I reveled in the calm and quiet of our daily life. We plowed the garden and readied it for planting, and we sat before a crackling fire on the still-cold nights. It was normal. Wonderfully, boringly normal. Lulled into complacency, I allowed myself to believe our ordeal was over. It had been three months and there had been no one. There had been no other children. I was so caught up in wishful thinking that I ignored certain signs and signals. The first of these was a picture.

"Ma, look at this," said Alex as he came into the kitchen and showed me a drawing he had made on a large sheet of white paper.

"What is it?" I asked.

"An indoor arena. A riding arena, you know, for horses."

I examined the picture closely. "Except for the wide doors, it seems more like a house. It's two stories high, and see these multipaned windows on both levels?"

He lowered his voice as if he were afraid someone might hear. "Ma, it is an indoor arena, and they did terrible things there."

"What kind of things?"

"I don't know, Ma. I don't know. Just terrible things."

The second incident was another trance.

"It's nothing," explained Alex, making light of the situation and giving me a convincingly embarrassed grin. "I was just trying to go into the castle this morning and it kind of backfired on me. I guess I need more practice."

I believed him. The cumulative effect of the atrocities had taken its toll. I needed to believe him. I tore up the drawing of the indoor arena. I crushed any suspicion there were more personalities.

But there were. And with their coming, he alternated between clinging to me like a small boy and spouting vile obscenities. Wild-eyed and disoriented, he raved on and on about Christine. "Nothing's happening to her," he shouted. "Nothing is going to happen to her! And look at me. . . ." His voice trailed off to a moaning sigh. "Look at me."

Two days later, Sam strode angrily into the house and deliberately placed a rifle and a half-dozen bullets on the dining-room table. His face was red and a purple vein throbbed in his forehead. "Jesus Christ, Carole!" he shouted. "Alex was on his way to Bainbridge. He was walking along the road carrying this gun and these bullets. I made him get in the truck, and he said, 'I've got to get to Bainbridge. I'm going to find Christine. I'm going to kill Christine.' That's what he said. Exactly what he said."

"Where is he?"

"Down in the barn. I yelled at him. He says he borrowed the gun from a friend. I have to return it. Good thing I saw him before the police did."

I mentally compared this situation with the moped escapade and how Alex had sounded like a little kid as he told the state trooper he was going to kill his parents. "Sam," I ventured, "listen to me. I don't think it was Alex."

"Dammit! Don't start!" he retorted sharply.

My husband did not want to hear anything about personalities, and there was no point in arguing. "Okay. But suppose Alex did get up to Bainbridge and shoot someone? Or worse yet, suppose one of them shot him? We have to do something."

"Yeah, like what?"

"We can have him committed. If he's a danger to himself or others, we can go to court and have him committed. I'm sure Bill and Dr. Kingsbury will back us up."

Alex was sent to a renowned psychiatric facility composed of both modern brick structures and old Victorian mansions that were named for their former owners. Alex was in the one called Blair House. When Sam and I went to visit him, he was having adverse reactions to the medications that had been prescribed for him. The symptoms included drowsiness, vision problems, palsylike shaking, and a cracked and swollen tongue. I was having second thoughts about the paper I had signed giving the hospital permission to administer drugs. "It hurts," he said. "I haven't been able to eat." Sitting down on the bed, he stared disconsolately at the opposite wall. It was hung with a championship horse blanket he had won at a show. The blanket was green with gold lettering and was flanked by an assortment of tricolor ribbons. In the center was a framed picture of Alex and Blaze. "That's the only thing keeping me from going crazy," he said. He looked at the beige-painted walls and tall, curtainless windows and he began to beg. "Mom, Dad, I want to come home. Please take me out of here. Please let me come home."

"Alex," said Sam, "we want you home. But we can't go on the way we have."

Sam was right about that. We couldn't. Even the most devoted parents couldn't be expected to endure the severity of the more recent spells. "Alex," I added, "you're in the best place in the world to work through your problems. These people are here to help you. Talk to them, Alex. Talk to them."

Alex gave me a pained look that was touched with contempt. "Mom, I can't. I tried. I tried to tell something to Jen, a counselor, and she said, 'Oh, come on.' Just like that. 'Oh, come on.' They don't believe me. And some of the stuff coming through . . . if I told them, they would freak out."

In spite of our repeated urging, Alex was unable to confide the content of his flashbacks to any staff member. But the following week, when he had gained enough privileges to accompany me on a drive through the grounds, he directed me to a secluded, forested area. After I parked by the side of the road, I asked him what was going on.

Leaning over, he placed his head in the hollow of my shoulder. I had a strong premonition this was the last time he would need to be held while he talked, and I put my arms around him. "There's more personalities," he replied.

"Oh?" I said, trying to sound as though it was an unexpected revelation.

"Yes," he went on. "There's an older boy who has something to do with drugs, and . . ." He left the sentence hanging, unfinished and incomplete, and then the words came in a rush. "There's another who does sex. His name is Goldstem."

Goldstem? Why was that familiar? For a moment, I couldn't place it. Then I remembered the sketches, the leering, horned devils Alex had drawn over eight months ago. "Goldstem" had been printed underneath one of those devils.

"It was my cult name, too," said Alex.

"What?"

"In the cult everybody was given a different name, and mine was Goldstem. They had a ceremony."

In spite of everything, I could not suppress a slight smile of satisfaction. According to Dr. Kingsbury, the personalities were all good. Each had its own particular function and had kept and saved for Alex an integral part of his self and of his past so eventually he could become a whole human being. The cult objective was to pervert and destroy his humanity. To learn how Goldstem, the product of a blasphemous christening in the name of Satan, had circumvented this objective was an ironic twist that gave me a great deal of pleasure.

"The personality, Goldstem, he told me—" Breaking off abruptly, Alex lifted his head and stared out of the window. "Look, Ma. Look!"

I followed his startled gaze to the edge of the woods.

Standing on a slight rise not ten feet away from us was a
fox. His ragged reddish fur was tinged with gray, and his
bright eyes were watching us with an intent curiosity. The
wild animals around here must be partially tame, I said to
myself. People probably feed them. But regardless of why
the fox was there, its presence helped to keep the sickening
perversions in some kind of perspective. It helped to keep
us aware of a part of existence not touched and tainted by
incarnate evil. It made it easier for him to speak and for me
to listen.

"Goldstem told me," said Alex, picking up the thread of
his thought and keeping his eyes on the fox, "about the sex
I had to do with Christine. I was eight that summer, eight
going on nine. We were naked, both naked. On a blanket. In
front of everyone. The whole cult. Watching. In the indoor
arena."

"Oh, Alex!" I said in an exclamation of sorrow, and not
knowing what else to say, how else to comfort, I held him
closer. "This arena—was it the same riding arena you drew
a picture of last spring, the one that looked like a house?"

"Yes. They had meetings there. It's where the apple orchard was. And the field where they did sacrifices. The field
was near the arena. And Ma, at the horse shows, whenever I
was in an indoor arena, I was really scared. The sex was
worse for me than the killings."

The fox was sitting on his haunches with his plumed tail
curved around his body and his tongue lolling. "If I get close
to a girl, Goldstem comes and takes over. Like when I tried
to kiss Mary after the dance. Somehow all I can see is Christine. Just the other day I went to hug a girl, one of the other
patients, and I saw Christine and shoved the girl away. I got
in trouble. I tried to explain, but . . ."

Alex gave a shrug of despair, and after a moment of contemplative silence, he said, "Ma, you know the box?"

"What box?"

"The box!" And with a show of impatience. "Long ago."

"Oh, yes. The box." The small, intricately carved box with

the tiny brass latch. The box that held and kept safe the little piece of love he had for Christine. The box that was still in Bill's office. Alex had insisted on leaving it there. Even symbolic love had been too dangerous to bring home. Why was he asking about it?

"It's yours," he said as if in answer to my unspoken questions. "It belongs to you. What's in the box belongs to you."

I had never thought of it in such a way, but it was so right. It was so perfect. This had been a missing piece in our bonding, and now it was whole and complete and he would be free to take another step in normal development. He would be able to go on with the process of separating from me. "Thank you," I said, biting my lower lip in an attempt to hold back the tears. "Is there anything else?"

Alex's eyes followed the red fox as he walked away into the forest. The fox paused once, looked back, and disappeared in the thickening dusk. "There's a door," Alex said in a hushed voice. "Goldstem showed me. There's another door in the castle, and behind the door there is something terrible, something that happened in the arena."

I took a deep breath and expelled it slowly. "Do you have any idea what it is?"

"No, I don't know what it is. All I know is I'm afraid. Ma, I am afraid."

What could it be? All the way home the question tormented my thoughts. What else had gone on in the riding arena? God knew the public sex with Christine was bad enough. What could be behind the door?

While the answer was moving toward cognitive awareness, Alex's life was fraught with fear, a fear camouflaged by explosive anger and desperate measures to gain control of his environment. This, of course, got him into more and more trouble with the staff and resulted in increased or different medications. The latest side effect from these drugs, an uncontrollable smirking and giggling, made it impossible for him to discuss anything of a serious nature. The periods of isolation were also extended, and Alex was spending more and more time in what was called the Quiet Room. The room was located at the end of a long hallway. Its single window was heavily screened and shaded by a large tree. Its only furnishing was a bare mattress.

Although Dr. Kingsbury had been making regular weekly visits to the hospital, Alex would not go into hypnosis. As always, he had the option of using his own skills to go into the castle and communicate with the personalities, but he wouldn't do that either. He seemed to have a need to feel a certain degree of safety before he could even enter the castle to find enough security to allow him to learn what Goldstem and the drug personality had to tell him. "If my mother can be there with me," he told Dr. Kingsbury, "I will do it. I will feel safe enough to go under."

And so it was that on July fifth, Thursday evening of the following week, I was in Alex's room at the hospital and was once again listening to the poetic cadence of the doctor's words. This time, he told Alex that inside the magic castle he would find a suit of armor he could put on for protection. As was his custom, he reminded the others he did not wish to have them eliminated and would not try to get them to tell secrets they were not ready to share.

Reclining against the pillows on his bed, Alex closed his eyes, and when he opened them, he was someone else. I gazed at the personality with mingled curiosity and awe, and I knew I had seen that face before. I had seen it in the televised photos of the Holocaust and of the Great Depression. I had seen it in the pictures of shell-shocked veterans and skid row derelicts. Burnt-out. Hollow-eyed. The hopelessness of just this side of death.

"Have you talked to me before?" asked Dr. Kingsbury, addressing the personality.

"No," he said, staring at the opposite wall.

"Is there anything I can do for you? I know you don't have to trust me. What should I call you?"

He hesitated for a moment before answering. His voice was tight and tense, with a slight raspy quality. "I don't care."

"Who are you?" continued the doctor, pursuing his line of questioning. "Are you the one who handles drugs or sex?"

"The drugs," he replied.

"How old are you?"

"Seventeen. I was five when I first came to Alex. I've been there all the time."

"Am I correct," proceeded Dr. Kingsbury, "in believing that when Alex was given drugs, you were the one who took over?"

"Yes, I took over what happened after they gave him drugs and I know what happened."

"Do you think Alex could deal with this information?"

"No, I don't," answered the drug personality. "And I can't help him. He has to do it for himself."

"When Alex was given drugs, were you able to protect him?"

"Yes, I did. I protected him and I have a lot to tell him."

"Do you talk to any of the others?"

"No, but I know about the Twin. He has given all of his strengths to Alex. I want to give my strengths to Alex."

So this personality, whose whole aspect up until now had been characterized by a total lack of concern and detached indifference, did care about something. He cared about Alex. I could not envision him throwing Alex into a trance as the Twin had done. Of course, he was much older and more mature, more in control.

Dr. Kingsbury gave a slight nod of his head in acknowledgment of the personality's desire. "Is Alex listening now?"

"Yes, but I'm tired. I want to go back."

I could see he was leaving. I could see the changes. The doctor spoke quickly. "You should know that someone who can keep an even keel, who can keep his balance, is a valuable asset. You have strengths Alex needs. And Alex, I want you to feel some pride that someone is with you who is able to handle things most adults cannot."

Several days later, Alex told me he knew what had happened. He could not yet talk about it, but he had been able to hear what the drug personality had to tell him. The seventeen-year-old alter's assessment of Alex's ability to handle the impact of this knowledge was fairly accurate. On Wednesday, July eleventh, the staff responded to the accompanying rage by administering more drugs. On Thursday, July twelfth, the charge nurse called to inform me my son had been placed in four-point restraints with both arms and legs strapped down and given a chemical restraint by injection as well.

That evening I met Dr. Kingsbury at the hospital and we went in to visit Alex. He had been released from the restraints and was presently in isolation. As we were walking down the corridor toward the Quiet Room, Dr. Kingsbury was speaking to the pretty young nurse who was in charge. "You don't give that drug to dissociative patients," he said. He sounded rather annoyed, but I didn't think anything of it. We entered the room, and although the afternoon had been gray and gloomy with a steady light rain, I was surprised to see how dark it was in there. My eyes fell on Alex's motionless form. He was lying on his left side on the mattress with a blanket covering his entire body.

Two chairs were brought in for the doctor and me, and the light was switched on. "Turn it off, please turn it off," Alex begged as he laboriously raised his right arm to pull the blanket over his head. "Oh-h," he groaned in distress. "I hurt so bad. My muscles are so sore. What time is it?"

"Six o'clock," said Dr. Kingsbury as he moved to turn off the light.

"Six o'clock! I must have slept all day. They gave me an injection."

The doctor made several attempts to talk to Alex, but he kept drifting in and out of a drug-induced stupor. "I understand you've told Carole you recalled something," he said, making one more try. "Do you care to share it?"

We waited. We waited to see if he could respond. For a long while there was only the sound of muffled footsteps in the corridor and indistinguishable voices fading in and out of hearing. "She sold me."

Three words. Three words so laden with grieving that it permeated the very walls of the Quiet Room and dripped with the falling rain from the leaves of the tree outside of the window.

"She sold me."

"For sex," said Dr. Kingsbury in a tone that was half statement, half question.

"Yes."

Like a piece of meat. Like an object, an inanimate thing, nonhuman.

Alex roused himself and, thrusting the blanket down around his waist, painfully turned onto his back. "I was about seven," he said. "Before I went to RFK. She drugged me first so I was unconscious. I saw her take money from people. I don't know how much. Mostly men, but some women."

How was this possible? I asked myself. If Alex was unconscious, how could he know what had happened? Then I recalled reading how a part of the mind is not affected by drugs. The personality whom we had seen and spoken to must have utilized that place in order to keep and save the information for him. "And the door, Alex," I said. "Is this what's behind . . ."

"No," he answered, cutting me off.

So it was still there, still to come.

"Sometimes these people picked me up," continued Alex. "And sometimes Uncle Ralph took me to them. He did it to me too. Along with the rest of them."

The second uncle. Brother to Christine. Brother to Harold. I added his name to the list of perpetrators.

While I had been listening to what Alex was saying I was observing his breathing with growing apprehension. The blanket was no longer covering him, and I could see the rapid movement of his chest. "I don't like this," I said, glancing at Dr. Kingsbury. "I don't like the way he's breathing."

But the doctor was already looking at his watch with an expression of alert concern. "Do you realize," he said to Alex, "that you are breathing sixty-six times a minute? Normal is between sixteen and twenty."

Alex did not answer.

XVI

Goldstem

I didn't know how sick Alex was until the Blair charge nurse called the next morning to tell me that my son had been taken by ambulance to Mount Auburn, a medical hospital in Cambridge. She couldn't give me any more information, so I got hold of Dr. Kingsbury. He told me that Alex's sore muscles and rapid breathing had made him suspect there had been an allergic reaction to the chemical restraint of Haldol and Prozac. After I left, he had had the nurse take Alex's vital signs, and when it turned out he also had a high temperature, the doctor ordered an IV and called the paramedics. They transported Alex to the medical hospital, where he was treated aggressively to prevent brain and kidney damage.

Alex had indeed suffered an allergic and potentially life-threatening reaction to the drugs. Haldol, I learned, is an antipsychotic, and since Alex was not psychotic, it evidently should never have been prescribed in the first place. And the Prozac? That intensified the effects of the Haldol. It made a bad reaction worse.

I was angry at the Blair staff for not seeing something was wrong when one of them was right in the room with him. I was even more angry when I found out there had previously been a similar, if less serious, reaction when they had administered Haldol. Why hadn't they heeded this warning? I felt relief and gratitude that Dr. Kingsbury had recognized the

symptoms of what they called neuroleptic malignant syndrome and had most likely saved Alex's life.

Just thinking about what might have happened brought
tears to my eyes. I began to cry, and once I started I couldn't
stop, because then I was crying for that beautiful little boy
who had to lie naked with Christine, on the blanket, in the
arena, while everyone watched. And for the selling. What
did they do? Line up, one after another, to sodomize him? No
matter how hard I tried not to think of it, it kept coming, coming, coming. The scene. The sounds. Did they laugh? Did
they make jokes? And the helpless child with only an invisible entity to protect him, to keep him from knowing until he
was old enough and strong enough to deal with it directly
and not in some way that was perverted.

Sam hated to see me cry, and he put his arms around me
and tried to comfort me. "It looks like they got it in time," he
said. "We'll go visit him tonight. I'm sure he'll be okay."

Physically, maybe, I said to myself. But what about trust?
What about the fragile, still-healing trust we had worked so
hard to build? In the past, before Alex came to us, whenever
he had trusted anyone to protect him and keep him safe, that
trust had been betrayed. Now, for whatever reason, for whatever excuse, here in this hospital that should have been a
sanctuary, that should have been, above all else, a place of
safety, there had been one more betrayal. The Quiet Room
had become a place of near death. It had become a place of
fear.

When Sam and I went in to Cambridge to see Alex, this
fear was readily apparent. It was in the slight quaver of his
voice as he greeted us, not with "Hi" or "Hello" but with "I
could have died. Mom, Dad, the doctor in the emergency
room said I could have died," and it was in his eyes as he
glanced at the intravenous tube taped to his wrist and the
black wires that went from his chest to a rectangular black
device with a number of knobs and dials. This machine was
to monitor his heart, he said.

We stayed as long as we could. At the end of the visiting

hours, I gave Alex a hug and waited by the door for Sam to say goodbye. Always embarrassed at any public show of affection, Sam pulled the curtain around one side of the bed. I waited for a long time.

Back at home, I called the hospital and told the doctor on duty that my son was not to be given any more drugs. "Just exactly what do you expect us to do if the patient becomes violent?" she said in a voice that dripped sarcasm.

I stood my ground. "You're going to have to find another way. No drugs! Is that clear, Doctor?"

Evidently it was, because when Alex was out of danger and returned to the hospital, no medications were ever again prescribed for him during the remainder of his stay.

Many members of the staff had been less than thrilled over Alex's insistence on telling only me and Dr. Kingsbury of the traumatic episodes disclosed to him by the various personalities. Whether they thought an outsider, a mother of all people, had no business invading the sacrosanct territory of their therapy or did not really understand Alex's primal need for safety, I did not know. But after they learned of my refusal to allow my son to be drugged, the vague irritation and dislike they had for me rose to a barely concealed hostility. I was unable to shake the feeling that some kind of battle line had been drawn.

On Monday, July sixteenth, I went in to the hospital to meet with Martha, the social worker who functioned as a liaison between the patients' families and the staff of the unit. She was genteel, well-spoken, open, and sympathetic. Everything about her seemed to flow: the way she moved, her clothing, her voice. I liked Martha. I didn't always agree with what she said, but I liked her.

Today's meeting was to discuss the decision to give Alex a male therapist. "His name is Mr. Evans," she said. "He's a psychology intern and I'd like you to meet him."

Martha had barely finished speaking when the door opened and Mr. Evans entered the office. He was an intense, somber young man whose muscular body was attired with impeccable neatness. I perceived a certain unsureness and lack of confidence, and the reddish beard shadowing his cheeks and chin appeared to be an attempt to make himself look older and more distinguished. "Mrs. Smith. How do you do?" he said upon being introduced. And indicating a folder of papers he held in his hand, he said, "I've looked over the record. You've done a good job. A very good job. But Alex needs to separate."

I'd heard rumblings of this separation business before. It was a big thing with the staff. He was referring to the process by which a child grows into an autonomous individual with his own values and his own identity. Every instinct I had cried out it was not yet time for this. Alex was not ready for it. I somehow knew that until his sense of safety came consistently from within himself, he could not break the emotional bond between us without irreparable damage. Dr. Kingsbury had tried to explain it to them. "Yes," he had said, "separation is important, but right now other things take priority." And to me: "The hugs you give him are worth more than any therapy."

There was something else, too. I did not believe they would understand, so I did not dare to say it aloud, but I trusted it to be true. Under normal circumstances, if a young child is cruelly and deliberately injured by someone, this child knows his mother's fiercely protective love, her bitter sorrow, and her burning outrage. It is a natural reaction and helps him to heal and to be whole again. Wasn't this what Alex was telling me when he said, "It helps me when you cry"? Wasn't this one more piece of the reparenting that was so important?

"He went through his first separation stage," I said, trying to explain, "when he was eleven. Eight years later than normal. Isn't it logical this phase should also be delayed?"

The intern's fixed stare, studied detachment, and refusal to enter into any dialogue on the subject made me feel frustrated and defensive. The message I heard was loud and clear:

There is no point in discussing this because I am right and you are wrong and that's all there is to it!

With the image of Peter flashing before my mind, I began to talk faster in a futile attempt to get some kind of reciprocation. I spoke of Alex's growing relationship with Sam and compared it to the small child's gravitation toward the father as he begins to separate from the mother. "Alex has to go back and pick up all the pieces he missed," I said. "It's all a part of the reparenting." I spoke of how the trust had to be complete before Alex could go on. "It just happened a short while ago." This comment elicited a raised eyebrow from Mr. Evans, so I elaborated on the fragment of love Alex had for Christine and its symbolic safekeeping in the carved box. "He gave it to me," I said, looking at Martha, because I had told her about it, about the day of the red fox, and she, too, was silent, and I had a sense of being abandoned and drowning in that silence.

When they finally spoke it was on a different subject, or maybe it was the same subject and they were just coming at it from a different angle. It was Martha who brought it up. "Staff reports Alex has been quite agitated today, and they have some concerns around this. He is telling us he wants to go back and live with his biological father."

"And you believe him?"

"There is the option of a residential treatment home."

I smiled incredulously at Martha and thought of how often I had heard Alex shout, "Call Ann! Get me out of this place!" He had never really wanted to leave. It was always something else.

"What exactly do you think the problem is, then?" asked Mr. Evans, with emphasis on the "you."

"Sometimes it's the only way he can feel he's in control, but I don't think that's what it is now. Two years ago, Alex ran away—he went as far as the barn—and he left a note on his pillow. It said, 'I'm leaving because I'm not fit for this family.' A particularly traumatizing event has been trying to

enter his consciousness for the past few weeks," I said as I remembered the thing behind the door. "I think it's come
through—that would account for the agitation—and it is so
totally disgusting and revolting he doesn't feel he's fit to live
with decent people."

At this point they brought Alex in, and I reminded him of
the note he had written long ago. "Is that what this is about?"
I asked.

His brittle posture collapsed and the stoic hardness of his
features melted into an almost tearful vulnerability. "Yes,
yes," he cried. "That's what it is. I don't want to live with
George. I want to come home, Ma, I want to come home."

When the meeting was over, Alex asked me to come to his
room. "Ma, I have to talk to you," he said, closing the door
and sitting down in a plain oak chair by the window.

I eased myself onto the edge of the bed with a feeling that
if I made a sound, I would break something. Alex grasped the
edges of the seat of the chair. His hands were clenched and
bloodless. "I know what's behind the door in the castle," he
began. "Not all of it. Just some. Goldstem—Goldstem
showed me. It was at the arena. Fourth of July weekend. I was
eight."

I thought of the nightmarish weekend four years ago.
Fourth of July: I felt the muscles in my back and stomach
tense and tighten.

"They led a horse into the arena and all of the men took off
their clothes and had sex with a horse. My uncles, Ralph and
Harold. They were there. They did it. There was a lot of
chanting. After they were done, the leader came up to me
and said I had to do it. They made me, Ma. They made me do
it."

I felt enveloped in a thick, smothering cloud of sympathy,
and I went over to him and I held his head close to me and I
stroked his brown hair that was stubby from a recent crew
cut. His shoulders trembled and his tears were wet against my
dress, and when I could, I moved in front of him and clasped
his hands in mine. "I am so sorry," I said, looking at him

through my own tear-flooded eyes. "This is so awful!" And again the fathomless question: "How could they? How could they? Alex, listen to me, to what I'm saying. Goldstem did whatever he had to do to save you. And besides that, he saved your sexuality. He did this for you. He wouldn't be letting you know this stuff if you weren't able to survive it."

The staff still had "concerns around" Alex's agitated behavior, so I tried to reassure them he would be okay. "It's always been this way," I said. "Once he's talked about it, he calms right down." Had I not been in such an emotional state, I would have realized that letting them know of this last disclosure was the worst thing I could have done.

"We'll see," said a young man with a ponytail. "We will see."

It was obvious he didn't believe me. But there was something else, something I didn't like, in his voice. At home, after such a revelation, we treated Alex as any parents would a child who has just been grievously wounded. His pain was real and fresh, and, to aid the healing, it was our custom to give him a time of nurturing and pampering, of leniency and understanding. I had a premonition Alex would get very little of that from the staff at Blair House.

On the afternoon of July twentieth, I received a telephone call. It was the intern, Mr. Evans. He began to speak about a decision the team had made in regard to Alex. "You and his father will be limited to fifteen-minute supervised visits."

Just like that. No explanation. No discussion. No consideration. And no sensitivity for my feelings.

It took a moment for the full impact of what he had said to hit me. I stood there clutching the phone, unable to speak. Finally I managed a faltering, "Why?"

"He has to learn to trust the staff," was the answer. And then, delivered in the same nonchalant tone in which a person might ask about the weather, "Do you have a problem with that?"

The naive, guileless innocence of this inquiry was too much. There was no way, absolutely no way, the man could possibly be so stupid. Shock gave way to a seething indignation. I picked up a pencil from the counter and wrote down everything he had said and was saying. "You know damn well I have a problem with that," I said bluntly. "Supervised visits are for perpetrators. Supervised visits are for parents who lose custody to the state because of abuse."

"Oh, it's only for the weekend," he countered.

"And what do you mean, he has to learn to trust the staff? They almost killed him, for God's sake. And you're going to take away Alex's contact with the two people he does trust so he will learn to trust the staff. That really makes a whole lot of sense."

The Blair worker who supervised my Sunday visit was a young black woman. She positioned herself less than five feet away from where Alex and I were sitting. Holding a pen and clipboard in her hand, she prepared to take notes on any subversive elements of our conversation. Somehow, she managed to look both hostile and pleased.

We turned our backs to her and attempted to speak of innocuous irrelevancies. According to a large clock on the wall, our visit had begun at seven-fifteen. At seven twenty-five the girl began a countdown. "Five minutes left," she announced. Then it was "Three minutes. Start to say goodbye." At the one-minute warning, she got up from her chair and stood staring at the clock.

I was pushed to the limit by this unnecessarily cruel treatment and whispered to Alex that I was going to stay an extra fifteen minutes.

His eyes grew round and his jaw dropped. "Ma, can you?"

"Watch me. They simply are not going to get away with treating us like this."

"Okay," the girl announced on the dot of seven-thirty. "Come on. Let's go."

"No," I said, "I am not going for another fifteen minutes. I'll be happy to leave at seven forty-five. And," I added generously, "you may feel free to write that down."

Alex clapped his hands to his face to muffle his laughter, and the girl scurried to the front desk. After presumably reporting her predicament to Mr. Evans and receiving instructions, she returned with the head nurse.

"You did say you would leave at seven forty-five?" said the nurse.

"Yes," I answered. "Seven forty-five." Since that was evidently the end of it, the Blair girl could do nothing but stand there fuming helplessly.

We could only guess at the reasons behind the provoking and punitive behavior of certain members of the Blair staff. Was Alex being punished for his disclosures to me? Were they trying to get back at me for my refusal to allow them to give Alex drugs? Were they misguidedly trying to force the separation issue by keeping us apart as much as possible? I suspected to some degree the answer to all of these questions was yes. How any of this was compatible with good psychiatric care was beyond my comprehension.

The humiliating experience of the fifteen-minute supervised visits resulted in Sam's and my firm determination to have Alex removed from the jurisdiction of the Blair staff and to secure his release from the hospital. Both Bill and Dr. Kingsbury were in full accord with this decision. On the following Tuesday, with the supervised visit order no longer in effect, I drove up to spend some time with Alex and tell him of our plans.

I was not alarmed when the secretary told me I could not go in until someone was summoned to supervise. "No," I said confidently, "there must be a mistake. That can't be right. Please check again." Some kind of mixup, I thought as I waited. Mr. Evans had even assured Dr. Kingsbury it was just for the weekend.

It was not a mistake. The fifteen-minute supervised order was still in effect. The Blair worker, a slender youth with a sparse mustache, came and unlocked the door of Alex's unit. I shot him a withering glance as I charged past him and headed for the telephone.

"Your fifteen minutes starts now," he said, holding out his arm and bending his wrist so he could stare pointedly at his watch.

"That's what you think," I retorted as I dialed Martha's number.

Her voice came over the line as a dull monotone, reserved and quiet. She dodged my questions, refused to elaborate, and would only say, "The team had a meeting and decided to continue the order for supervised visits."

"Visit is over," said the Blair supervisor.

Slamming down the receiver, I whirled to face him. "I haven't even seen Alex yet."

"You have to leave or I'm calling security."

"Well, you go right ahead and do it," I told him, "because I am not leaving. You are going to have to drag me out!" Turning my back on him, I found Alex and we sat down in the lobby.

There was a flurry of excitement at the nurse's station, and I noted the appearance of a burly, uniformed security guard. Alex saw him too and, conspicuously flexing his muscles, gallantly prepared himself to defend me. "Ma," he said, "if he so much as touches you, I'll . . ."

"You'll do nothing," I said firmly, and as I watched the guard out of the corner of my eye, I explained the concept of passive resistance to Alex. I also spoke to him of Gandhi and Dr. King, but that was more for my benefit than his. Thinking of myself in such company helped to strengthen my resolve.

Nothing happened. No one came near us. Within the hour, however, I saw Mr. Evans hurriedly approaching. His countenance was wreathed in forced conciliatory smiles. "Oh, I'm so sorry," he said somewhat breathlessly. "I haven't had a chance to get up to Blair to change the order, but I just came from there and it's all set."

Fixing him with an icy stare, I said, "I don't believe you didn't have the time. You had all day yesterday, and Martha told me there was a meeting at Blair this morning and the team—that does include you, I presume—decided the fifteen-minute supervised visits would continue." Mr. Evans neither confirmed nor denied this, so I reached into the pocket of my dress for my notes and smoothed the crumpled paper on my lap. "Last week you told me over the phone we were limited to fifteen-minute supervised visits so Alex would learn to trust the staff."

"No, I didn't," he responded. "You misunderstood."

Oh, my God, the man was lying through his teeth. "Don't tell me I didn't hear what I heard! I wrote it down, and you did say it. And when I asked about the other times I have contact with Alex, you said in regards to the family therapy"—here I read from my notes—" 'We'll see. It has to be reassessed.' And to my question about the hypnotherapy sessions with Dr. Kingsbury, you said, 'We'll have to take another look.' It's right here. I wrote it down."

Although somewhat disconcerted, the intern still continued to deny everything. "You have it all wrong. What Dr. Kingsbury does is entirely up to him. Alex, can we go somewhere to talk?"

"Are you kidding?" said Alex with exaggerated contempt. "If you think I'm going to talk to you, you're nuts."

"Now you listen to me," said Mr. Evans. "You—"

"No!" I said, cutting him off. That he could even think of taking an authoritative stance after telling such bald-faced lies was more than I could bear. "You listen to me! How can you possibly expect Alex to respect you or have any trust in you after what you've done? You blew it, Mr. Evans. You blew it!"

Alex was released from the hospital on the sixth of August, and when he got home he told me he now knew the location of the indoor arena and asked me if I would help him find it. At first I didn't want to do this. What if it was there? What if it was near apple orchards as he said it was and looked like he said it did? Such a discovery would give all the more reality to the alter's tales of cult meetings and abominable sexual acts and ritual sacrifices. I believed Ricky and Gold-stem were telling the truth, but this was too much and too close, and I didn't think I was ready. It was important to Alex, however. Very important. Because if the arena was there, it was some proof that he was not crazy.

So four days later, Alex and I went to Bainbridge. "It's right around here somewhere, Ma," he said as we drove slowly down a country road. Just being anywhere near the place seemed to have a devastating effect upon him. Tight-lipped and pale, he hunched himself down in the seat. His eyes darted fearfully out of the window. Fine beads of moisture gathered on his brow in spite of the cool comfort of the car's air-conditioning.

A stretch of thick woods gave way to gently rolling hills, and I saw that the hills were covered with apple trees. On the left, partially hidden by the rise of the land, was a fairly new housing development. "I don't understand," said Alex when we reached the end of the road without spotting the arena. "I was so sure . . ."

"Well, maybe we missed it. Let's go take another look." I turned around, and about two miles back, just past the devel-opment, I noticed a woman working in a garden next to her house. It wouldn't hurt to ask, I thought, pulling into the driveway.

The woman, dark-haired and deeply tanned, looked up and approached the fence. "Can I help you?" she said.

"I don't know. I'm sorry to bother you," I apologized. "But we were trying to find an indoor arena that is supposed to be around here. Would you happen to know where it might be?"

"There was one. It was right over there," she said waving her arm in the direction of a field behind her home. "It was torn down several years ago when the developers bought the land. A shame, really. It was a beautiful place, very expen-sive."

"Oh, you know what it looked like then?"

"Yes, absolutely. It was two stories high, and it had everything: a heated viewing room, tack room, living quarters."

"Living quarters?" My eyes met Alex's. Could we be on to something?

"Yes, an apartment along one side." She went on to describe the building exactly as Alex had drawn it, and then she began to speak of the owner. "His name was Frank Hanlon," she said. "He was married to this rich woman. They were odd people. He was sleazy, dangerous, and very violent. The neighbors were all scared to death of him. They never did do much of anything with the arena. There was no business to speak of. Trained a few racehorses. That's about it. Oh, they called it October Farm."

October. I felt my blood run cold. Halloween was the most important date on the satanic ritual calendar. Halloween was in October. Was this name some kind of private joke only those who belonged to the cult would understand? I wanted to stay and talk to the woman, but Alex couldn't take being near the location of the arena any longer. "Get me out of here," he hissed through clenched teeth. "Please, Ma, get me out of here!"

My next step was to contact the developer who had bought the land from these people. He reiterated much of the same information and described how he had observed Frank Hanlon being cruel and abusive to horses. "Once I saw him push a stick into the rear end of a horse," he said. "They were terrified of him and would tremble in their stalls if he came close. I recall that my engineer found the body of a dead horse while walking the property. Hey, what can I say. The guy was disgusting—even had the nerve to offer us a chaw of tobacco in the lawyer's office at the real estate passing."

A chaw of tobacco. Frank Hanlon chewed tobacco. What was it Alex had said about one of the cult leaders? Something about him spitting all the time. People who chewed tobacco spit a lot. Was it possible Frank Hanlon and the leader of the cult were the same person? Or was it all conjecture and coincidence? The only certainty was that the indoor arena Alex had sketched last March actually had existed.

The rest of the days of August, hot and thick with humidity, were uneventful. Alex happily renewed his relationships with his friends, successfully competed at the last horse show of the season, and prepared for the beginning of the school year. Fortunately we had been able to enroll him in an excellent alternative program. It was close enough so he could be bused and small enough to provide him with the academic and emotional support he needed in order to get his education back on track. Alex's feelings about this fluctuated between elation that he did have a school to attend and despair that it was not a regular high school.

Late in September, he confided to me how he had become sexually intimate, once and briefly, with a girl from this school. Her name was Heather, he said, and he sounded troubled and distressed, as though he wanted to say more but couldn't. Bill and I had always known any such experience would be very difficult for Alex. Never before had we so underestimated the severity of a trauma.

Alex went into a deep depression, and his stability deteriorated rapidly. The old and by now terribly familiar behavior: the agitation, the need to be in control, the lying, and the irresponsibility appeared like signposts to the gateway of hell.

The call came just as I had finished flouring and flattening biscuit dough on the kitchen counter and was ready to cut it into small circles. It was the school principal. "Alex has been suspended for two days," she said.

I wedged the receiver between my head and my shoulder while I rubbed the dough from my hands onto a towel. "What did he do?" I asked wearily.

"Well, it started with the girl."

"Heather?"

"Yes, Heather. There was an angry verbal exchange between the two of them. Heather said, "Why don't you kill me?" and Alex just went out of his mind. He shoved her away from him, broke a table and a chair, and called me names. I'm sorry to have to say this, but if there are any more such incidents, Alex will have to leave the school."

Hanging up the phone, I cut the biscuits and put them in the oven and sat down at the table to think things through. Alex had told me he knew only part of what was behind the door. This had to mean there was more. Goldstem had something else to tell him. But the destructive behavior shouldn't have to happen. Alex should have been able to use the skills Dr. Kingsbury had taught him to communicate with Goldstem without losing control.

I was in the living room cleaning out the fireplace when he arrived home from school that afternoon. He dropped his books on the hall table and came toward me. I emptied the last shovelful of cold ashes into the bucket. A gray puff of dust floated upward. Still holding the shovel, I said, "Alex, I have to talk to you. The principal called. You're on the verge of getting kicked out. Do you know how hard I worked to get you into that school? Letters! Lawyers! Phone calls! Hours and hours of time! If you're having problems, you know what you can do. Whatever is going on, you know you can handle it by going into the castle."

I saw his composure fall away from him, and he collapsed in a crumpled heap on the couch. After a moment he lifted his head and looked at me, his features twisted with a harrowing, racking pain. "I can't, Ma," he said in a tone of intense despair. "I can't go into the castle."

"Why?"

"It fell down, that's why! It's a pile of rubble. It's gone."

I drew in my breath with a sharp utterance of surprise and shock. What could be so terrible? What could have had the power to destroy the castle?

"That castle simply wasn't strong enough," Dr. Kingsbury explained when we went to him and told him. "Alex can build another castle, a stronger castle."

And he did. With his customary courage, he tackled the

task of building a castle that would be able to hold the coming horror. While Goldstem, the personality who handled sex, came to him and showed him the past and what he had done for him, I could do nothing but watch as Alex suffered through the nightmares and the nausea marking the span of time between the accessing of the information and the ability to verbalize it.

Finally when I could not tolerate any more, I confronted him.

"Why can't you talk about it? You've always been able to before. Why not now? What did they do? What did they do?"

"All right," he agreed. "I'll tell you what they did." And, unable to stand or to sit, he paced the living room in an erratic pattern of circles and lines. "In the hospital, you know how I told you they had sex with the horses?"

"Yes."

"After they had sex with them, they killed them."

"What else did they do? What else, Alex?"

He wheeled about and glowered angrily at me. "Isn't that enough? Isn't that bad enough?"

"No. Not for what you've been going through it isn't. Did you think they would do it to you?"

A piercing, screaming "Yes!" was torn from his throat. "Yes! They said they would! They said they would if I didn't do what they wanted!"

"Which was . . ."

There was no sound, no movement now, as we faced each other. Only a strange calm, an infinitude of silence waiting to be shattered by the words that followed.

"Have sex with the babies and then kill them."

A wave of dizziness. Whirling. Spinning. Don't think. Don't think about this. Don't feel. Whatever you do, don't feel. Not now. Not now.

Alex walked away from me, through the entry hall, into the dining room. I could not see him but I could hear him speaking in a low, choked whisper. "I was supposed to kill them."

"Who?" I said, staying where I was, still not seeing him. "Who were you supposed to kill?"

"Girls. I was supposed to kill girls."

"What girls?"

"They told me. They kept telling me. When I grew up. After I had sex with girls—I was supposed to kill them. That's why when Heather said in school about why don't you kill me—that's why I lost it."

No wonder the castle had not been strong enough. No wonder the castle had fallen down.

XVII

The Halloween Child

Having given Alex this information, Goldstem's task was finished. His function was fulfilled and he was now able to become integrated. But the implications of that hellish brainwashing sent my senses reeling. What would have become of Alex if Goldstem had not been there for him? Had the cult made a deliberate attempt to turn him into a serial killer? What else could it be? I took some comfort in what I had learned about programming from Dr. Kingsbury. Once the process of being programmed is recalled, it no longer has any effect. It is stripped of its power.

In the late summer of 1990, our son Eddie was laid off from his job and was being forced to give up his apartment in Worcester. He called us to ask if he and his dog, a golden retriever named Major, could come home for a few months. Sam and I were, of course, delighted to help him out, and we looked forward to having him back.

My one concern was his likely reaction to the personalities. Whenever one of the older boys had come to visit, Alex had fortunately been in a period of normal functioning. Eddie, however, lived within twenty miles and frequently spent weekends with us. On more than one occasion, these weekends had coincided with the times a personality was in control, and Eddie was shocked and angered by the boy's behavior. I tried to explain about the alters, about Alex's condition, but like most people, he did not understand and equated it to "something like mood changes."

Shortly after Eddie moved in, I took Alex to see Dr. Kingsbury. This was a precautionary measure, as there were no apparent problems at the present time. During the course of the session, however, Alex complained of an ominous sense of foreboding. "There's something else coming through," he said. "I can feel it."

"Prepare for this," cautioned the doctor. "Replenish yourself. There is much work ahead. Remember your safe place is a part of you and will always be there."

Despite the doctor's warning, there was no way any of us could have been prepared for what happened during the early hours of a day in September. The morning dawned bright and sunny with just a hint of fall in the air. Sam left for work, and at eight o'clock I was in the kitchen taking plates and glasses out of the dishwasher and setting them on the counter. I looked up to see Eddie coming toward me, and I knew from the haggard expression on his face something was wrong. In a low, husky voice he said, "There were real strange goings-on around here last night, Ma. Did you hear anything?"

"No," I answered, already alarmed. And then quickly, "Why? Why? What did you hear?"

He did not reply directly but after a moment managed to say one word: "Babies."

"Babies? What do you mean, babies?"

"Babies crying, Ma. Little babies. And there was this terrible, screeching howl in the background—like some kind of animal. It started when I went to bed. I was up late, so this must have been around two o'clock. It lasted for half an hour."

"Oh, Eddie," I said with a scornful laugh. "It was probably cats fighting or noises carried by the wind."

"No, Ma," he replied decisively. "I know what I heard. Nothing else sounds like that. I have friends who have a baby. It was not cats! It was babies, I tell you, and it wasn't carried by the wind. It came from Alex's room!"

I tried to conceal the cold, prickly sensation crawling up the back of my neck behind an angry retort. "Why in the name of heaven didn't you check it out? Why didn't you call me or Dad?"

"I was afraid," he said, his face flushed with embarrassment. "There was something about the cries. Ma, I just froze under the covers."

Such a difficult admission from the strong, stalwart young man standing before me banished my annoyance and displeasure and left me face to face with a set of circumstances that defied logic and reason.

He went on to speak of his dog. "Major was in my room. He didn't bark, and you know what a good watchdog he is, so there wasn't anybody outside. But Ma, he kept whining and once he tried to crawl under the bed. And the horses. They were nervous, too. I had my window open and I could hear them down in the barn stomping and kicking at the walls."

While Eddie fixed himself some breakfast, I sat down at the table with a cup of coffee and tried to figure out what was going on. I knew my son, and he was not given to flights of imaginative fancy. I had to believe he was telling the truth. I did wonder if the sounds had actually come from Alex's room. Or had some cult member discovered he was talking to the police and tried to frighten him by playing a tape near the house? If so, why hadn't the dog barked? Could another personality, another of the secret selves, have been the source of those ghostly cries and howls? A quick, flashing vision: Dr. Kingsbury's office, Alex being sodomized by the uncle, and the shrill whistling of a teakettle. A personality had not only held the physical pain of a past trauma, it had held the sound associated with that trauma. Could this be a similar situation?

And if Eddie had heard the cries of doomed babies, who or what was responsible for the screeching howls? These questions, along with a fear and dread of the answers, caused a feverishly churning turmoil in my mind, and I stared numbly into a cup of coffee that had long since grown cold.

At ten o'clock, Alex emerged from his bedroom, and I told him of Eddie's baffling experience. He denied everything. "Ed's hearing things," he said with a derisive laugh. "He's cracking up. Babies crying. Give me a break!" It wasn't until late the next day that he tearfully admitted he, too, had heard the sounds. "I thought they were in my head, Ma. I thought they were in my head. How could Ed have heard them?"

I didn't know. And a greater problem was how a personality could have created both the crying and the howling at the same time. I called Dr. Kingsbury and he didn't know either. But he consulted with experts in the field, and he learned that it was possible, that the human voice box was capable of extraordinary feats.

Eddie stayed with us throughout September and October, and there were no further incidents. After the night he heard the crying of the babies, I did notice a slight change in his attitude toward Alex. There was a certain tenderness, and it was as though the reality of his experience had given him a stronger tolerance for the boy's problems.

In November, when the trees were newly bare of foliage except for a few skeletal remains that rattled in the colder wind, Alex was helping me plant eight new shrubs in front of the house. "I got these on sale," I said to him as I knelt down to firm the soft, dark earth around the roots of a rhododendron.

Industriously wielding his shovel to deepen and widen the hole for a grayish-green juniper, he said, "That's because it's so late in the year. They'd cost twice as much in the spring." With a casual indifference, he added, "I used to do a lot of digging."

"Oh?" I said, mildly curious, because I hadn't heard him mention it before. "Where?"

His right foot pressed down hard on the sharp-bladed shovel. "That should be deep enough."

"Where, Alex? Where did you do all this digging?"

"I don't know where. It was long ago. I had to help bury the babies."

My hands gripped the rough, woody base of the juniper. I hadn't worn gloves, and the prickly needles bit into my fingers. The chill November wind picked up and I watched a nearby pile of dry, fragile maple leaves blowing about in eddying circles, and I wondered what else had happened. Had they stopped with having him help dig the graves? Or was there more? If there was, Alex didn't know it. And whoever did know was only going to give him this brief glimpse. For now.

And so we went into the winter to enjoy another one of those blessed periods of respite. Having learned from past episodes, I was not so quickly lulled into thinking our troubles were over. Even at the happiest moments of holidays and gift-giving and of our pride in our son's academic achievements as he flourished in the tutorial environment of the special school, there was a shadowy veil of apprehension. Elusive pinpricks of thought kept going back to the cries of the babies, that unearthly howl, and the digging of graves.

The only instabilities marking this interlude focused around the conflict between Alex's childlike dependency upon Sam and me and his growing desire for normal autonomy. One minute he would be clinging to me and saying, "Ma, I need a hug. I need a hug," and the next he would be vociferously demanding more freedom. If we didn't give it to him, he would walk out and go where he wanted to go, and if he found this freedom to be frightening to him, we were to blame for not stopping him from leaving.

In spite of Alex's neediness, he was able to take another step in separating from me. We were in the living room and he was standing by the window, staring disconsolately at the frost-browned fields below. "I'm feeling different about you, Ma," he managed to say. "And I don't like it. It scares me. It makes me feel—you know—like I used to. Abandoned."

"It must be very hard for you," I said gently. "Alex, you're sixteen years old. It has to happen. It's part of growing up and it has to happen."

He turned from the window and gave me a soulful look.

"It's still the worst, Ma. Worse than anything else. The abandonment."

My mind went back to the little boy who completely disintegrated and became incoherent, irrational, and physically ill if I left him. And to that flashback before our trip to Washington. I saw Alex sitting cross-legged on the floor, not knowing me and making those sharp, high-pitched cries of unreasoning terror and panic. "She left me there on the sidewalk," he had said when he came out of it. "She just left me on the sidewalk. And I'm afraid you're going to do the same thing. I'm afraid you'll leave me."

I steeled myself against the tender, protective feelings these images evoked. This was no easier for me than for him, but I knew it was time. It was not forced but occurring as the result of a natural process. "It has to happen," I said again.

Throughout the winter, Alex struggled with his fears of abandonment. If he didn't come home when he was supposed to and I didn't run right out to find him, his perception was that I didn't care about him, and he would be overwhelmed by fear. He worried himself sick over the possibility of something happening to Sam and me. "I couldn't handle it," he said. "I would have nobody. I would die."

"You will not have these feelings when you are older, when you are a grown man with a family of your own," explained Bill during a therapy session.

"Oh, yes I will," Alex insisted with firm resolve. "I will have them when I'm forty."

Since these beliefs belong to a much earlier age, this was but one more example of Alex's uneven emotional growth. Yet another was his conviction that I could read his mind. If I picked up clues and was sometimes able to figure out what was going on before he actually told me, Alex was sure it was because, as he put it, I could see inside his head. "This," said Bill, "is called magical thinking. A young child really believes his parents are like God and have the power to see into his mind. He thinks his mother and father know everything and can do anything."

It was late February of 1991 when the real problems began. At first it was the counselor from the school calling to report highly inappropriate sexual remarks and behavior. And there were the elaborate scams and the need to be in control. A particularly strange matter involved a phone call from Lori, his girlfriend of the moment. I came in while he was talking to her, and putting the phone on hold, he looked at me with a strained expression of great anxiety. "Lori's been getting these weird phone calls on her answering machine. I want you to listen." Releasing the hold button, he asked the girl to play the tape again and handed me the receiver.

I held it to my ear and I heard the drawn-out words spoken in a deep, threatening voice: "I'm—watching—you. I'm—going—to—get—you. I'm—going—to—get—you."

"How scary," I said to Alex after he'd hung up the phone. "Has she reported it to the police?"

He didn't seem to hear my questions. "Ma. Ma," he said imploringly. "That voice. Could that be me?"

My hand pressed against my lips. "Oh, my God, Alex! It's a personality, isn't it?"

"I don't know."

Yes, he does, I thought. And aloud, "Will you please tell me what's going on?"

"Ma, I need to see Dr. Kingsbury."

I made the appointment, and at the end of the week we drove into Boston. The doctor was happy to see him and to hear about the new horse he was riding at a local stable. "He's outgrown his own horse," I said, "so he's taking lessons on one of those fancy, high-action park horses."

After filling us in on his most recent speaking engagements and professional publications, the doctor peered speculatively at Alex through his thick glasses. "What can I do to help you?" he asked.

"There's someone else," said Alex with a self-conscious smile. "I need to go into the castle and I guess I'm a little rusty. I haven't done it for a while—not since last fall."

Dr. Kingsbury settled himself into his swivel chair and folded his hands casually in his lap. A personality? It was all in a day's work. "So you want to brush up on your skills."

Reassured to hear the conviction and determination in Alex's affirmative response, I began to relax, but when he told us he wanted to meet with the alter alone, I felt a twinge of discomfort. "I don't know, Alex. I'd feel better if Dr. Kingsbury spoke to him." As soon as I said it I was ashamed I had doubted my son's ability to do this on his own.

The doctor read my fears, and his intelligent, probing eyes rested on me for a moment. "It's all right. I'm going to give Alex some questions to ask him." Turning to Alex, the doctor said, "Listen carefully. These are the questions. How old is he now? How old was he when he first came? Does he have a name, and, if so, what would he like to be called? What are his needs? What can you do for him?"

Alex repeated the questions until he had them committed to memory. When that was done, he stretched out his legs, placed his hands across his abdomen, and followed the doctor's voice to the sanctuary of the castle, to the safety of the room, where he would meet yet another self.

We waited for Alex to do the work, his own work. His breathing was deep and even, and every so often the barest hint of a frown flickered across his features. What was he seeing? I wondered. What was he hearing? I scanned the titles of the books on the shelves, the high ceiling, the tall windows. I shifted my weight restlessly. The sounds of traffic came from the street below. What was he seeing? What was he hearing?

I brought my attention back to his inert form. After fifteen or twenty minutes there was an almost imperceptible movement of the right index finger. Rousing himself, he yawned and blinked and shook his head. He seemed strangely distant, as though part of him were still inside the castle.

"So how old is he?" queried Dr. Kingsbury.

"Seven. He first took over at Halloween. I don't know why. He was seven then and he's seven now."

"Does he have a name?"

"No," replied Alex, and, after pausing to reflect, "he looks like the Twin, only he's not. He's smaller."

"Were you able to find out what his needs are, what you can do for him?"

Alex gave a scarcely audible sigh and stared out the window before he answered, but when he did speak his voice was firm and forthright. "He's in terrible pain," he said. "The only way out of the pain is to kill George and Christine. He was the one who took the gun. And Ed's moped. To find them and kill them. If he can't kill them, he has to kill himself."

I shivered involuntarily and swallowed hard against the sudden dryness in my throat. Why was this boy trapped in such pain that the only escape was through murder or death? And what did this tormented Halloween Child have to tell Alex? Was his experience similar to Ricky's? Had he come for the same reason?

The doctor was nodding his approval. "You've done well," he said to Alex. "Very well. It is important for you to continue this communication on your own, at home. You must tell him things have changed. You must tell him of the love and kindness you have known these past years and that your life is not the same as it was at seven. You must help him to understand."

"I'll try to talk to him," replied Alex. "But it's awfully hard. He's only seven. His vocabulary isn't too good."

Alex's behavior while he underwent the difficult task of communicating with the seven-year-old was more unbearable and insufferable than ever. Each attempt to get him to accept the consequences for even the most minor of transgressions at school or at home resulted in threats of violence and damage to property. When I reported this to Bill, he gave a possible explanation. "Maybe," he said, "Alex is afraid that if he takes the consequences for small, relatively unimportant things, he might have to take the consequences for something so terrible he wouldn't be able to live with it."

This irresponsibility also extended to his language. My

efforts to give meaning to his words were futile. There was
nothing there, nothing to hold on to. It was like trying to
catch a will-o'-the-wisp. But worst of all was his fear of having me find out about anything he was doing that was wrong.
When the school counselor called to tell me Alex had been
neglecting his work and was failing in most of his subjects,
he went completely out of control and trashed his room. His
stereo, tapes, alarm clock, and some furniture were destroyed
and his posters were ripped from the walls. It had been years
since we had seen a tantrum of such proportions, and our
concern deepened.

On Easter Sunday, Alex wanted to go to church. He hadn't
been in quite a while, and I thought it was a good sign. "I
want to go every Sunday, Ma," he said. "I want to get back
with the friends I had there." So we went to church, Alex
and I, and we sat in the antique pew with its narrow seat and
red horsehair cushions. We admired the white lilies that were
banked around the pulpit and we sang the familiar hymns
and listened to the minister deliver the traditional messages
of everlasting hope and renewal and rebirth. Toward the end
of the service, Alex leaned over and whispered in my ear,
"Ma, I don't feel good. My stomach. I need to get out of here.
Can we go?"

I was somewhat puzzled by this sudden illness, but he did
look pale and distressed. Just a touch of flu, I told myself as
we got up to leave the church. A bug he'd picked up somewhere. An intestinal virus of some kind.

To add to the confusion of symptoms, Alex also was becoming nauseated around the horses. It was happening at the
stable when he went for his lessons, and it was happening at
home. I watched him one day as he groomed Blaze. He had
the body brush in his hand, and he brushed the crested curve
of the gelding's neck, the long, silky length of his mane, and
the smooth flanks and strong, straight legs. He brushed until
the horse was sleek and glowing, his coat shining like dark
satin.

And then Alex was sick, retchingly sick. Stumbling from

the stall into the aisle, he doubled over and heaved and vomited until he lay spent and limp on the floor. "Oh, my God, Alex!" I exclaimed as I knelt next to him in the shavings. I placed my hand against his brow to see if he had a temperature. He didn't. He felt cold and clammy. And I wiped his mouth with some tissues I'd taken from the pocket of my jeans. "What is wrong with you? This has gone on long enough. I'm getting you to the doctor."

"I'm okay. I'm okay," he insisted, not looking at me, not meeting my eyes. "It must be something I ate."

"I don't think so," I said with a touch of suspicion. Was this really physical? Or was it connected to what the seven-year-old Halloween Child had to tell him? "We'll see. If it happens again, we have to check it out."

Alex made such a fast recovery that I decided to postpone any medical intervention, and it wasn't long before he came to me and announced cheerfully, "Ma, I'm going to be the best kid you ever saw. You just wait. I'm going to go down to the barn and clean the tack room and the stalls. You and Dad will be proud of me."

This was said with such honesty and sincerity I had a tiny glimmer of hope everything might be all right. Maybe Alex had gone into the castle and accomplished the necessary communication. I went over to the window in the living room that looked down over the pasture, and I saw him unlatch the gate and go over to Blaze. He put his arms around the gelding's neck and gave him a hug. It was a heartwarming sight, and with growing optimism, I watched Blaze affectionately nuzzle the boy's smiling face.

Within minutes Alex burst explosively through the front door. His eyes held a flint-hard coldness and his features were twisted into a mask of heart-searing rage and hatred. "It's you!" he shouted. "I can't live here. It's you! You're the problem. We have to get away from you."

"Alex, who are you talking about? What do you mean by 'we'?"

His voice dropped to a venomous hiss. "Me and him. The

one who came at Halloween. He's afraid you'll guess his secrets. He made another personality to protect himself from you. We have to get away from you!"

To know an alter was into the magical thinking and believed I had the power Bill spoke of, the power to read his thoughts, was a shock. But the realization that one personality was itself capable of creating another personality was mind-boggling.

This same pattern continued throughout the following week. One day Alex would be a normal teenager with hopes and dreams and plans for the future, and the next he would be caught in a web of fears and terrors from the past. When Sam and I could not survive one more hour of this dizzying roller-coaster ride of emotional heights and drops, we considered a short-term hospitalization. Both Bill and Dr. Kingsbury agreed, and we took Alex to the emergency room to be evaluated for admission. Once we were there, however, he was so rational that the mental health worker who conducted the interview gave me an odd look and said, "I'm sorry, Mrs. Smith, but this young man is simply not committable."

"Not committable!" yelped Sam on hearing this. "I suppose if he knows the name of the president and doesn't go around saying he's Napoleon, he's okay. Well, Carole, you know who's going to be committable if this goes on much longer? I am. That's who, Carole. I am!"

Since we were unable to have Alex hospitalized, we did the next-best thing. We got him to agree to stay at a local Department of Mental Health shelter, a secure, locked facility, where he could go under and communicate with the personalities. While he was in the shelter, I decided to tackle the chaotic condition of his bedroom. Scattered on the floor amid the dirty socks, candy wrappers, and moldy remnants of things once edible were his English text and a notebook. I picked up the blue-covered notebook and turned the pages. Some of the entries were on current affairs, and some of a more personal nature were remarkably creative. I'd seen this notebook before on several occasions when Alex had proudly

Year End Awards

Predisclosed Drawing, April 1991

shown me his grades and the teachers' comments. I don't know why I hadn't noticed it then. The handwriting! I looked at it again, dumbfounded and stunned. It was different. It was all different.

On some pages, the writing was tiny, close, and cramped. On others, it was slanted to the right with long, graceful loops or slanted to the left with letters that were broad and round. All of the creative work, I observed, was written in the same style, a spread-out, carelessly formed script. The last of the variations was wild and erratic. It was barely legible and full of dagger-sharp points. As I studied the pages, I realized that what I had here, although I had no idea who had written what, was the handwriting of the personalities.

There were also two mysterious items tucked into the notebook. The first of these was a slip of paper with a crude figure drawn in sky-blue crayon. It was overlaid with scrawled lines in black ink that formed an uneven circle joined by a triangular shape. These lines extended outward from both sides of the triangle. The second was the program from our horse association's year-end awards banquet. A graceful sketch of a high-stepping horse decorated the front cover, but the horse's eye had been colored over with red ink so it appeared evil and slanting. The ears had been made to look like a long, red horn, and the genital area was also colored in red. Just above the horse's rump there was an enclosed five-pointed star. A pentagram.

At the end of the fifth day, Alex called me from the shelter. He wanted me to come and get him. He wanted to come home.

"It's done," he said, looking at me through bloodshot eyes and rubbing his hand over a scraggly growth of beard.

"When?"

"Last night. I'm so tired. I kept going into the castle while I was in the shelter."

"It must have been hard to communicate with him. You said he had a limited vocabulary."

"What do you mean, 'limited'?" snapped Alex, jumping passionately to the defense of the Halloween Child. "He could talk as good as any seven-year-old."

"Oh, I'm sorry," I said, somewhat taken aback by the fervor of his response. "At Dr. Kingsbury's office you said—I thought you meant—I'm sorry," I repeated, deciding it wasn't worth an argument.

Accepting my apology, Alex went on to describe what had happened in the room in the castle. "I told him how things were better," he said, "and about you and Dad, the changes, all the good stuff, but he wouldn't believe me. He still wanted to kill them. He still wanted George and Christine dead. I had to make a deal with him. I worked it out so if he could see George—I couldn't find Christine—and know we are a lot bigger now and stronger than him, he would give it up. I called Sandra. He hated her, too. And I got her and George to come to the shelter and trick the people into letting me go with them for the afternoon. Only it wasn't me, it was him, and when he saw them and knew there was no way they could hurt him anymore, he came in."

I experienced a moment of panic that Alex, or worse yet, a personality with deadly revenge on his mind, had been near George and Sandra. If there had been a confrontation of some sort . . . My thoughts shied away from the possibilities.

While I listened to what Alex was telling me about this personality, I realized that he had gotten to know the boy quite well and that during the process of communication he had learned to understand him and care for him. He was obviously relieved to have the seven-year-old now a part of him, but there was at the same time, as with the Twin, a feeling of deep sadness. It wasn't until later on in the week that he shared the child's story.

I went to Bill. I took it to Bill. He knew why I was there. He knew it was something so awful I couldn't tell Sam. Sam couldn't handle it. And Bill didn't look as though he was too sure he could. I sensed a protective guardedness about him. But I had to tell someone. It was the only way to ease the pain—that and the writing, the blind transcription of details to be locked away in a desk drawer until enough of my own healing had taken place.

It was almost dusk when I entered Bill's new and more spacious office, and I could see the slices of gray sky through half-opened blinds. His desk, cluttered with evidence of a busy day, was bathed in soft lamplight. "Maybe you recall," I began, "I told you how Alex used to insist he had a baby brother when he first came to me."

A worried frown creased Bill's forehead. He tapped one hand against the desk and nodded. "I do," he said.

"And the house, the one in Bainbridge where he was sexually abused? Christine lived there with her friends the Hendersons. Alex called it the House of Horrors."

"Yes, of course. I had it in my report. He was able to pinpoint the location when the detective drove him around the neighborhood."

"That's right. He gave her information about both the interior and exterior, and it proved to be correct. Well, after he saw the house and told the detective there was a closed-in patio at the back, he remembered that the baby, the same baby he thought was his brother, had slept in a small crib on that patio. I checked the records, and there was no baby born to either Christine Mercer or Patsy Henderson around that time. I didn't think any more of it, because I figured they were just taking care of someone else's baby and Alex had jumped to the wrong conclusion."

I felt a strange rigidity in my arms and legs and a pressure across my chest like steel bands being pulled tighter and tighter. Light-headed and finding it difficult to breathe, I forced myself to push forward. "Bill, they were taking care of someone else's baby. They were taking care of it for the cult! During the summer of 1981, someone came to the house with a baby and gave it to Christine and Patsy. Alex really believed the baby was his brother. On Halloween, Alex and the baby boy were brought to the indoor arena in Bainbridge. There was a cult meeting on that night, and a hooded figure led a horse into the arena. Another cult member took blue house paint and painted satanic symbols on the horse. The horse's legs were hobbled. It was thrown to the ground. It couldn't move. A personality, the Halloween Child—he came and they handed him a knife. It was very sharp and they had him use it to cut the horse's genitals.

Bill flinched and paled and looked away. When he could speak, he said, "And the baby?"

"The same." Quickly, mercifully, avoiding detail. "The same." We sat as though caught in a witch's spell, like statues, the weight of the horror bearing down upon us. My mind went to that karate lesson, Death Night at the dojo, to the look on Alex's face as he gazed at the blood on his sleeve. And Jack's jeering question: "Haven't you seen blood before?" And Halloween of 1986. Was it this alter who had dissected the frogs?

Bill broke in, "Maybe it didn't happen?"

"Maybe. But could imagination or trickery explain away the sounds Eddie heard? Alex says the cries were made by the baby, and the terrible screeching howl was made by the horse when he was castrated. He never heard any of it until last September."

"It would account for him getting sick around the horses," observed Bill.

"And it also explains why giving Blaze a hug triggered such bizarre behavior, and I'm sure that's what was behind the red-ink defacement of the horse on the awards banquet program. There's—" I hesitated, and Bill raised his eyebrows expectantly. "There's something else he told me. He was supposed to be a leader when he grew up. They were training him. They were teaching him to be the leader of a satanic cult. That's why they had him wearing the red robe with the embroidered satanic emblems. He still doesn't know when or how he got it."

Bill expelled a deep breath and shook his head slowly. "It is what they would do, isn't it? Take the brightest and most beautiful child . . ."

"Yes," I said. "Lucifer was the most beautiful of the angels. Oh, and the consequences, Bill, you were right. When he told me, we were in my pickup and he kept banging his fist into the dash and screaming, 'I killed the baby! I'm a murderer! I killed the baby!' Since he couldn't accept the consequences for that, he couldn't accept them for anything."

Bill's face was still colorless. "We can talk about that," he offered. "If he did do it, he has to understand he wasn't responsible. They used his body. He was just a tool. The personality did it because he couldn't. Did he say any more about that other personality?"

"You mean the one this seven-year-old created to keep Alex away from me so I couldn't guess his secrets?"

"Yes."

"Alex says he was integrated along with the Halloween Child."

"Maybe this is it," said Bill hopefully. "Maybe this is the last of them."

I stood up to leave. "I don't know." I opened my hands in a gesture of emptiness. "Dr. Kingsbury says we shouldn't be surprised if there is another."

When I got home, I took out the scribbled drawing I had found with the awards program. Could it be? Was it possible that the triangular shape represented a torso and the circle a head? Was it possible that the extending lines were meant to be arms and perhaps a leg and—? I looked more closely. A knife? I didn't know. I couldn't tell.

XVIII

May 1991

Easter Boy

"It will be over," Dr. Kingsbury told me. "It did end at one time, and it will be over." I held these words close to my heart. They gave me hope. They kept me going. "It did end at one time." This was true. The abuse had stopped before Alex's ninth birthday. The children who had suffered that abuse would no doubt continue to come forward to tell him of their pain. When, at some point, there was nothing else to tell, when the past and the future came together, it would be over.

After the Halloween Child was integrated, Alex returned to the stable to prepare for the first horse show of the season. Unfortunately, he had only two short weeks before the appearance of the next alter. It happened on a Saturday in May. As Sam was finishing his breakfast that morning, I poured myself a second cup of coffee and took a small pad of paper and a pencil from a drawer in the kitchen. "I've got a lot to do today," I said, sitting across from him at the trestle table. Pencil in hand, I began making a grocery list. "Let's see: bread, orange juice, eggs . . ."

"We need pepper. We're out of pepper."

"Okay. Pepper." Sam liked a lavish sprinkle of pepper on his food. "Besides the groceries, I have to go to the bank and the post office and get your pants from the cleaners. Oh, and I have to take Alex for his lesson. Ben, his instructor, says he'll be all set to show the park horse he's been riding by the middle of next month."

"I don't know what the hell he needs with those fancy horses. What good are they? They have to be kept in a stall. You can't take them on trail rides or let them out to pasture because they might trip over those five-inch hooves or ten-foot tails."

My husband's rather sarcastic comment alluded to the practice of wrapping the tail so it would grow longer for the show ring. It was not uncommon to see a tail that had to be carried like the train of a bridal gown. As for the hooves, the extra length helped the horse achieve the desirable goal of lifting its feet higher. "But they are beautiful," I retorted. "And it's not like we're going to buy a park horse. We're talking about lessons."

Sam snorted in disgust, set his plate on the counter, and headed for the door. On his way out, he paused and called over his shoulder, "Carole, don't forget to have Alex move the pile of manure with the tractor, and if he wants me to put up the basketball backboard, make sure he digs the hole for the cement. It has to be three feet deep and two feet wide."

I didn't think Alex would need much urging to do this digging. Although the school he attended did not have a sports program, he still loved basketball and would spend hours shooting hoops. The one fastened to the front of the barn had fallen down, so we had bought him a brand-new backboard and pole.

By eight-thirty, he had taken care of his chores and was anxious to leave. "Come on, Ma. Let's go," he urged impatiently. "I don't want to be late. I promised Ben I'd help him before I rode today."

"I'll be with you in a second," I said, thinking how good he looked in his white turtleneck jersey and the tan jod pants that accentuated his slim-hipped, athletic build. His hair, cut stylishly short on the top and longer in the back, had darkened, and the dimple in his chin had deepened. Going on seventeen and almost grown, he was quite handsome.

Within two and a half hours, I had finished my errands and was on my way up the winding, wooded roadway leading to the stable. Maybe if I hurried, I could catch the end of Alex's lesson. I drove by a row of white-fenced paddocks where mares and foals cavorted in the spring sunshine, rounded a curve, and climbed a steep hill. At the top of the hill stood a weathered gray building. This structure housed both the horses and the indoor arena. Over to the right, a man on a tractor was busily bringing buckets of sawdust to be used for bedding into the stall area. At the other end of the parking lot, a young girl was walking a recently bathed chestnut mare toward the barn.

I left my car next to a white trailer and entered the observation room. Separated from the arena by a wall of glass, it was luxuriously furnished with brown leather chairs and thick gold carpet. A massive fieldstone hearth, featuring an oak mantel covered with gleaming silver trophies, dominated the outside wall. I looked through the glass and I could see Alex sitting tall and straight in the saddle as the black gelding, its feet snapping up at each flashing step, moved out into the trot. The instructor, thin and thirtyish, was in the center of the arena turning in small circles to keep horse and rider in his line of vision. For another ten minutes, he guided the pair through a series of upward and downward transitions: walk to trot to walk to canter. It took a number of tries, but when Ben was satisfied and praised the results, an expression of immeasurable pride brightened Alex's features.

During the drive home, he could hardly contain his excitement. "Ben says I'm doing real good, Ma. I feel great! You know, I have to have a saddle suit for that show. Do you suppose we can get it next week?"

Alex was referring to the riding attire worn in the park saddle classes. The suit, always a conservative color for men and boys, consisted of a longer-than-normal jacket and pants, low-cut boots, and a straw or felt hat. I gave him a smile and said, "How about Friday? We can go shopping for your saddle suit on Friday."

At approximately two o'clock, Alex went down to the flat, level place near the front of the barn where Sam planned to set up the basketball backboard. I could see him from the dining-room window. He was industriously using a sharp-pointed shovel to pile the excavated soil in a growing mound to one side of the hole. An hour later he returned to the house, and I noticed the change had come over him. There was a far-away look in his eyes, he did not know what either of us had said moments earlier, any question or comment brought a completely unrelated response, and he seethed with an intense energy that seemed to burst through his skin. These were all indications of the presence of an alter, so it was with deep misgivings I yielded to his pleas for permission to go to the Roller Palace.

I spent a tense, uneasy evening. I must have checked the clock every fifteen minutes before it was time to pick him up. I somehow knew he wouldn't be there, and it was no great surprise when he wasn't. As I was about to leave without him, a group of his friends and acquaintances approached me. There were ten in all. They stood in a light rain around the side of my car. The neon reflection of the roller rink sign gave a reddish tinge to their angry faces. "Mrs. Smith," said a dark-haired boy named Roger, "Alex is not right. He was not himself. He was hitting people and attacking girls."

"Yeah," chimed in a barrel-chested youth wearing a black leather vest and a gold earring. "I'm gonna kill him if I find him. He got rough with my sister."

"And he kicked me!" yelled one of the girls.

"We don't want him here anymore," cried another.

"There is something wrong with him," added Roger. "He just wasn't himself."

Going back to the house, I walked into the living room. Sam was watching television.

"Where's Alex?" he asked.

"I don't know. It looks like he's taken off. Some of the kids at the skating rink told me he wasn't right. He was violent. He was hitting girls."

Sam shot a quick glance at the picture window and the blackness beyond. "Damn!" he said.

I went to my husband, to the safe circle of his arms. "Where could he be, Sam? Where could he be? He's in no shape to be out there."

Sam did his best to reassure me. "Alex will be okay. We can find him in the morning. Carole, look at me," he said, taking a step backward. "Listen to me. There's nothing we can do right now. We might as well go to bed and try to get some sleep."

I did go to bed, but I kept remembering what Roger had said. "He just wasn't himself." If Alex wasn't himself, I wondered, who was he? I could not sleep, and three times I got up and checked his room to see if he had slipped in without being heard, and three times I saw his bed was empty and felt the chill of the night air in the very marrow of my bones.

We didn't find him in the morning. Or the morning after that. We reported him missing, and the agony of the waiting, the not knowing, lasted for five days. On Thursday, I received a phone call. "Mrs. Smith?" said the voice on the other end of the line.

"Yes."

"This is Sergeant Lanigan, and we have your son here at the station."

"Oh, thank God!" I exclaimed in a flood of relief. "You found him."

"Well, yes. He's been arrested for stealing and vandalizing a car. You'll have to come down and bail him out."

"Bail him out?" I had to give this some thought. I was certain that Alex needed another hospitalization. If I took him home, he would most likely run away again and get in more trouble. "What happens if I don't post bail?" I asked.

"We'd have to keep him in jail until court tomorrow. We don't want to do that. He's a juvenile. We'd need to pay an officer to guard him all night. It's the law."

It was one of the hardest decisions I ever had to make. "Keep him," I said.

The next day, Sam and I went to the district courthouse. Upon our arrival, we were told Alex was being held in a cell in the basement. "I'm going down," said Sam. "Do you want to come?"

I shook my head. "I can't. I can't bear to see him there." And I took a seat on a polished wooden bench in the lobby and looked about me at the marble pillars that rose from the green-tiled floor to the high ceiling. Next to one of the pillars was a social worker who was speaking in Spanish to a mother with two small children. Under a row of gracefully arched windows, a matron brushed a piece of lint from her son's suit and told him to straighten his tie. "You go in front of the judge," she said, "you show respect. You hear?" Across from me, a well-dressed father did not speak to his son at all but stared past him in tight-lipped embarrassment.

I turned away and sought other distractions, anything to keep from thinking of how I had left Alex behind bars, locked up with God only knew who. I watched the lawyers huddled in corners busily conversing with clients, the clerks hurrying to and fro carrying documents, the line at the pay phone, the uniformed officer by the courtroom door. Then Sam was back.

"I feel so sorry for him," he said. "They put him in handcuffs when they brought him out, and this sheriff's deputy stood right over him while we talked."

I reached for straws of comfort to ease my guilt. "At least he's safe, Sam. He needs to be confined. If he isn't, he's only going to run from his fears and make things worse. How—how is he holding up? Is he all right? I'm sure he must be angry at me for leaving him there overnight." Not that it mattered. He would hate me anyway for putting him in a hospital. And even for whatever past horror that was coming through. When he was like this, everything was my fault.

"It's hard to say," answered Sam. "He didn't say much. He seems numb. His voice is flat. No emotion. Look, Carole, they don't hear juvenile cases until after the regular session.

By the time they get a doctor here to examine Alex—well, it will take all day. Do you mind if I go to work?"

I would have liked to have Sam stay with me, but I said, "No, of course not. I'll call you when I know something."

Sam was right. It did take all day. The doctor, a harried-looking man with a German accent, showed up at three o'-clock. I nervously paced the lobby floor. It was empty now. Everyone had gone home, and if the doctor wasn't ready to make his recommendation within the next forty-five minutes, the judge would also go home and Alex would have to spend another night in jail.

At exactly quarter to four, the doctor, Alex's court-appointed attorney, and I were called to appear in front of the judge. Except for a portrait of George Washington, the state seal, and an American flag, the court was starkly functional, with bleached wood paneling and modern furnishings. From a stairwell in the corner of the room, Alex and his deputy guard emerged to stand under more of the arched windows. My son wore a sullen expression on his face, his eyes were downcast, and the light from the windows glinted on the steel handcuffs fastened on his wrists. I tried not to look.

The doctor was the first to speak. He told the judge he had examined Alex and had spoken with his psychiatrist, Dr. Kingsbury, and his psychotherapist, Bill Conti. Based on their concerns about safety issues, he said that he would be in favor of a ten-day observation in a secure facility. The shaggy-haired young lawyer's declaration of his client's opposition was little more than a formality. The judge signed the order.

As soon as the arrangements were made, I went to the pay phone in the lobby to call my husband. "We did it," I said. "The ambulance is on its way to take Alex to the hospital. They tell me I have to go there and fill out some papers. If I leave right now, I won't be too late getting home."

"If you want to wait awhile, I can go with you."

"I've had enough of waiting. I just want to go and get

back. It would help if you could take care of the horses for me."

"Okay," replied Sam. "You got it."

An hour later I was sitting in the admitting office of a small psychiatric institution composed of several old brick mansions surrounded by shaded clumps of rhododendrons not yet in bloom. This office, a gracious room with oriental rugs, antique furniture, and fresh flowers, was on the ground floor of one of the buildings. A friendly receptionist offered me a cup of hot black coffee. "I just made it," she said. "You look tired."

"Thank you," I replied. "I am."

"I'm afraid you'll have to wait."

What else is new, I thought. Taking a sip of the coffee, I leaned my head back and closed my eyes. Now Alex was safe, I could relax enough to try to retrace the events of last Saturday. What could have caused the cheerful, optimistic boy I had brought home from the stable to become an out-of-control car thief? I was fairly certain that whatever it was, it had triggered the takeover of another personality. Could it have been the riding lesson? He had spent three hours around horses. But since the integration of the Halloween Child, being near horses had not been a problem. What else? He had done some chores: cleaned Blaze's stall, used the tractor to move a pile of manure over to our vegetable garden, dug the hole for the basketball backboard.

The hole. Could that be it? It was supposed to be three feet deep and two feet wide. I had noticed the change after the digging. The digging! It came together. All at once. Last November. Planting the shrubs. Alex saying, "I've done a lot of digging. I had to help bury the babies." Easter Sunday. Alex's illness in church. And last Saturday. The hole. There was only one logical conclusion. Logical? Only the presence of the receptionist behind her desk kept me from laughing aloud at the obscene irony of the word "logical" used in connection with such unthinkable acts.

The scene flashed before my eyes in living color and with ghastly vividness. My breath caught in my throat and I felt an oppressive and smothering weight as the pictures assaulted my mind. Oh sweet merciful God! Easter and that gaping hole, the deep dark depths of that grave. The black-garbed leader calling forth the evil of the Stygian pit to transform a Christian celebration of renewal, of life from death, into further proof of Satan's power.

Yes, Alex did have to help bury the babies. Only my guess was they weren't dead. They were alive and kicking and screaming as the shovelfuls of fresh earth fell on their eyes and mouths and blocked their nostrils.

It was seven days before Alex worked through his anger at me and was able to realize I had done what I had had to do. He wanted to see me, he said in a phone call. He needed to talk to me. I understood this to mean integration had been accomplished and he was ready to talk about it. Sometimes the putting together of clues, of having advance knowledge, was helpful to me. But not now. All the way into the hospital, I could not shake the fear and the dread. The closer I got, the worse it was. And as I made my way from the pine-tree-bordered parking lot to Alex's unit, each step took tremendous effort. I focused my attention on the ground under my feet. Brown, winter-darkened needles scattered helter-skelter. Long slender cones, some half-chewed by squirrels. Last year's dead leaves of grass intermingled with the new growth.

I reached his room, and he stood silently, no greeting, no smile, only a dam of tension and a quickly closed door. My eyes traveled from the unmade bed to the now lush and purple rhododendrons outside the window, and finally it was not only what he said, it was the shuddering agony of his distorted and crumpled features and the harrowing pain in his voice. "Ma, while I was digging that hole for the basketball backboard, I went blind. All of a sudden. I couldn't see. I was so scared. I didn't know what was happening to me and I stumbled around in the dark. I was crying and it seemed like forever but in about twenty minutes I could see again and he was there."

"Who?"

"He was five. He came at Easter. There was a hole in the ground. Ma, it was . . ." He paused and squeezed his eyes shut. There was no blindness now to shield him from that image, and the words came ragged and torn and held a mournful horror, the like of which I'd never heard before and hoped never to hear again. "When—when I took—when I took the babies out of the grave . . ."

Babies. Grave. Tiny limp forms. His face blurred as the dread vision exploded senses. I sought to pull solace for him and for me from the spinning black vortex of my mind. Finding nothing, lost in helplessness, I reached out to him.

Since the Easter Boy had taken the babies out of the grave, I assumed he had put them in. I never questioned why Alex had skipped over that part. And after Alex left the hospital, Bill repeated once again the all-important message, "It wasn't you. You didn't do it. You couldn't do it." Alex had to understand that no matter what the personalities had done for his survival when he was a small child, he was not responsible.

Besides his regular therapy, Alex continued to go to Dr. Kingsbury. At the first session he told us the five-year-old alter had saved and kept for him his ability to experience deep, warm feelings. This was evident. I could tell from his eyes. They were different. There was a softness, a gentle quality. "I don't want anyone to see my eyes," he said, peering at Dr. Kingsbury and me through shielding bangs. He gave an embarrassed shrug and ducked his head. "I don't want people to see me crying. I cry so easily." What he was saying was true. He cried over everything: sun, sky, river mist, a cloud, a book, everything.

Before long, I noticed one more difference. It was in the way he moved, unsure and tentative. It was in the way he paused to examine a daisy or to run his fingers across the smooth surface of an oak leaf or the rough bark of a tree. He was like someone who had been blind and had just regained his sight. Someone who was seeing, really seeing, for the first time.

By the end of May, Alex had returned to school to finish out the year. He seemed to be exuberantly happy, and in a visit to Dr. Kingsbury he explained why. "That personality, the one who came at Easter, he told me he was the last and there were no more. I feel whole," he said joyfully. "I'm free!"

"Be careful," cautioned the doctor. "You have done much good work. But the personalities do not always know of the existence of others."

XIX

June 1991

The Old One

Part of me tried to reject Dr. Kingsbury's warning. Alex was thriving. Easter Boy was the last of the children. He said he was. He had to be. But I could not dismiss the stern gravity of the doctor's voice or ignore the significance of his words. So when two more alters did come forward, it was not completely unexpected.

My initial meeting with the first of these was early in June of 1991. I had gone down to the pasture to fill the horses' buckets. Leaning across the fence rail, I put the hose in one of the pails and watched the water make a miniature whirlpool before it flowed over the sides. Blaze and Roxy were grazing nearby. Blaze, always looking for a treat, ambled over to me. His hooves made a sucking sound in the surrounding mud, and his tail swished at the flies. He pricked his ears forward, whinnied softly, and rubbed his head against my arm. "I don't have anything for you," I said, laughing and pushing him away.

As I was twisting the brass nozzle to turn off the hose, a series of loud, cracking noises from inside of the barn startled the horses. Wheeling about, they galloped to the other end of the field. I dropped the hose and hurried through the barn to the tack room. I flung open the door to find a wild-eyed, red-faced entity beating violently against the walls with a black whip. The floor was a chaos of harness and bridles, and two saddles were leaning upside down against a trunk. Other items, including a can of fly spray, a curry comb, and a jar of hoof dressing, were strewn about. A bottle of leather cleaner lay shattered under the window, its contents slowly oozing across the pine boards.

"Oh, my God," I said. "Alex"—not knowing what else to call him—"stop it! Stop it this minute! What are you doing? What's wrong?"

He stared at me with strangely unfocused eyes. "Murderer!" he screamed. "Murdering bitch! You're going to pay! You're going to pay! Murderer!" With that he dumped out the contents of a brush box and ran from the room.

Although I was sure this was not my son, the terrible accusations left me stunned and shaken. While I pulled myself together, I placed the saddles on their racks, straightened out the tangle of harness, and put the scattered brushes back in the box. Taking a roll of paper towels from a shelf, I tried to soak up the spilled leather cleaner. Calmer now, and having returned the area to some semblance of order, I went searching for Alex.

He was in the hayloft, and in the meager, dust-laden light that came through a web-curtained window, I could see he had curled up on a bale of hay and fallen asleep. It would be best to let him sleep, I decided, but as I turned to leave, he stirred and opened his eyes. "I'm sorry," he said, raising himself to a sitting position. "That—in the tack room—it wasn't for you."

"Do you want talk about it?"

"I was—I was brushing Blaze and I saw a little scratch over his eye. I put ointment on it. That's when it came."

"What came?"

"Christine. She was one of the leaders in the cult. A kind of priestess. It was September. Just before dark. In the apple orchard. I remember the trees. A lot of them had so many apples they almost touched the ground. There were mostly kids. Christine had on her black cloak and she was carrying this stick. It was burning on the end. A torch. Like a torch. She made us follow her. We went up a hill and there was a horse lying on the ground. It was dead. We got closer and I could see the bullet hole behind its ears. Its eyes were open. Anyway, Christine said, 'This was a bad horse. He refused to obey. He would not do what he was told and he deserved to die. This is what happens to those who do not obey.' Then she took the torch and burned out the eyes—and she burned its penis."

My knees felt as though they could not support my weight, and I slowly lowered my body onto the sweetly fragrant hay. There was more. I could tell there was more. I waited.

"She killed babies."

"She what?"

"Christine—she killed babies."

"You watched her kill babies?"

"Yes," he said. And in answer to questions I was not able to ask, "I don't know how or why."

"You will, Alex. Someone knows. Someone will tell you."

"No, no! It has nothing to do with a personality. They are all integrated. It was just a flashback."

Oh, sure, I thought. There was no point in arguing the matter. I had dealt with enough of Alex's dissociative experiences to know this was not a flashback. We spoke no more of the incident. I could not bear to think about Christine and the babies, and since this did not yet have any reality for me, I had no difficulty shutting it out of my mind.

Nothing further occurred until the twentieth of June. It was the evening of the summer solstice. The house was stifling, and to get a breath of air, I went outside to sit on the front steps. The repetitive cry of a whippoorwill was coming from the woods beyond the stone wall. Agile brown bats, barely visible against the black sky, were circling and swooping over my head. And down in the barn, Alex was finishing his chores.

It was hot. Too hot to work. I would go to him and I would tell him he didn't have to do any more. When I got there, a bright, fanning light was shining through the open doors. It cut a swathe in the darkness, and I could see the green-and-yellow John Deere, its bucket overflowing with fresh clay. Alex was shoveling the clay into a wheelbarrow and emptying it into Blaze's stall. I watched him curiously, this man-child in the pale green body shirt and the many-pocketed jeans gathered at the ankle. Something was not right. His movements were rapid and jerky, like a robot's. I walked closer, and he stopped working. The space about him fairly crackled with a frenetic energy, a powerful and consuming force that seemed to emanate from every pore. "Ma," he said, leaning the shovel next to the wheelbarrow, "I'm going to change. I don't want anyone to care about me. If people care, they will be hurt."

The despair was taking the light from his eyes, cutting deep furrows into his smooth features. "Alex, what are you talking about? What—"

He cut me off and his voice was more insistent. "I know I'm going to change! There's—more of them. Two more of them."

It was said. Flat out. Faced. And for that I felt a measure of relief. As always for Alex, the first and often the toughest part of dealing with the personalities was to admit to their existence.

His lower lip quivered and he came to me in a rush. Throwing himself into my arms, he pressed his head against my shoulder. He was crying and I could feel tears seeping through the thin material of my blouse.

"I want to die, Ma. I just want to die." Gray words reaching for oblivion, peace, forever peace, and nothingness, the blessed, blank cessation of pain. "I want to die." Tortured words lacerating the soft summer air.

The other, different, not the one I had seen in the tack room, came fast on the heels of his desperate wish. He lifted his head and placed his face within inches of my own. His brows were arched and closer together, his features lengthened, cheeks hollowed and sucked in. "I'm old. Can't you see how old I am?" he said with fierce intensity.

"Who are you?"

He stepped away from me. "Look, look how strong I am. I have the strength of ten men." Holding up his right arm, he flexed his biceps. "I weigh a hundred and ninety-one pounds," he added proudly.

Alex weighed 150 pounds.

"Who are you?"

"I hold the future," he replied. "I must go. I have a mission." He took my hand tenderly in his and, in a courtly gesture, raised it to his lips. Then he was gone. He was gone into the night and I was alone.

Alex had no memory of my encounter with the Old One. Any mention of him was met with confusion and bewilderment and "Ma, are you okay? You must be imagining things."

On the third morning after the appearance of this personality, I was folding laundry from a pile on the dining-room table. Alex was in the kitchen fixing himself some breakfast. I could hear the splash of running water, the clink of silverware, the clatter of dishes—and a high, thin voice saying, "I'm going to kill myself."

Dropping a sheet in midfold, I rushed into the kitchen. The alter was standing by the counter between the stove and the sink. A top drawer in the cabinet was open and there was a sharp, gleaming butcher knife in his right hand. He held it over his left wrist so the point was touching the pulsing blue artery. "I'm going to kill myself," he repeated gleefully in the manner of a small child who had made a delightful discovery. He lowered the blade of the knife and began scraping it back and forth along the inner side of his arm from his wrist to his elbow. I saw blood oozing from the white skin. Not a lot. But there was blood.

Help. My only thought was to get help. Suppose this child carried out his threat? A little more pressure, one slip of the knife . . .

I turned to the phone on the kitchen wall. There was no emergency 911 number in our town. All I could do was call

the police station. As I was talking to the dispatcher, whoever
it was that stood before me gave a contemptuous laugh. The
voice changed, became deeper, more resonant. "The police
can't touch me," he said.

I hung up the phone and studied his features, and I saw the
lengthened face, arched brows, and hollowed cheeks of the
Old One. "I am more powerful," he continued. "I am stronger
than they are. I have a gun. I have it hidden. If they come, I
will shoot them. I will kill them."

A flash of fear. A gun? Was there any truth to this? If
there was a gun, he couldn't get to it as long as he was with
me. The police would be here soon. I had to keep his attention. I had to keep him talking. "Where did you hide it?"

"Where you'll never find it," he answered. "I am smarter
than you are. I am stronger than they are."

While the Old One was repeating his bragging, power-
laden statements, he was carefully placing the knife back in
the drawer. What else could I say? The questions! I would ask
him the questions. "What is your name? What would you
like to be called?"

"I am old. I am very old."

"How old were you when you first came?"

"I was always old."

"How old was Alex?"

"He was seven."

"What did you do for him?"

"I kept him from committing suicide. I kept him from
killing himself. I hold the future. I can see into the future."

I heard the cruiser, the crunch of tires on the crushed stone
of the driveway, and minutes later, the police knocking at
the door. "Come in," I called, not daring to take my eyes
from the alter. "It's open." I held my breath as the two uniformed officers entered the house and walked through the
dining room to the kitchen. They were wearing guns, and I
was afraid of how they would react if they were greeted with
threats to shoot them and kill them. But then my son was
saying, "Ma, what have I done?" and I knew I didn't have to

worry. For all his bravado, the Old One had gone and left a perplexed Alex to face the consequences.

It was so hard for me to think clearly while I was in the midst of all this turmoil. Police, guns, knives. It was all I could do to take a few notes. After Alex was once again hospitalized—this time in a city near Boston—I spread them on the trestle table and tried to make some sense out of what the Old One had said and done. I picked up a scrap of paper. On it was written: "I kept him from committing suicide. I kept him from killing himself."

Of course! The eve of the summer solstice. Down in the barn. As soon as Alex had told me he wanted to die, the Old One was there. And in the kitchen, a child—possibly the same boy I'd seen in the tack room—was drawing blood with a knife and this ancient protector had taken over and put the knife back in the drawer.

Next question. How? How did the Old One accomplish his purpose? The answer was right in front of me. "I hold the future." I read it aloud. "I can see into the future." Having dealt with the inexplicable and mysterious energies possessed by alters who had in the past created being and motion and sound, I was not about to discount his claim. There were people with such psychic abilities. Why not a personality?

Did the Old One really have the gift of clairvoyance? Or did he paint a false picture of an imaginary future, a future of shifting shadows that masqueraded as reality? Was he a master of illusion, a sorcerer who did tricks with mirrors? And even if it was all magical make-believe, what did it matter? It worked. It got Alex through the desolate aftermath of a trauma. Someone who thinks he has a future is not likely to take his own life. And neither is someone who believes he is all-powerful, an omnipotent being, a superman who can perform extraordinary feats.

Before the week was out, I met with the hospital therapist. Her name was Dorothy. Black hair, coffee-colored skin, lips a slash of red, gold hoop earrings, green jersey top, red-and-yellow skirt. She looked more like a gypsy fortune-teller than a professional woman, I thought. Although I didn't believe she really understood Alex's condition, I admired her confidence, and I had some faint hope that the free-spirited statement of her unconventional attire might be an indication of an open-minded and flexible approach.

"I don't want to see him," I said to Dorothy. "You have to understand the anger he has for what Christine did to him. He—and they—give it all to me. It all goes through me. I can't handle it right now. I'm feeling too—well, too vulnerable. These last few weeks have been rough."

The red lips parted in a friendly smile. "We have these family meetings for parents and kids on Wednesday night at seven o'clock. I'd really like you and his dad to come."

I didn't want to tell her Sam wouldn't come. He'd had it with Alex for a while. Even though he knew there were others inhabiting Alex's body, when one of them lashed out he could not see past the physical presence. As far as he was concerned, it was Alex who was screaming the terrible names and vicious insults. Sam dealt with this by not speaking to the boy or acknowledging him in any way. I didn't blame him. I had to support his entirely justifiable actions. But still, it broke my heart to see Alex's distress over the consequences for unknown and unremembered behavior.

During Alex's recent instability, there had been a painful confrontation between the two. Sam retaliated and traded insult for insult in an exchange that culminated in an angry ultimatum. "It's either him or me, Carole!" he shouted. "Him or me! It's your choice. I shouldn't have to take this, and if he stays, I'm out of here." Had Alex not been hospitalized within a few days, I was sure he would have had to leave our home.

"My husband won't be able to make it," I said.

"You come then. You should come. I can't be there, but I will tell the group leader about the problem. If Alex becomes abusive, you can ask for a time out."

On the strength of Dorothy's promise, I did go to that meeting. There were nine adolescent boys and girls, almost as many counselors, and a half-dozen parents in attendance. We sat in a circle, and the comfort of the upholstered chair I settled into did nothing to ease the knots of tension in my stomach. Alex was sitting directly across the room, his eyes fixed on me in a stare of piercing hatred. I cringed before the withering intensity of his loathing. A counselor passed me an attendance sheet, but my trembling hands could barely sign my name. Couldn't anyone see? Didn't anyone notice? I looked pleadingly at the group leader, but she was busy organizing a game. She wanted us to pantomime our favorite activity. This only made it worse.

The contrast of a silly frivolity with the palpable wrath bearing down upon me made it worse. I tried to pay attention. Prior to the game, the patients were supposed to introduce family members that were present. They went around the circle. It was Alex's turn. He said, "My mother," and the words were followed by a battering barrage of malicious taunts.

"I need a time out," I managed to say, and I fled from the room.

"Go apologize to your mother," I heard as I closed the door behind me. They were sending him out after me. I couldn't believe it. I was leaving the meeting to get away from him and they were sending him after me.

He rushed from the room and I was caught in his merciless, sun-blackening rage, crashing against me, thundering about me. Footsteps. Running. Voices. A nurse led him down the hall to a door at the far end. Another helped me to a nearby chair. "What's wrong, Mrs. Smith? What's the matter?"

It was several minutes before I could speak without giving way to choking sobs. "I—I told Dorothy. I told her what would happen. She—she promised. Why? Why didn't they know? Why didn't they stop him?"

The apple-cheeked young nurse didn't have the slightest idea what I was talking about. It occurred to me she probably thought that I was crazy, that I was the one who should be locked up. She took my hand in hers and studied me with long-lashed, serious eyes. "Mrs. Smith, the problem here is trust. You need to learn how to trust Alex."

It was just as well that the secretary summoned me to the telephone before I could respond to this bit of advice. There was a call for me from my husband, she said.

Wondering why Sam would be calling, I went to the front desk and took the phone. "Sam? What's going on? Are you okay?"

"Of course I'm okay! Where the hell have you been?"

"What do you mean, where have I been? I've been right here at the hospital. Why are you so upset?"

"Because I was worried sick. I thought you were in an accident or something. I was checking with the hospital to see if you'd left a message. Did you just get there?"

"No. I've been here since seven. What makes you think I wasn't here?"

"Alex called. Ten minutes ago. He said you never showed up."

"He said I never came to the meeting?"

"Yes."

It took only a moment for me to understand the meaning of this, and I let my breath out in a great sigh. "Sam, I'll explain more when I get home. But it was Alex who wasn't there. It was Alex who never came."

Lee

"Alex has had a seizure." It was the fifteenth of July, 1991, and the call was from a medical doctor at the hospital.

"A seizure!" I exclaimed as I pictured some kind of epileptic fit. "How is he? Is he all right?"

"He's awake now. We have him down in Neurology. We've given him a CAT scan and a couple of other tests. So far the results show no abnormalities. It seems he was carrying a tray into the dining room when he suddenly fell to the floor. He could not talk, and the only movement was a slight jerking of his head and one leg."

Alarm gave way to relief as I realized that in all probability, Alex had just gone into a trance and did not have a serious brain disorder. After a second, very similar episode, however, the doctor left orders for him to be confined to his room. "We were worried," the charge nurse told me. "He might injure himself if the spells were to continue. Mrs. Smith," she added, "he wants to see you."

It had been two weeks since one of the alters had unleashed his rage upon me at that family meeting, and I had neither called nor visited. But maybe it was time. I went in the next day and found him lying on his bed. He was fully clothed—white shorts, brightly striped shirt—and had his hands behind his head. "Look, Ma," he said, staring upward at an array of silver paper stars and moons and planets pasted to the ceiling. "They glow in the dark. I go there at night."

"Safety?"

"Yes, I go under and I go to the stars."

I pulled up a chair. "Are you okay?"

"I'm fine," he answered, and rolling his eyes in the direction of the nurse's station, "but they don't think so."

We talked. Idle chitchat. He showed me a painting of intertwined color he had done in art class, a basketball sports poster on the wall, and a collection of photographs of himself and Blaze he'd taped to the door. He asked questions. How was Dad? When was he coming? Was I taking good care of Blaze?

I didn't have the heart to tell him I was going to sell his horse. The gelding was too small for Alex to ride and too good to keep for a backyard pet. Instead I said what I'd been wanting to say. "The trances. Did you find out anything?"

He knew what I meant. He spoke cautiously, as though he were afraid someone might be listening. "He's seven. His name is Lee. It's something to do with a birthday. He hasn't told me anything yet except it's the seventh birthday. That's important with the cult. They have a big ceremony."

Alex had once before mentioned a ceremony when they had given him his cult name. "What kind? What did they do?"

He did not elaborate. He fastened his eyes on the silver stars, and there was a long pause. "Ma, the other one. I'm afraid to integrate him. He keeps me from killing myself."

"I know."

"How?"

"He told me. And last month, in the kitchen, before the police came. I saw him take the knife from—well, it sounded like a child. I doubt if it was you."

Alex's brows came together, and his eyes narrowed in a slight frown. "It wasn't. It was Lee. He invented him. But he's there for me, too."

"You mean Lee had to invent a superbeing to keep him from committing suicide?"

"Yes, he did."

"And you don't have any idea what happened? What made him want to take his life?"

"Only that it's terrible and it has to do with the seventh birthday."

Whatever the reason, I was sure it involved Christine and Lee had been confusing me with her. Or maybe, to him, all mothers were the same. It must have been Lee who had been so incredibly hostile at the family meeting. It must have been Lee who had trashed the tack room. The tack room! What had he called me? "Murderer! Murdering bitch!" And up in the hayloft. Alex had revealed to me that Christine had killed babies. He did not know how or why. A shudder passed through me, icy cold, sucking the heat from my body. Lee? Was it Lee who held that information?

I turned my attention back to Alex. "What else?" he was saying. "What else did he tell you?" There was a caustic note in his voice. He obviously did not want the alters talking to me.

"Not much. He's very old and very strong and powerful. Or at least he claims he is. He came when you were seven. Oh, and the future. He can see into the future. I think you're right about not integrating him right now. It's too risky."

Alex let out a half sigh, half groan. "Ma," he said, "I have to see Dr. Kingsbury."

"I'll do what I can. We need to get permission from the hospital for your doctor to come in. I have an appointment with your therapist, Dorothy, in a couple of days. I'll talk to her about it."

Dorothy sat across from me at her desk. She had on a red-and-pink floral-patterned dress and dangling jeweled earrings. The red lips merged into a straight line of thoughtful concern. "We are trying to arrange it," she said in response to my request. "We have to be careful. If anything were to go wrong, we would be responsible."

"What could go wrong?" I was genuinely puzzled. "Alex

does it on his own. The doctor is just a guide. He will help Alex communicate with the personality. We've done this many times at his office."

"I'm sorry," she replied. "We can't take the chance."

Translation, I said to myself, "We don't understand and we are afraid."

Dorothy examined a calendar on her desk, lifted her eyes, and said with cheery enthusiasm, "Alex is looking forward to his seventeenth birthday next week. July twenty-sixth falls on Friday. You're welcome to come and bring any presents you may have for him if you like."

I stared at the therapist through a haze of rising panic. Her face was a barometer of her expectations, and she was waiting for me to say, "Oh, how nice."

I tried to explain. "There is no way you could know this, but Alex has already had his birthday. We have it on the anniversary of the day he first knew Christine sexually abused him. That was the beginning of his healing and of his life."

"Alex is looking forward to his seventeenth birthday next week," she repeated, shaking her head just enough to cause the earrings to sway back and forth. Her expression told me she thought I was making a mountain out of a molehill. "We're going to have a cake and candles and sing 'Happy Birthday.'"

So much for flexibility, I thought. And aloud, "Dorothy, you can't! Don't do this. That date has always been so stressful for him. He says something terrible happened. Ten years ago."

She got to her feet and took a case-closed, end-of-discussion stance. "Each patient is entitled to a birthday party if he so desires. It is hospital policy. Alex has specifically asked for a celebration."

"I don't know who wants this birthday. But I can tell you one thing," I said as I prepared to leave the office, "it sure isn't my son."

By Wednesday, the twenty-fourth of July, Alex was beginning to fall apart. He called me in the morning and again, with great urgency, asked to see Dr. Kingsbury. "I have to see him, Ma. I have to. Please. I need Dr. Kingsbury!"

"I know, Alex, I know. I just talked to him. The hospital has given the okay, but he has to leave town this afternoon. He can be back by Sunday. He'll be in to see you then."

"That's too late, Ma. Sunday is too late." Sunday was the twenty-eighth, two days after the birthday.

He kept calling throughout the afternoon. By nightfall, nothing he said was related to anything I said. His speech became increasingly disjointed and incoherent and was littered with expressions of mortal fear. Lee was growing stronger. He was taking over and would run away if given the opportunity. I telephoned Dorothy. "He's going to run," I warned her. "The signs are there. I know he's going to run. Can you have him confined to the unit until after he sees Dr. Kingsbury?"

There was a lilting reassurance in the voice on the other end of the line. "Alex is fine. He's a model patient. He's doing very well. Now don't you worry about him."

I heard from Alex several more times on Thursday. He seemed hardly able to speak. Sometimes he could only manage a strangled "Mom" or "Save me" before the phone went dead.

I tried again to caution the hospital. A young male counselor came on the line. "Mrs. Smith," he advised in tones of condescending patience, "you must learn to trust Alex."

"If I hear that once more," I retorted angrily, "I swear I will scream. You do not know anything about this! Leave a message for Dorothy. Ask her to call me."

Friday. The twenty-sixth day of July. The tenth anniversary of Alex's seventh birthday. The moon was full. I felt a great foreboding. Heavy. Immobilizing. It was coming. Cake and candles. Hospital policy. It was coming. Happy birthday, dear Alex. Hospital policy. An express train hurtling through tunneled blackness. I was powerless to stop it.

Dorothy did call. Friday. The twenty-sixth day of July. The tenth anniversary of Alex's seventh birthday. The moon was full. "Mrs. Smith," she said, "I'm afraid I have some bad news. Alex is gone."

Sam arrived home within the hour. I was sitting in the chair by the fireplace, trying to ease the tight knots of worry in the pit of my stomach with the rocking. "They wouldn't listen, Sam. They wouldn't listen. Alex has run away from the hospital."

"How?" His lips hardly moved.

"They were . . ." I swallowed and took a deep, conscious breath. "They were coming back from an outing. He just took off. The counselor—I hope it was the same one who advised me to trust him—tried to catch him, but—" The ring of the telephone interrupted me.

"I'll get it," said Sam.

A quick surge of hope. I stopped rocking. Maybe it was the hospital. Maybe they had found him. I couldn't hear.

My husband came back into the living room. "Guess who that was?"

I looked up, questioning, expectant.

"Sandra, of all people," he said. "That was Sandra."

"Sandra! What did she want?"

"Alex is in Bainbridge. He just left her apartment. She sounded frightened. Says she threw George out and she's all alone."

"How did he get there from the hospital so fast? It's what—twenty, twenty-five miles?"

"He drove. He was driving a small brown station wagon. He had the keys. She saw them."

We both said it at the same time. "He's stolen another car!"

Sam suppressed a slight smile, but he could not hide the glint of amusement in his eyes. "Carole, get hold of Alex's unit. See if anyone is missing a small brown station wagon."

I did and no one was. No one knew anything about it. Until Sunday night when a nurse called from the hospital. "I just checked the parking lot down the street where we keep the vehicle we use to transport patients," she said. "It's not there. I heard you had asked if anyone was missing a car."

"What kind is it?"

"A station wagon. A small brown station wagon. A Chevrolet, I think."

"Alex was seen with a car answering that description."

The nurse's voice echoed her disbelief. "Alex stole the unit station wagon?"

I couldn't resist the temptation. "Well," I said, "I warned them. I warned them he was going to run and I was told he was a model patient, but yes, it certainly looks like Alex stole the wagon."

"How?" she replied. "There are only two sets of keys, and we have both of them. He must have hot-wired it."

"No, he had keys. He was seen with keys. There had to be a third set. Have you reported this to the police?"

"We can't," was the astounding reply. "The license plate number is locked up and we can't get at it until security comes in tomorrow morning."

I had to explain to Sam why a vehicle stolen on Friday could not be reported until Monday. After making a number of colorful and uncomplimentary remarks about the competency and intelligence of the hospital personnel, he commented on the mystery of the keys. "Why can't those birdbrains figure out that someone on the staff had an extra set of keys made so he or she could have the wagon for personal use? The only mistake this idiot made was leaving the keys in a car full of mental patients."

Sam was right. A few days later, Alex was arrested by the police, and we learned he had indeed taken the keys from the glove compartment.

Although we firmly believed Alex could not be blamed for what the alters did when he was a child, this was a very different situation. He was much older now, and if he was not held legally responsible for their acts, he would have less motivation to keep them under some measure of control by using and perfecting his communication skills. I suspected it was Lee who had stolen the station wagon, but I did not get far in my efforts to have Alex pay a penalty or suffer some kind of consequences. The hospital was not interested in pressing charges.

Our son was sent to yet another psychiatric institution. It could not hold him. He kept on running. To come home, he told us. And by the end of the summer, Sam and I agreed to let him stay. "What else can we do?" I said to Bill. "We have no choice. He's managed to escape from most of the locked facilities in this part of the state. It's either home or the street."

Life with Alex during August of 1991 had an unreal, nightmarish quality. As before, words were nothing, language was meaningless. He never knew who said what or who did what. His inability to recognize people and places that should have been familiar resulted in a plethora of cover-ups. And he was seldom without the energy I had felt when I first met the Old One. It swelled under his skin. It poured from his eyes.

He did admit that Lee had taken the station wagon to go to Bainbridge. "Why?" I asked.

"I don't know," he said. "I've lost the time. I can't find the time."

He was usually able simply to go under and fill in the pieces, and I wondered why he could not. Further questioning got me nowhere, so I let the matter drop.

While Alex was in this mercurial state, we found a buyer for Blaze. When the new owner, a woman from Vermont, came to take the horse, he insisted on helping. He attached a green lead line to Blaze's leather halter and led him out of his stall. Slowly, somberly, the boy walked up to the low ramp of her waiting trailer. The gelding planted his feet and resisted. He knew this wasn't his trailer. "Come on, Blaze," said Alex coaxingly, his voice breaking.

Reluctantly the little horse moved forward. The bars were fastened; the ramp was lifted and latched. The escape door at the front was open, and I could see Alex with his arms around Blaze's neck and his face pressed against his silky coat. Fighting to hold back his tears, he stepped down and out of the trailer. There was one final look and a low, answering whinny before the woman closed the door and drove away.

I told Alex again how sorry I was. "He's too talented and too valuable to keep for a pet," I said, trying to justify the check for seven thousand dollars I had in my pocket. "He's going to a good home where he can continue showing. We can go visit him if you like, and maybe someday you'll have another horse." I could have told him I hadn't been able to depend on him to feed and care for this horse, but I didn't.

That evening, Alex's fifteen-year-old girlfriend, a vivacious brunette with Dresden-blue eyes, stopped by the house. Her name was Carla. She also was very much involved with horses, and, thinking she might be able to console Alex, Sam and I left the two of them alone in front of the television.

We were both in the kitchen when Carla burst through the doorway. "Come, come quick!" she cried in distress. "There's something wrong with Alex! There's something wrong! I can't wake him up."

We followed the girl into the living room, and we saw him reclining on one end of the couch. "Alex?" I said hesitantly.

"I'm not Alex!" he spat the words out indignantly as though I should know who he was. He certainly seemed to know who I was. Carla and I knelt down beside him. Sam stood nearby, watching intently.

"It's a personality," I said to Carla. She had been going with Alex on and off for the past year. She knew about the personalities. I studied his face. The features appeared to be rounded, especially the eyes. Round and wide open. A look of innocence. "Who are you? What is your name?"

The only response was an impish smile like that of a child who has a secret, so I continued, "How old are you?"

"Ten." This time the answer was prompt. "I'm ten years old."

"How old was Alex when you first came?"

"Ten. Alex was ten."

Ten? Alex wasn't in the cult when he was ten. He wasn't with Christine. He was right here with Sam and me. There had been no abuse. I didn't know why he would have had to create an alter. Next question. "What are your needs? What is it you want?"

"I want to play," the boy said plaintively. "I want to go out and play."

His reply caught me off guard. It was—it was so normal. "Play? Why can't you play?"

"Alex won't let me." His voice was petulant, like the complaining of a wronged sibling. "Alex stops me. I want to play."

"I could have Dr. Kingsbury talk to Alex about this. He might be able to do something. Do you want to see Dr. Kingsbury?"

"I don't know him. I don't know who he is."

"He's a doctor who helps Alex. He might be of help to you, too. What did you do for Alex? Why did you come?"

"I came to comfort him. I came to give him courage." The boy sat up straight and looked around the room with an expression of approval and pleasure. His gaze lingered on the antique rocker by the fireplace. It was almost as if he were laying claim to his surroundings.

I began to feel uneasy. "Listen," I said. "Maybe you should go now."

"I'm not going anywhere," he replied with a stubborn conviction that I found disconcerting. "I'm staying. I'm staying right here. I'm never leaving!"

"Carole," said Sam, "what are you going to do? Maybe you should call the doctor."

While I considered Sam's suggestion, Carla reached out to touch the boy's arm. "It's all right," she assured him. "Everything's all right."

He jerked away from her and gave her a startled glance, as though he hadn't been aware of her presence. "I don't know you!" he exclaimed. And in desperation, "Mommy, Mommy. I want my mommy." Tightly gripping my hand, he brought his face closer to mine, "You killed my security," he said more in sorrow than accusation. "You killed my security."

He closed his eyes and leaned against the pillows, and I puzzled over his words. What could he be talking about? What security had I killed, and how had I done it? I was at a loss for an explanation. I could feel his hand in mine, pulsing and throbbing. After a while the trembling ceased. The hand lay limp and quiet, and I released it.

"Why don't we let him sleep?" whispered Sam. He picked up an afghan from the other end of the couch and carefully placed it over the boy.

The three of us went to the kitchen and sat down at the trestle table. Sam was visibly shaken, and his face was the color of putty. He was the first to speak. "Carole," he said, "all this time you've been telling me about these personalities and I never—I never really believed—hell, what I'm trying to say is, I guess I must have thought it was some kind of act, a way for Alex to do and say whatever he wanted and blame it on a personality. What I just saw in there was no act."

"It was the same with me—about the believing, I mean," said Carla. "Alex has told me about the personalities, but until I saw it . . ." She lowered her head and brushed away a tear. "He didn't know me! He didn't know me."

We waited about forty-five minutes before returning to the living room. Carla went to Alex, saying his name softly. He opened his eyes and, momentarily embarrassed, hid under the afghan. The girl pulled it down and took his hands in hers. "Who was he, Alex? Who was that little kid?" she asked with a childlike candor and sooner than I ever would have dared.

"He didn't have a name," replied Alex, swinging his legs over the side of the couch and getting to his feet. He paced slowly back and forth as he spoke. "Ma, do you remember when I first came and you put me on a horse? You had me ride Roxy?"

"Yes, of course," I said thinking of his poise and balance, the promise of talent. "You did very well."

"No. I didn't. It wasn't me. Ma, I was scared to death of getting on a horse. I had someone else do it for me. I invented a personality."

I was astonished. I'd had no idea. Although I suppose I should have considered it strange that so disturbed a child was able to perform in high-level competition. I recalled those early riding lessons and how he would cower behind the fence and then suddenly become filled with confidence. It was the personality! "That's what he meant when he said he gave you courage?"

"Yes. I learned to ride, too, later on. It wasn't always him."

"He said I killed his security. What was he talking about?"

Alex didn't answer right away. He looked from me to Sam and back again. "You sold Blaze," he said. "You took away his reason for being. He's gone, Ma. He came in."

The throbbing hand holding tightly to mine. He was leaving. He was integrating. Good, I tried to tell myself. Alex didn't need him any longer. Alex had his own courage. It was a good thing the ten-year-old was gone. But why did I have such a feeling of sadness? I had just learned a little over an hour ago of this child's existence. And there was something else. Guilt. A pervasive, inexplicable feeling of guilt.

Given Alex's still unstable condition, I objected strenuously when Sam announced in early September he had taken a masonary job out of state and would have to be away for the weekend. "I have to go," he argued. "Carole, these people are good customers and I've been promising them all summer I'd get up to New Hampshire to work on this house they own up there. Now, I've already talked to Alex. I figured he'd be better off if he kept busy, so I gave him a list of chores to do while I'm gone. He's supposed to mow the lawn, take out the rubbish, and weed the garden." Reaching in his pocket, Sam took out a slip of paper. "Here, here's a phone number. I told him he could call me anytime he wants. He said he would be fine and sounded like he meant it."

Alex's resolve rapidly diminished in the hollow helplessness of Sam's leaving. Sam was safety. Sam was strength. With him gone, the boy was left stripped and vulnerable. Toward evening, his fear intensified and he took vigil by his bedroom window. What ogres were lurking in the cavernous pits of darkness that lay between and beyond the trees? What demons were waiting to slither out from under the great granite boulder at the edge of the woods?

He called Sam and took what solace he could from hearing his voice. But it wasn't enough. He insisted on sleeping in the living room, the telephone at his fingertips. To get the police if he was attacked, he said.

In the morning, Alex was unable to follow any of the instructions. He could not mow the lawn. He could not take out the rubbish. He could not weed the garden. Any reminders of his promise to Sam were met with an imperturbable silence. Staring through me and past me, he moved like a sleepwalker, down the hallway to his room. I listened for the blare of the radio. He always turned on the radio and I always yelled, "Turn that thing down!" I heard nothing.

He had left his bedroom door ajar. I went to it and I looked in. Wearing a dark blue T-shirt and faded blue Levi's, he was on his bed lying on his right side with his knees pulled up to his chest and his head resting on the pillows. He was facing toward me, and I was struck by his eyes. They were extraordinarily wide and unblinking. I said his name. "Alex?" There was no answer.

Going farther into the room, I made a closer inspection of the boy on the bed. The cheeks and nose were broader and wider and the lips were fuller. It was not Alex. "Who are you?" I asked. "What do you wish to be called?"

Swallowing hard, he closed his eyes and made a guttural sound.

"Who are you?" I repeated. "What can I call you?"

He struggled to speak, and when he did, I was not sure I understood. He said it again. His name. "Lee."

Blood rushed to my feet. There was a tingling in my arms and fingers. A sudden weakness came over me and I sat gingerly on the edge of the mattress. My mind was blank. This was not the same as talking to those alters who had not suffered pain and trauma. This was not the same as talking to the Old One or the Equestrian. And it was a far cry from the clinical setting of the doctor's office.

Then, without warning, an impassioned cry. "She killed the babies. Christine killed the babies."

For one brief instant, I felt an instinctive dread of being alone and seeing and listening to someone whose age and experience were frozen in the past, someone from another time and another place. My suspicions about Lee had been correct. He did hold that information. He had been there when it happened. He knew how. That was my next question. "How?"

Lee did not hesitate. His speech was clear and precise.

"She drowned them. She buried them."

"Why? What did she say?"

"She said, 'It is what life is all about.' She said, 'It is what I will do to you if you tell. It is what I will do to you if you do not obey.' "

I reached out to him in a rush of sympathy and took his limp, cold hand in mine. This was the core of what really lay behind Alex's terror of a mother. Worse than the sex abuse. Worse than the selling. Worse than the unspeakable things the cult had forced him to do. This was the ultimate horror. Mother. Mother was the negation of being. Mother was the antithesis of existence. Mother was death.

"Christine can't hurt you anymore," I assured him. "You are safe. Never again. She can never hurt you again."

"I have to return," he said with difficulty, "I have to go back."

"It's okay, Lee. You can talk. It's safe to talk. Where? Where do you have to go?"

"The cult! I have to return to the cult. That is my destiny. That is how I will be somebody. That is how I will have power." And in a low, moaning chant, "I have to kill, I have to kill, I have to kill."

Oh my God. What kind of monster had they conceived? The shock was an almost physical force. But I did not pull away. I stayed with him, still cradling his hand in my own. "Lee, do you want to see Dr. Kingsbury?" It was all I could think of to say, and it was a mistake.

"No!" he said with an angry defiance. "I hate Dr. Kingsbury! He took my people away."

"What people?"

"My personalities! He took my personalities."

My people? My personalities? What did he mean? Was Lee some kind of ringleader who had authority over the others? Their integration clearly caused him to feel threatened.

"Christine controls me," he said unexpectedly. "She controls everything I do."

No wonder, I thought. Look what she was doing to keep that control. And again I heard the awful chant: "I have to kill. I have to kill. I have to kill."

This time, however, I was not frightened. I began feeling more comfortable, more relaxed. Perhaps I was becoming accustomed to the strangeness of the circumstances. It struck me that although I was dealing with a rotten little sociopath, he was still only seven years old. "Oh, really," I commented lightly. "What about me? Do you want to kill me?"

"No!" he spat out as though against his will, as though such an admission might ruin his tough-guy image. "Not you."

"Well," I said, "thank God for small favors."

Almost immediately, Lee gave a sharp cry of terror and turned to press his face into the pillows. "Don't bury me!" he shouted in a plea that tore at my heart. "Don't bury me!"

"She can't," I said, stroking his back, wanting to console him. "You're safe. She no longer has the power—"

I was interrupted by another outburst. "We're going to

kill him next. Alex is next. We are going to kill him. Leave
me now. Leave me alone."

I would do as he wished. I took a light blanket from the
end of the bed, covered him, and left the room. My first object was to find a pen and a notebook. I had to get it down
on paper. Right then. Right away. Everything he had said. If
I did not, I wouldn't be able to remember the details of a conversation that was like none I had ever known.

As soon as I finished, I read over the last lines. "Don't
bury me." I did not understand. Was it somehow connected
to the sunrise service? But how? Easter Boy was only five
and Lee was not with Alex when he was five. And what did
he mean by "We're going to kill him next. Alex is next"?
Who wanted to kill Alex?

With two pages of notes in my hand, I called Dr. Kingsbury to tell him what had happened. The occurrence had been
so far removed from reality that I felt the need to ground it by
sharing. While I had the doctor on the phone, I set up an appointment for the following week. If I could get Alex in there,
it might help.

Later, when I thought about it, I realized I was in a most
uncomfortable predicament. I knew about Lee's fears and
Christine's power over him and about his compulsion to return to the cult. I knew how he felt about my son and Dr.
Kingsbury and myself. And although I didn't have the par-
ticulars, I knew how and why Christine had killed the babies. But I could not tell Alex. He had been annoyed to find
out the Old One had spoken to me. His reaction to this
would no doubt be worse. And why not? What must it be
like to have someone take over your mind and body and,
without your permission, reveal secrets you don't know you
have to someone else? I would wait, I thought, until we got
to Dr. Kingsbury's office. Perhaps that would be the place
to do it.

After fourteen hours of sleep, Alex was able to achieve a
fragile stability. Making no mention of anything that would
upset him, I fixed his favorite breakfast of pancakes and

syrup and kept up a nervous facade of cheeriness. "Well, you slept a long time. How do you feel this morning? I think it's going to be a hot day. Do you have any plans?"

Maybe it was too transparent. Maybe I tried too hard. Or maybe it would have happened anyway. At approximately three o'clock in the afternoon, Alex went into the bathroom off the entrance hall. Ten minutes later, it was Lee who came out. I was in the dining room and I automatically retreated from the apparition coming toward me. Black streaks of mascara were slashed across his face to form long, slanted marks on his cheeks and a deep V on his forehead. Riveting me with a penetrating glare, he shouted, "I'm returning to the cult! Is that what you want? Do you want me to return to the cult?"

My hands gripped the top of one of the ladderback chairs by the table and I stood speechless as the bizarre scene unfolded before my eyes like a movie playing on a screen in a theater. He began to bang his head against the doorjamb, harder and harder, until the layers of paint cracked and loosened and fell to the floor. Then he looked blindly around as though searching for someone or something and asked again in a howl of frustration, "Do you want me to return to the cult?"

Staggering to the living room, Lee fell on the couch, slumped against the pillows, and went into a deep sleep. When he awakened he was Alex, and when Alex looked in the mirror, he gasped in horror at the ugly black streaks on his face. "Oh, Ma," he said, as he vigorously scrubbed them off. "I have to keep the appointment with Dr. Kingsbury. I have to communicate with Lee. I have to work on this problem."

I believed him. I believed it was what he really wanted to do. But what about Lee? I suspected the last thing he wanted was to participate in a session with Dr. Kingsbury. He hated the doctor for taking away the personalities and was surely afraid he would meet the same fate. I wished I had explained to him how the doctor only desired to help him and would not try to destroy him.

To be honest, I couldn't say my own motives were that generous. Yes, I felt sorry for Lee, and I was truly grateful to him for what he had done for Alex. Obviously, a child who lives in fear that his mother will cold-bloodedly murder him can have no trust in anyone at all. He would not be able to function. By taking over and keeping this knowledge, Lee had saved the ability to trust. It wasn't perfect. It wasn't complete. But it was enough to ensure survival.

It didn't matter. I wanted him gone. I wanted him out of our lives.

On the afternoon we were to go into Boston, Alex begged to be allowed to drive. "Can I, Ma? Please, Ma, can I drive to Boston? I know what I have to do, and it's not going to be easy. If I can drive, it will keep my mind off it. I'll be careful. I promise."

"Alex, you know what's been happening lately," I argued. "He keeps—"

"No, Ma. I'm in control. I'm determined to go through with this, and I am in control."

I handed him the car keys.

During the ride to the city, Alex chatted happily about his plans for the future. "I want to go to public school again," he said. "I need to go to the special school for a while longer. I need to prove myself and I'm going to do it. I'll be the best kid they ever saw."

Lost in my thoughts, I did not notice that Alex had fallen silent until too late. It was so quick! The road curving ahead, the car going straight, the tree, closer, closer, closer; a scream that seemed separate and apart.

With not a second to spare, he came out of it and slammed on the brakes. The car lurched to the left and came to a stop in a pile of underbrush. The rough-barked trunk of a hickory tree was barely two inches from the right front fender. For a moment I was only aware of the furious pumping of my adrenaline-charged heart and the cold numbness of my nose, lips, and fingertips.

"I'm sorry, Ma," said Alex in stunned apology. "I must have fallen asleep. I guess you'd better drive."

Asleep? No way. It was Lee. He had taken over again. He was going to do everything he could to keep Alex away from Dr. Kingsbury, and he didn't care if he killed Alex and himself and me in the process. This seemed rather contradictory behavior for someone who was worried about committing suicide, but I doubted if he realized just how much his life depended upon Alex.

I was tempted to turn around and go home, but I couldn't give up. It would be a mistake, I felt, to let Lee have his own way. And there was always the chance that if I could just get him in to see the doctor, he might listen and forget about returning to the cult.

We parked near Fenwood Road and walked toward Dr. Kingsbury's office. Alex exuded confidence and his step was light and springy. "I'm definitely going to work on this, Ma. I am," he assured me as we passed an attractive cement planter filled with petunias, geraniums, and trailing ivy. Having survived an early frost, the flowers offered a bright contrast to the otherwise dismal surroundings. Over to our right, a sleeping homeless man was wrapped in a cocoon of tattered blankets. At the bottom of an embankment, a polluted stream flowed sluggishly through a wooded area. In the middle of the stream, a mottled-brown mallard attempted to navigate around the debris. Alex cast a pitying glance at the homeless man and he commented on the plight of the duck. "How can she swim in such dirty water?" he said.

This compassionate and caring frame of mind disappeared as soon as we entered the familiar office and sat in the chairs opposite the desk. Dr. Kingsbury put down a book he had been reading, adjusted his glasses, and studied Alex's face and demeanor. In a tone of reflective sincerity, he asked, "How can I help you?"

Alex did not answer. He stared sullenly out of the window.

The switching usually meant he was not there, but hoping he could hear me, I tried to talk to him. "Alex, before we left and again a few minutes ago, you said you were going to work with the doctor today."

"Me?" he bellowed, leaping to his feet and standing before me in a challenging posture. "I'm not working on anything!" His voice was high-pitched, accusing, condemning, his eyes black fathomless pits of hate. "You! You're the one. You're the one who's crazy. You're the one who should be committed!" And with that, he flung open the door and ran from the room.

Dr. Kingsbury nodded toward the open door. "He needs to be hospitalized," he said with certainty. "He's out of control."

I was crying. Whether it was the aftereffects of the close call with a hickory tree or the result of an emotionally ravaging week, I didn't know, but I felt I could not handle one more drastic change from calm reasonableness to rabid, irrational fury. "How?" I sobbed. "Can you do something? Can you hospitalize him from here?"

"No. I'm sorry. There are legalities. It has to be done from your own area. Just get him into a hospital. I don't care how you do it. You have my beeper number. Have the Mental Health people call me."

Armed with a prescription for Ativan, a medication that might quiet Alex down if I could get him to take it, I went into the street to find him. Catching a glimpse of his red T-shirt behind a parked car, I called to him. His only reaction was to crouch lower so he was completely hidden from my view. I walked slowly toward my car. From time to time, I threw a quick look over my shoulder, and I was encouraged to see that he was following.

He stayed about fifty feet from me, dashing from one vehicle to the next, often coming perilously close to oncoming traffic. When we approached the banks of the stream, he ran across the sidewalk and into the woods. I could see him hunched down behind a tree, peeking stealthily in all directions. Like a commando approaching an enemy position, he darted to a concealing clump of bushes.

Reaching my car, I got in and waited for him. He had left the protective underbrush and was standing by the stone bench near the flowers. His gaze traveled from me to the great brick and granite buildings looming skyward in all directions, and I tried not to worry about what I would do if he disappeared into the streets of Boston.

Five minutes went by. He did not move. It was time to raise the stakes. I slid the key into the ignition and started the motor. It worked. Faced with a choice between the terrors of the big city and coming with me, he evidently concluded I was the lesser of the two evils. Hesitantly, fearfully, he came to the car and got in.

Lee pressed himself against the door. I kept my left hand in the vicinity of the electronic lock button, just in case. Before long, he fell into a deep sleep, and the situation became less tense. As I maneuvered through the traffic, I tried to unscramble the chaotic disorder of my thoughts. I had to figure out a way to get Alex into a psychiatric unit. Admission had to be done through our local emergency room. But Lee was a strong and dominant personality. He would not give up without a fight. If I tried to bring Alex anywhere near the hospital, Lee was certain to take over and run. If I could just get him to the house. If I could get the medication down him. If I could deal with this in the morning. If I could . . .

"Ma, I'm hungry. Are we almost home?" It was Alex. "I'm starving," he persisted. "What's for supper?"

Supper? Cook? I rubbed the taut muscles in the back of my neck. "Promise me you won't run," I said, "and I'll stop and buy a bucket of fried chicken." Alex's promise would mean nothing to Lee, but I knew that right next to the fried chicken establishment, at a nearby shopping mall, there was a pharmacy. It was the best chance I would have to get the prescription filled.

"Ma, I'm not going to run," he replied innocently. "Why would I run? I want to go home and watch the Red Sox game on TV tonight."

I decided to take the risk. I turned into the mall, and after picking up the chicken, I went into the drugstore. Two customers were ahead of me, and I fidgeted nervously. From where I was standing, I could see Alex quite clearly through the display window. He had the car door open and was absentmindedly fiddling with the radio. He seemed to be okay. The clerk called my name. The prescription was ready. In forty-five seconds, a minute at most, I had paid for the pills and returned to the car.

It was empty! He was gone. I ran to the left, frantically searching behind the row of vehicles. Nothing. I circled to the right, my eyes sweeping the parking lot. No sign of him. I stamped my foot in frustration. Lee was responsible for this! I called out his name. No answer. I called again. No answer. "He's not going to get away with it," I hissed through clenched teeth. "That horrid brat is *not* going to get the best of me." Determined not to be outwitted by a seven-year-old, I got back into the car.

I had to think. I had to have a plan. But my head was throbbing. My nerves were frazzled. The pills. I still had the medication clutched tightly in my hand. I removed the plastic lid from the small vial and took out one of Alex's Ativan tablets. I held it up in front of me. It was quite small and had a hard surface. "Why not?" I said aloud. "Why the hell not?" And I popped the pill in my mouth and gulped it down.

For half an hour I drove through the streets, hoping to find him. It was Friday night. Where could he be? Friday night. Of course! The Roller Palace. I began to laugh. I had him. Whether he was Alex or Lee, sooner or later, on any given Friday night, he would go to the Roller Palace.

I went to the skating rink and stood on the edge of the darkened floor. A cacophony of discordant sound assaulted my ears as I scanned the faces of the teenagers who sped by in a colorful blur. He was not among them. But he would be. Before the night was over, he would be there. Having no desire to wait around, I arranged to have the manager notify me as soon as he showed up.

Back at home, I had hardly finished telling Sam about my dreadful day when the call came. Alex had just entered the Roller Palace. "Carole," said Sam, "why don't I get him? I think you've been through enough."

I readily agreed to the offer. "You'd probably have better luck, anyway," I said. "If he's Alex, he'll feel safer and be less likely to switch. I'm not sure about Lee. He'll come if he has no-place else to go. That's what happened in Boston. He was afraid to be left alone in the city."

It was good to be able to talk to my husband like this, to freely discuss the personalities and their characteristics. It lightened the burden. It eased the pain. And in less than an hour, I looked out of the living-room window to see him walking toward the house with the boy following meekly be-hind.

"How did you do it?" I asked Sam while Alex was in the kitchen rummaging through the refrigerator.

"He was out in front of the skating rink. I put my hand on his arm and he felt cold and stiff. Then he changed. He got all excited and went on and on about a dollar bill he'd found. So help me God, Carole, he sounded just like a little kid."

"Who knows?" I let out my breath in a despondent sigh. "Maybe he was. He seems to be himself right now, but how long will it last?"

"It won't," said Sam, lowering his voice. "Here's what we're going to do. I want you to crush up one of those pills and put it in some juice. I'll get him to drink it, and after he's asleep, we'll take all of his shoes and sneakers out of his room. First thing tomorrow, we'll call the police and have him taken to the emergency room. They can hospitalize him from there."

In the morning when I went into my son's bedroom to wake him up, a uniformed policeman was standing in the doorway. "You been having blackouts, Alex?" the young officer asked in a kindly tone.

Alex raised himself to a sitting position and draped a quilt around his shoulders. He looked from me to the policeman, and I saw confusion in his face. But I saw something else there, too. Relief. "Yes," he said. "I've been losing time. It's scary. It's so scary."

The Magical Thinking

Two weeks later, Sam and I were on our way to visit Alex at Westboro State Hospital. Although the hospital had an excellent reputation, everywhere I looked, the surroundings bespoke decay and neglect. The grass was unmowed and littered with cigarette butts, the courtyard was choked with weeds, the asphalt roads were crisscrossed with crevasses. And at the top of a hill, its windows boarded, its chimneys falling down, stood an old abandoned building. Other buildings, equally ancient but still functional, loomed on either side of the driveway. "I've heard," I said to Sam as he carefully avoided the potholes, "that there are underground passages lined with cells where they used to keep the worst cases."

Sam stopped the car. "I must have taken a wrong— What's that noise? It sounds like a damn wolf!"

"It must be one of the patients. Alex isn't in with those people," I added quickly. "His unit is on state hospital grounds, but it's run by the psychiatric department of U. Mass."

"Well, which way do I go?"

"Let me see," I said, searching for a familiar landmark. "I've only been here once since his admission. I had to attend a meeting with Alex and the social worker. You'll have to turn back. I think it's over there past those trees."

"Jesus, Carole, that howling gives me the creeps. Are you sure this place is all right?"

"It's not as though we had any choice," I retorted. "No one else would take him. And Alex does have a very good doctor here. He says nothing else has worked, so he's going to allow Bill and Dr. Kingsbury to be involved in the therapy."

Heading the other way, Sam parked in front of the building that housed Alex's unit. I opened the car door. I paused for a moment. I closed the car door. "I've changed my mind. You go in alone. I'm not ready to see him yet."

"Why not?"

"At that meeting I went to. I didn't tell you. I couldn't talk about it. Sam, he was so infuriating. It wasn't one of them this time. It was him. Since he doesn't want to face the real issues, he throws up these smoke screens, blaming me for all his problems. The social worker—Pam, her name is Pam—and the people on the staff actually believe his lies! They think I'm the one who abused him. They look at me like I'm a criminal. It's not fair, Sam. You and I both have been victims of Christine and her brothers, just as Alex has. We've suffered because of what they did to him. And then to be treated like this! Do you want to hear what the social worker said? I realize she's young and inexperienced and means well, but she said, 'Doesn't Alex have a right to be angry at you?' And the answer is absolutely, positively no. I didn't beat him and burn him and rape him. I've done nothing to deserve that kind of anger. I'm so sick of it. I hate him for making me pay for what Christine did to him."

"Tell him," said Sam, who had sat in silence throughout my tirade. "Why don't you tell him how you feel?"

I thought about it. While Sam was visiting Alex, I sat in the parking lot listening to those drawn-out wolflike howls, and I thought about it. I wanted to. And at the next hospital therapy session, in the bland colorlessness of one of the conference rooms, I did exactly that. Bill was there, and the social worker: doe-eyed, square face framed by long, auburn hair. But it didn't matter. "I hate you!" I yelled at him. "I hate you for every single filthy, rotten name you have ever called me, every trust you have ever betrayed, every bit of tenderness and affection and love you have thrown back in my face. I hate you!"

I let it come, welding and fusing into a billowing, skin-splitting fury, a glorious passion that was burning and purifying and cleansing. I stood over him, cherishing this moment, this exquisite release.

He moved his chair away from me. In his eyes, a flash of fear, a change, the other. Lee was listening, too. Good. Good! Let him hear this. Let him hear.

"I hate you!" Again the words screamed from my throat, emptying, purging that which had been held in too long. He turned away from me, his face a mask of studied indifference. "Look at me!" I shouted. "Feel my pain. I want you to know what you have done to me. I want them to know what they have done to me. Know my pain!"

Overcome by a trembling, a weakness, I stepped back and collapsed on a couch in front of the window wall. No one moved. No one spoke. In the calm of spent emotion, I said to him, "When you and they can understand finally and forever that it was Christine who was responsible for what happened, maybe, just maybe, you can stop making me pay for the things she did. When you are ready to do whatever you have to do to deal with my pain, you let me know. If you can't, I never want to see you again."

Getting up from the couch, I strode purposefully across the room, and as I was leaving I heard him say, "Go to hell."

I glanced over my shoulder. "Hell? I'm there, Alex. I'm already there. I am trying to get out."

I'd barely gotten beyond the locked doors of the unit before the social worker, in a flurry of agitation, caught up with me. "Are you ever coming back? Suppose he doesn't do what you want? If my mother had ever talked to me like that when I was his age . . ."

I felt as if I were listening to a foreign language, and I could do nothing but stare at her. What, I wondered, what in the name of heaven did that have to do with anything? What need or right would her mother have to the kind of anger I was experiencing? Presumably this young woman had come from a normal home and had lived a normal childhood. Why did these people keep trying to plug this into normal?

"I've simply drawn a line," I said. "I've set a limit. We do this sometimes in an unbearable situation. It's a calculated risk, but our relationship cannot survive if Alex does not deal with my pain and my anger. There is no way I can bring him home unless he does. And he will," I added with a rueful half-smile. "He will."

Pam's features were overcast with doubt. She gave a solemn shake of her head. "You're an optimist," she said.

In less than twenty-four hours, Alex called me. Probing, reaching, tentative, conciliatory. "I know you don't want to talk to me. I just wanted to find out if you'd heard anything about Blaze. I miss him. How is he doing? Did Dad finish that job? Have you heard from Eddie?"

My answers were brief and cold.

"Ma, please, Ma! I'm not going to call you bad names anymore."

"Oh? Why not?"

"Well, what you said. Do you know how long I've waited for you to say that, that you hate me? I'm so tired of hearing people tell me they understand. I wish you'd done it a long time ago."

"I couldn't. You weren't ready. And Alex, maybe you won't do it again, but what about him? What about Lee?"

"I don't know. All I know is I want to see you."

"I am not going up there to risk being humiliated in front of the staff."

"Ma, what we say has nothing to do with you."

"The staff don't know that."

"They will. I'll tell them the truth."

"I need for you to understand my pain."

He gave a sorrowful cry. "I can't, Ma. I can't feel it. I always feel like a victim. I can't get past feeling like a victim. Ma, I love you."

I hardened my heart. "I can't go on like this."

"I'll try."

"At the next therapy session?"

"Yes, at the next session."

This meeting was scheduled for the following day at two o'clock. Wearing an oversized, multicolored sweater, jeans, and high-top sneakers, Alex sat across from me on a plastic-upholstered chair. His fingers were tightly interlaced, and he leaned slightly forward with his hands between his knees. Bill and Pam were seated to my left.

"I—I'm afraid," began Alex. "Ma, I'm afraid you don't really love me. Sometimes I think you're only interested in me as a case, because of the personalities."

"In the beginning," I replied, "you were a client. I got very well paid for working with you. And it is true there have been many occasions when, for my own survival, I was forced to distance myself from you and see you as a case. But even then, you were also my child. There was an immediate sense of kinship. You were like me in a lot of ways. We shared some of the same interests. We shared some of the same characteristics, like strength and not giving up. Can you imagine? Can you imagine what a great feeling that was?"

I held his eyes with mine and went on talking, softly, gently. "And all those things I did for you, all of those lessons—the karate, the dancing, the horseback riding. They weren't only for you. They were for me, too. I got so much pleasure from watching you learn and grow. I loved going to the dance recitals and the horse shows. I was very proud of you. You were my child. I held you. I rocked you for hours on end and you told me of the terrible things that had happened to you and we both cried."

Alex was listening, really listening. He pulled the sweater up over his face, hiding the swelling empathy.

"I'm almost finished," I said. "Do you remember the flashback where you first knew of the sexual abuse? You were driving your head into the wall like it was a battering ram. For over an hour, I wrestled with you to keep you from injuring yourself. And when it was over, we were both exhausted and drenched with sweat. I've never told you about it, but something happened to me that night. It was very like a birthing experience. Afterward, for days afterward, I had the same feelings a mother has for a newborn baby. I felt the overwhelming tenderness; I felt the fierce protectiveness. Alex, you are my child."

"You're going too fast," he said in a voice choked with sobs and muffled by the still-shielding sweater.

Too fast? It couldn't be helped. For us, for Alex and me, there was no more time. He let the sweater slide down. He let me see his tears. "Why are you crying?" I asked him. "Why, Alex?"

"For what I did to you. For how I hurt you."

Given my son's past history of escaping from locked facilities, it wasn't until mid-November that the doctor granted him a two-hour pass to leave the hospital. I picked him up and I took him to dinner at a Chinese restaurant, and I took him shopping for some tapes of his favorite rock groups. By seven o'clock, we were back at the unit. As I hurried across the parking lot to the front entrance, I closed my coat against the sporadic gusts of cold wind. Low hovering clouds held a threat of snow, and I hoped it would hold off until I'd gotten home.

"Ma," he said as he was checking in at the nurse's station, "visiting hours aren't over till eight. Can you stay for a while?"

I sensed it was important. He had been strangely preoccupied all evening. "Just a few minutes," I answered, thinking of the impending storm.

We went into the kitchen, an immaculately clean room, barren in its neatness. The door was closed. No one else was around. A faint tapping sound caught my attention, and I walked toward a row of casement windows over the counter. Icy bits of hail mixed with the beginning snow were hitting against the glass, and in the headlights of passing cars I could see the frenzied motion of fast-falling flakes.

We seated ourselves in orange plastic chairs at the Formica table. Alex was describing an incident that had recently taken place on his floor. He was in the middle of a sentence when he cut himself off. "Ma," he blurted out, "there is one reason why I get angry at you. I'm sorry I couldn't talk to you about it before."

"What?" I said, already defensive.

His face was an agony of frustration. He appeared to be torn between staying and bolting from the room. "It's not your fault. You can't help it. But you know things. You know more than my doctor. You know more than my therapist. Ma! You know more than I do."

"Of course I do," I tossed off lightly, trying to shield my discomfort, trying to pretend I did not understand he was most likely referring to the secrets Lee had shared with me. "Of course I do. We've been very close for eight years."

"Ma!" he cried out, cutting through my charade of ignorance and leaping to his feet so quickly that the orange chair spun around and fell over backward. "Ma, I know he talked to you. I don't know what he said, but I know he talked to you. I'm so afraid you might tell me. Don't tell me. Please don't tell me!"

The anguish of his plea cut to the very soul of my being, and I wished he never had to know. I wished I could stop it and block it before it emerged from the bowels of that hellish past.

He stepped back and away from me as if I were someone dangerous, someone to be feared. "Please, Ma. Don't tell me," he repeated.

"I will not tell you, Alex. I promise I will not tell you."

I was committed to keeping my promise. The only one who could give Alex this information was Lee. I had to trust that Lee would know when Alex was ready to listen. In the meantime, while we waited for this to occur, something else happened. Something that made the existence of the cult more real and more frightening than ever.

Sam and I were in the living room watching the evening news on television when the phone rang. The man on the other end of the line identified himself as a police officer, a member of a local satanic task force. During an investigation of cult activity, he explained, his task force had come across a name. "Christine Mercer," said the officer. "Do you have any information concerning a Christine Mercer?"

I jerked the phone from my ear and clapped my hand over the receiver. "Sam," I whispered. "It's the police. They want to know about Christine. The cult."

Sam was instantly alert. He got up from his chair and hurried toward me. "Don't say anything. Get a number. Check it out and dial them back."

The call turned out to be legitimate. It had originated from the Bainbridge police station. "The residents," the officer told me, "have been seeing people in black hoods at night in the woods, and they found stone altars that had been used for some kind of sacrifices. There was blood, but they don't know if it was human or animal."

"Christine Mercer," I told him, "is my son Alex's biological mother. According to him, she and her brothers were members of a satanic cult."

"Well, we'd certainly like to interview him."

"Alex suffers from severe psychological problems because of what they did to him. He's hospitalized. He's in Westboro, the U. Mass adolescent unit. And besides, he hasn't had any recent contact with them. He doesn't know anything about now."

"Ma'am," replied the officer, "we think he does. We think he knows more than he's saying."

My sleep that night was haunted by a dream of a child standing under a full moon in a red sky. The child was dressed in a red robe, and all around him there were skeletal, dead trees like those that are left after a forest fire. I saw three apples hanging on the blackened branches of one of the trees. The apples were ripe and ready for harvest, and I was on a ladder trying to climb the tree to pick the apples. As I got closer to them, I heard a humming sound. It came from the sky. It came from the ground. And it grew louder and louder, and then the apples began to shrivel and darken and change into black arrows with sharp, gleaming points. They quivered like living things and they broke loose from the tree to fly swiftly downward to find the heart of the child, to pierce the heart of the child. And his blood became one with the red robe.

I woke up, sick and nauseated and drenched in sweat. The evil, even in a dream, clung to me like some insidious film. As soon as I could, I contacted Alex. I had to ask him. I told him of my conversation with the police. "Alex, they not only believe the cult is still in existence, they think you know about it."

"I do."

"You what?" My heart skipped a beat.

"I do. I went to a meeting. That is, Lee—Lee went to a meeting. On the birthday. Lee held the programming. He had been programmed to return to the cult on the seventeenth birthday."

So that was it! Why Lee wanted to have the birthday. Why it was so important. And why he stole the station wagon from the hospital. I should have guessed. Lee had come right out and said it: "I have to return to the cult. That is my destiny. That is how I will be somebody. That is how I will have power."

"Where?" I asked after I had recovered from my initial shock. "Where was this meeting? What went on?"

"I don't know, Ma. I'd like to help the police, but I don't know. I'm too afraid to go under and find the lost time."

"Do you want to see Dr. Kingsbury? Can he do anything for you?"

"Yes."

The doctor did come to the hospital, and in a small, lamp-lit conference room he once more guided Alex down the long, deep staircase and into the magic castle. "Attend to—the quiet—and peace," began Dr. Kingsbury in the familiar rhythm of the three-to-five syllable phrases. "Memories come—in bits and pieces—puzzle pieces—turned upside down. The pieces—of the puzzle—are the meeting—with Christine—and others. Turn over—only the pieces—that will allow you—to remain safe—as you see—and you feel—and you know. Go deeper. Feel safer. Turn over a piece—and feel safe."

Alex made no movement. He sat perfectly still as he concentrated on the task at hand. "Some don't seem—" the doctor continued, "to fit together. Slowly others—will fit with others. From the castle—you can see—the puzzle. Relaxing—more and more—as you feel—your own strength. You prove yourself strong—as you turn them over—and face them. What you couldn't—do then—you can do now. And it is good—to have—your memories—to hold—to control."

Within three days the safety of the castle allowed Alex to have this control and to know what had happened. "Ma," he said in a phone call, "the police have been talking to my doctor and they're coming to the hospital to see me. Before they come, I want to tell you about it. Can you take me out tonight?"

Alex was given a pass, but when I picked him up, he did not want to leave the grounds. Following his directions, I drove down a dirt road in back of the institution and bumped my way through the darkness. We stopped at the top of a hill that fell away in rain-rutted, rock-strewn steepness to the shores of a lake or reservoir. In the light of the waning moon, the water below had the look of molten silver. Staring straight ahead, Alex began to speak in a melancholy monotone. "The cult meeting Lee went to—it was at the lodge where they hung out and played pool and drank beer. It wasn't a regular meeting. They weren't wearing cloaks or anything. Whenever I—actually it was Lee—got close to them they stopped talking. I heard little bits and pieces, enough to know they were making plans for Halloween. I found out Christine was in the room upstairs. The barkeeper said I couldn't go up there, so I had to sneak past him when he was busy. She was sitting at a table with the Hendersons and some other friends of hers. She recognized me right away and motioned for me to come over to her."

"Was she surprised?" I asked. The thought of either him or Lee being anywhere near that woman made me sick to my stomach.

"No," he answered. "No, she wasn't. It's like I was expected. I was standing there and this man got up from the table and came over to me. I didn't know who he was, but he knew me."

"Oh? What did he look like?"

"Late forties, well-dressed, tie, business suit. It was gray. And he had brown hair, kind of receding in front, and a mustache. He walked like he thought he was tough and important. Macho. Anyway, he said, 'Good to see you. Are you ready to return to the cult?' "

"So what did you—I mean Lee—say?"

"It was what Lee wanted. To get back to the cult. So he said, 'Yes, that's why I've come.' The man gave him a piece of paper with his phone number and said, 'Halloween. Dusk. Be here. Be sure to call me at this number the night before. I'll be expecting to hear from you.' "

Fear struck like a thunderbolt, and it was only later, much later when I was back home with Sam, that I could speak of it.

"Hell," said Sam, putting some kind of perspective on the situation. "There's a good reason why Alex didn't recognize this guy. He's probably never seen him without his costume. There's no need for him to be afraid of those bastards now. Alex isn't a little kid anymore. They're just a bunch of yellow-bellied cowards hiding behind their damn silly-looking cloaks."

"But Sam," I argued, "suppose he did contact this man? Thank God he came to himself and got out of there. And of course the programming doesn't work once he's aware of it. But suppose he did call and go to the lodge? Do you believe for one minute those people have forgotten what Alex has done? They must know he's been trying to prosecute Christine for sex abuse, and I'm sure they've figured out his talking didn't stop there. They've got to suspect he's betrayed them and everything they represent. Remember, Sam, to them this betrayal is a thousand times worse because the traitor is someone who was raised in the image of Satan and was being groomed for leadership. If they had gotten their hands on him, who do you think would have been the Halloween sacrifice?"

And who, I asked myself, would have done the honors? I could hear Lee's voice telling me what Christine had said when she killed the babies. "This is what I will do to you if you tell." But I was unable to speak the words out loud. Over the years, there had been so much else. I wondered if Christine's fear of Alex's telling had been the motivation behind the attempted kidnapping at the horse show six years ago. What was it Alex had said she was going to do? Something about hiding him in the woods where no one could find him. If he had gone with her, would anyone ever have seen him again? I recalled that night in the emergency room when a five-year-old alter had let Alex feel the pain of a beating. "She wanted to make sure I didn't tell, so she beat me." And it was Christine who had reinforced the programming of the confessional in the Catholic church. "If you tell, the devil will take your soul, and when he does, you will know. You will know because you will lose your image. You will not be able to see yourself in the mirror."

When Lee allowed Alex to learn about the programming, he was essentially giving up his single-minded and fanatic quest to return to the cult. This weakening of a position that was the very mainstay of his existence fostered a much different relationship between the two. In December, Lee was able to tell what had happened on the seventh birthday. All of it. On the day this came through, I went up to the unit for a visit. As I walked down the long hallway to check in at the nurse's station, I had to pass by the open door of the common room. It was a spacious, sunlit area, decorated with patient-created artwork and furnished with assorted couches, chairs, game tables, a television, and, in a corner to the right, a Christmas tree. A group of counselors and teenagers on the other side of the room caught my attention. They were clustered around someone. It was Alex! He was in a chair, rocking himself back and forth, back and forth, with jerky motions. He had his face buried in the brown plush fur of a large teddy bear he held in his hands. It was the same bear, minus the karate outfit, I had given him on that first Christmas.

The rocking motion stopped and he doubled over, crushing the bear between his chest and the upper part of his legs. His arms hung limply with his fingers touching the floor. It was a trance. I knew it was a trance and I wanted to go to him and comfort him.

The charge nurse came in and ushered the boys and girls out while two male counselors pulled Alex to his feet. Supporting him under his arms, they half-walked and half-dragged him across the hall to the Quiet Room. As he came out of the trance, I could see him inside the room, pacing rapidly from one wall to the other. All of the color was leached from his skin, and his eyes seemed twice their normal size. He still had the teddy bear. Through all of this, he had the bear, clutching it tightly against his body. There was nothing I could do, and unable to watch any longer, I turned away and I left.

Because of the erratic and unstable behavior that followed the trance, Alex was confined to the hospital for the holiday. When I arrived at the unit to bring him his gifts, he was himself. But in the common room, after opening the packages of mostly clothes, Lee was there. He regarded me with a dark, hostile look and demanded I play cards with him. I told him I didn't feel like it. I was tired. It had been a long day. To the accompaniment of loud accusations and hateful insults, the new clothes, boxes, and an open pack of cards were hurled angrily at the Christmas tree. The commotion caught the attention of a counselor. "It's all her fault!" Lee yelled to him. "I want her out of here!"

"I didn't do anything," I said, trying to explain. "I didn't say anything."

"Well, something sure upset him," the counselor replied.

The counselor was right. Something had upset him. And later in the week, during another visit, I learned what it was. "I can't talk about the birthday yet," Alex said. He was sitting on his bed and I was in a chair near the desk. "But I want to tell you, and Bill when I see him, about the Christmas. It was the last thing Lee had to show me. I was seven and I was living with George and Sandra at her parents' house. Christine came in a taxi to pick me up. She wanted me to spend Christmas with her. She took me to the Hendersons, and after she gave me my presents, she sexually abused me. Five times, Ma. Over that weekend, she did it to me five times. So when you gave me my presents . . ."

Here was one occasion when Christine's access to the child was easily checked. A date. A place. And a witness, Sandra. Except for that chance meeting in the hospital seven years ago, the only contact we'd ever had with her was when she talked to Sam on the night of the birthday. That was the night Lee stole the station wagon and went to Bainbridge. I remembered she had told my husband that she had gotten rid of George, so I was quite sure she would be able to speak freely. She would be able to provide the verification I needed. Although I had mixed feelings about getting in touch with her, I had to take into consideration that Sandra's participation in the abuse was minimal in comparison to what the rest of them did. She did hold him down while George beat him but under what circumstances did this happen? She was seventeen years old and under the control of an extremely violent man. Alex had once told me how George had hurt her so badly she had to be carried from the house on a stretcher. It seemed to me that Sandra was also a victim. I decided to call her.

She did remember Christmas of 1981. "Christine," she said, "came to my parents' house in a taxi. She picked up Alex and took him to the Hendersons', where she was living. When she brought him back, he was a disaster. He was off the walls. He was always out of control after she had him. And he had this thing about candles. He would walk around carrying a candle and saying these weird words."

Sandra went on to talk about the many visits Alex had had with Christine during the summer prior to that Christmas. This was the summer Assistant District Attorney Paul Phillips had claimed they could not get an indictment for until they could prove Christine had access to him. My son was in no condition right now to go forward with his case. But under the law, he had until he was twenty-six years old to prosecute Christine. Perhaps when he was older and stronger and all this was behind him . . .

There was something else that was very important in Sandra's substantiation. The details of Lee's report of being picked up by Christine were entirely accurate. The time, the place, the taxi. Did not this give a little more credibility to his accounts of past events?

Over the next eight days, Alex undertook the difficult and delicate task of communicating with Lee. How he persuaded this alter to surrender his independence and his very existence, I do not know. Along with all of the skills Dr. Kingsbury had taught him, he must have had to use his own considerable ingenuity. So it was that on January third of 1992, Lee came in. He had been a worthy adversary, and in spite of his Machiavellian methods, I was thankful to him for the part he had played in saving my son. But I would not miss him.

As for the Old One, Alex quite literally owed him his life. Although this ancient protector may well have been a charlatan, he had creatively fulfilled his purpose. He had helped

Alex to survive his seventh birthday, then and now, and he, too, became integrated.

In February, Alex was released from Westboro. We said our goodbyes to the staff. I must admit that of all the hospitals, this one had been the best and the most flexible in meeting Alex's needs. The ride back was slow. An early morning ice storm had made the roads slippery. When we reached the house it was almost noon. I parked in the driveway behind Sam's truck, but before I had a chance to shut off the ignition, Alex jumped from the car and half-slid across the lawn to the front door. I caught up with him in the dining room. He was running his fingers across the table and the chairs and the dark pine hutch. "I'm home. I'm home," he repeated joyfully. "I'm home."

My husband emerged from the kitchen, a half-eaten sandwich in his hand. "Where the hell do you think you are?" he said in a gruff covering up of feeling. And to me, "Look, I've got to get to work. I'll see you tonight."

After Sam left, I followed Alex into the living room. Subdued now, his expression serious, he paused to gaze out the window overlooking the woods and the snow-patched pasture. A sudden wind howled around the chimney and whipped the branches of the trees to shatter the frozen sheathing and send it crashing to the ground. "Ma, I need to talk to you," he said. He went to the old rocking chair by the fireplace and eased himself into it as though his body were sore and hurting. "I want to tell you about Lee."

I sat on the end of the couch, tucked my legs under me, and wrapped an afghan around my shoulders to ward off the chill. We'd be needing a fire later.

Alex was rocking with quick, jerky motions. He stopped and looked directly at me. "Lee didn't come when I was seven."

"I thought . . ."

"No. He was the first. He'd been with me the longest. Since I was three going on four. He was stronger than the rest of the personalities. If there was something the others couldn't deal with, he would take over. Like at the sunrise thing. When Easter Boy realized what they were going to do, he refused. He couldn't handle it and Lee had to come. Lee got the punishment for what Easter Boy did. They put him in the grave and Christine told him they would leave him there if he didn't obey. It was just for five minutes, but it seemed like forever. When they took Lee out, Easter Boy came back, and this time he did help them shovel the dirt over the babies. In about half an hour, they made him pull them out."

"Well, that explains why you only knew Easter Boy's part in this at first. And why Lee cried out 'Don't bury me!' when I spoke to him. So it was Lee who put the babies in the grave?"

"No. It was Christine. Lee had to keep me and Easter Boy from knowing about it."

Christine. Yes. It fit with what Lee had said. I could hear his voice: "She buried them."

"It's okay to talk about it now. I know what Lee told you. I know how she killed the babies. That morning, that same Easter morning. Just before sunrise. There was a lot of chanting. Some wore robes. Some didn't. Christine picked up the babies, two of them, and she just tossed them into the grave. Like it was nothing. Lee didn't let Easter Boy take over until after she had done it."

Alex stared at the half-charred remains of a log in the fireplace. "I'm cold," he said, and getting up from the chair, he crumpled several sheets of newspaper, took a handful of kindling from a basket on the hearth, and arranged the paper and wood in the fireplace. "Do you have a match?"

"On the mantel. In that bowl."

He took a wooden match from the polished pewter trophy he had won at a horse show. There was a grating noise as he scratched it on a brick, and it flared briefly to ignite a crescent of flame along the edge of the paper.

As the kindling sputtered and snapped, he sat on the raised hearth and began to speak again. "Ma, there was one thing you did to help Lee integrate. Do you remember the therapy session when you went on about how you hated me for what we'd done to you?"

"I'm not likely to forget it. Lee came, didn't he? I could tell."

"Yes. Lee thought all mothers were like Christine, so when he saw a mother could be that angry and not want to kill, he knew he could tell me what Christine had done. He knew I wasn't in danger anymore. It was safe for him to leave. Ma, he really did like you."

"Oh? How come he treated me so rotten then?"

Alex's lips parted in a slightly sardonic smile. "He didn't want to kill you."

"I know. He told me. And he also told me—Alex, he said Christine—he said she drowned babies."

"She did. One that I saw, anyway. It was in the daytime. A meeting in the woods. Near a stream or small river about ten feet wide. The leaves were falling off the trees into the water. Uncle Ralph was there. I hid behind a tree and watched, and Lee took over. There was the usual, the chanting, the glory be to all-powerful Satan crap. She walked into the stream. She wasn't wearing her cloak. She had the baby in her hands. She held it under the water, like in a baptism. Only she never brought it up. Until it drowned. But the worst was the birthday."

If I had paused to dwell on the drowning and picture it in my mind, I wouldn't have been able to hear anymore. "The seventh birthday, Alex?"

"Yes. Christine came to Sandra's parents' house in the morning. She stood on the sidewalk out front and kept calling me. The windows were open and I could hear her. She wanted to take me with her. George didn't want to let me go, but she was making a scene, saying she had a right, till he gave in. Christine brought me back to the Hendersons', and it started out okay. Her boyfriend came over and took me bowling, but he left around four or five o'clock, and then things went downhill. I went with Christine to the lodge and the Hendersons followed in a separate car. Partway there, Lee came.

"They had a cult meeting that night in honor of my birthday. I saw my sister Debra and Uncle Ralph. The leader got up and talked to everyone about me, how I'd proved myself worthy to be a Prince of Satan and about my destiny in the cult. He made a big deal out of giving me the name Goldstem.

"They started the stuff about returning to the cult in exactly ten years. No matter where I was or what I was doing, I was supposed to return to the cult on the seventeenth birthday. Lee wouldn't cooperate. He didn't really rebel. He just got stubborn and refused to swear allegiance to Satan. The leader had already made this big speech about me, so he got mad and told me I was going to belong to Satan one way or another."

Alex got to his feet and picked up two logs from the hearth. When he placed them on the fire, their weight crushed the burning kindling. But then the flames wrapped themselves around the logs and I could feel the warmth. Turning toward me, he said, "After the Twin. You know, the candle and how the doctor found marks on—on my penis?"

What did that have to do with now? "As I recall, he described them as oblique. Slanted red marks."

"They weren't made by the candle."

"What? What did make them?"

His face darkened and the words spilled out. "It's what they did on the birthday. They held Lee down and pulled off his pants. He was kicking and screaming. Everybody watched, Christine, Debra, everybody, while the uncle took a branding iron and branded him. There. With the sign of Satan. The pentagram."

I stared into the fire, deep into the glowing orange-red coals. The familiar numbness permeated my being and walled off the horror. At last it was Alex who broke the silence. "Even Lee couldn't handle that. He wanted to die. He wanted to kill himself."

"So he invented the Old One?"

"Yes."

"Alex, when they took you back to George and Sandra, didn't anyone see this? Didn't you tell anyone?"

"What was I going to say? I didn't know who did it or how. They would have thought I was crazy. When I was myself again, I was in pain, but Sandra wasn't too observant. Anyway, a few months later, they convinced Lee to go along with it. There was another ceremony. This time he swore allegiance to who they said was the only true God. He faithfully promised to obey Satan and to dedicate his life to his service. He vowed to return to the cult on his seventeenth birthday. There were more speeches, and Christine came out with the red cloak. The rest of them chanted while she dressed him in it."

"That's why Ricky and the Halloween Child didn't know how they got the red robe?"

"Right. They weren't there. At the hospital, when the birthday came, I didn't want to go to the cult. I tried to resist. I tried to fight Lee, and he threatened to kill me. He said he was going to get the others to help him."

The hospital. Alex begging to see Dr. Kingsbury. The fearful desperation of his cries. And Lee: "Alex is next. We're going to kill him next."

"Did he actually do anything? I haven't forgotten that it was the Twin who almost stopped your breathing."

"Well, it was him when we were going to Boston and came close to crashing into a tree. Ma, Lee didn't really want to hurt me. He thought my life depended on him. He thought he was saving me by forcing me to go back to the cult. He really believed they would kill me if he didn't. He was afraid Dr. Kingsbury would get rid of him, so that's why he had to do whatever he could to keep me away from him and that's why he made the threats."

"These others, Alex. Are there others? Are there more?"

"I don't know. I'm not sure. Ma, there is something else. I have to ask you something. At the hospital—in the kitchen—do you remember? I told you how I was angry because you knew things."

"I remember. You were afraid I would tell you before you were ready."

"Well, there is one more reason why I was angry at you."

"What?" My response was short and clipped. "What now?" I scanned his face for a clue.

"That day you told me how you hated me, you said you wanted me to stop making you pay for what she did. Well, you didn't know me back then. Part of me understands that. You didn't know I was alive, but . . ." He hesitated. A faint flush of pink touched his cheeks. "But the reason I was making you pay was—this doesn't make sense—I've felt for a long time you should have protected me when I was little. I've been blaming you. I've been blaming you for what happened to me."

Casting aside the afghan, I got up from the couch and stood before him. Alex looked at me with soulful, gold-flecked green eyes and his words came into my heart. "Ma," he said. "Where were you? Why didn't you save me? You are my mother."

As I began to understand the full implications of what he was saying, as I began to understand the depth of his bonding, my defensiveness melted away and I gloried in the triumph and joy of that moment. We had come full circle. This was the magical thinking Bill had told me about. I remembered his explanation of how young children think their parents know everything and can do anything, and I knew that only a child who is truly one's own could be angry at his mother for not protecting him. The lengthy, piecemeal process of rebirth was complete. What my son was telling me did make sense. It made all the sense in the world.

EPILOGUE

For years, I've wanted to kill my perpetrators. There were a lot of nights when I couldn't get to sleep because I was just lying in bed trying to think of a way to pull it off. It got so bad, and I wanted it so much, that I had to do what I had done many times before. I concentrated real hard and went deep inside of myself and said, "Help me, help me, please come," over and over like a prayer or spell. Then I was gone and one of the personalities would be there to handle my need for revenge.

Christine does not know how close some of these alters came to killing her. They would stalk her, following her at night, waiting for an opportunity to strike. Sometimes one of them would go to her house and try to catch her off guard by pretending to be friendly. Before anything happened, I was able to take over my body. It was horrifying to find myself there and I got out fast. I didn't want to spend the rest of my life in jail for murdering Christine. She wasn't worth it.

I was feeling really good when I believed the criminal justice system was going to put Christine behind bars. It didn't work out that way, but I can still press charges in a civil suit, and I may decide to do that. Even though she doesn't have anything, it would give me some revenge. This book is also a part of that revenge, although my mother isn't using the perpetrators' real names. But my best revenge is the "living well" that Dr. Kingsbury spoke about so often. Christine, her brothers, and the rest of them tried to destroy me and it didn't work. They did not succeed.

My troubles weren't over with the integration of all the personalities from the past. Creating personalities to handle stress was such a habit that I kept on doing it. By the time I was twenty-one, I realized they were more trouble than they were worth and learned to deal with problems on my own.

The people who have helped me the most are my parents. They were the first ones I could trust, and no matter how bad I got, they would be there for me. If it wasn't for my mother and father, I would be dead or locked up. I didn't always show it, but I love them dearly.

Bill Conti, my therapist, was also there for me and my parents whenever we needed him. At first, Bill didn't know that much about dissociation and personalities but he stayed in there and he learned. I couldn't have gotten a better therapist. He knew what to say and how to say it at the right time. He was patient and caring, and I could always trust him.

Dr. Kingsbury helped me with the things that were more advanced, such as dealing with the personalities. He taught me how to go into the magic castle, where I could feel safe enough to overcome my fears and face the past. He taught me how to integrate my alters rather than fight with them. He also made it clear to me that being a multiple was a way of survival and not a sign of insanity. Without him I would not be the person I am today, and to me he is a superhero.

I have come so far in so many ways. I do not use drugs or alcohol to hide from my problems, and I don't lose control if I get angry or frustrated. I have recently been able to have some money, and I have proven I can be dependable and trustworthy. It took a long time, but I feel completely normal. In some ways, I'm ahead of my friends because I've learned how to talk about my problems and emotions. I'm still living at home; I'm working with my dad, and I'm doing great.

There are a lot of people, including doctors and mental health workers, who do not believe multiple personalities exist. I have met quite a few of them. I hope this book helps them to understand what multiples go through. I also hope it helps them to understand that with the right treatment, we do get better.

Alex Smith
February 17, 1997

AFTERWORD

Steven J. Kingsbury, M.D., Ph.D.

I was honored when Carole and Alex asked me to write my comments, and I would like to say that I believe the story to be true. I am equally convinced that Carole and Alex are certain of the truthfulness of the events and memories recounted here, but I wonder whether some readers will discount them as very dramatic fiction. So rather than trying to convince anyone of the truth of what is described here, I hope to give a perspective that will briefly discuss some of the ways to view the problems and some of the ways to view the therapy. The story clearly stands by itself. These pages may be extraneous to some and safely skipped.

There are many aspects of Alex's tale that raise some of the most controversial issues in the mental health field today. Multiple personality disorder, despite the increasing scientific literature concerned with it, is still a condition that some respected and noted psychiatrists and psychologists think does not exist. Rather, they believe such dramatics are a product of some type of nonconscious collusion between the therapist and the patient.

Similarly, hypnosis has been a part of the healing skills of professionals (and charlatans) for hundreds of years, and has had periods in which it has enjoyed greater acceptance from mental health professionals and lesser. Again, in present-day psychiatry and psychology, there are those respected authorities who denigrate its usefulness for actual healing.

Fortunately for the victims, over the last several decades

the existence of the sexual and physical abuse of children has been more acknowledged. Satanic cults, however, are much more controversial, and the actual existence of such organized groups is denied by some professionals.

Since Alex's history has these three elements as prominent foci—multiple personality disorder, hypnosis, and the existence of satanic cults—each needs some comment. Actually, these areas are not as discrete as the labels might imply.

Multiple personality disorder is a condition that has been known for hundreds of years. Although the diagnosis has found favor in scientific circles at some times, it has virtually disappeared at other times. Although there is much that is unknown or controversial about the disorder, it seems clear that a major cause is early childhood trauma, typically taking the form of repeated sexual and/or physical abuse. Trauma later in life or trauma that is not repetitive may certainly have long-term serious effects on a person's ability to cope with a variety of stressors, but it most usually does not lead to multiple personality disorder.

How trauma leads to the creation of multiple personality disorder is also only partly understood. The most often used concept to explain this fractionation of the self is that of dissociation, a term denoting a splitting off of consciousness. Perhaps the simplest way to view dissociation in this context is to think of a situation so horrible and so different that it cannot be integrated into everyday consciousness. Unlike what we had for lunch last Tuesday, which becomes part of the general mass of memories, some of which are more easily accessed, some of which are less so, these memories are separate from the normal streams of consciousness. As such, the memories of such awful events are not accessible to normal consciousness.

That does not mean that such memories are forgotten or that they have no influence upon normal consciousness. If the conditions are such as to approximate the state that is dissociated, a "flashback" may occur in which the mind replays the event in vivid detail. If enough abuse occurs in which the individual is repeatedly in this altered state, the altered state may develop a "history" with a store of memories separate from the main personality. In the book, I explain to Carole and Alex about this by talking about islands of memories separated from the main continent of consciousness.

Alex's history is somewhat different from the typical case histories of multiples in several respects. First, he is a male, and most known cases of multiple personality disorder are female. One explanation for this may be that females are abused more than males, although some experts suggest that the number of male multiples is much larger than current clinical reports would suggest. Due to social pressures, male multiples may more often act out aggressively or antisocially than females and end up in the prison system rather than the mental health system. Certainly, the meaning of being a helpless victim and the steps believed necessary to prevent such future victimization may be different for males and females in our society. Some of Alex's behaviors could have led to greater involvement by the courts if it hadn't been for the interventions of Carole and Bill, Alex's therapist.

Secondly, this history begins (and ends) at a much earlier age than the stories of many multiples. In fact, reading such histories, it is often surprising how little mention is made of the adolescent years. My suspicion is that for most of the cases, the teens were a time of more of the same chaos in the victims' lives as well as a time when the multiple personalities were continuing to become more distinct and autonomous. The total separateness shown by some adult multiples would be difficult for an adolescent to show, since society does not allow adolescents to live and function as autonomously. Some authorities suggest that treating multiples while they are younger, if they can be identified, shortens treatment. In any case, the dramatic, often extended shifts into other personalities shown in some popularized accounts of adult multiples are not present here.

Dissociation, however, is as central to understanding Alex's problems as it is for other multiples. This splitting off of a stream of consciousness has been seen for many years as a type of self-hypnosis, in which the shock and arousal of the event creates an altered state in the victim. The connection between hypnosis and these altered states had been written about by such early physicians and psychologists as George Gilles de la Tourette, Pierre Janet, and Josef Breuer long before modern scientists demonstrated a link in research. In such research, it is shown that multiples and other trauma victims with such diagnoses as posttraumatic stress disorder are almost invariably hypnotic virtuosos who quickly enter into a profound state of hypnosis as measured by hypnotic susceptibility scales.

In my work with trauma, I, too, have found this connection between hypnosis and trauma, and I consider it central to therapeutic work with these individuals. With Alex, my hypnotic induction was often no more elaborate than "Why don't you close your eyes, and go into a deep trance." Obviously, I was using his excellent hypnotic skills rather than relying only on my induction techniques.

Perhaps there is no clearer example of the overlap of multiple personality disorder, dissociation, and hypnosis than the episode in which Alex was unable to see himself in a mirror for several weeks, although everything else was reflected accurately in the mirror. Technically this is known as a negative hallucination, the not seeing of something that is there. Interestingly, the concept of negative hallucinations does not appear in the literature on psychopathology, but appears repeatedly in the hypnosis literature, where the creation of negative hallucinations is often used as a marker for greater hypnotic susceptibility.

Therefore, although the induction of hypnosis was simple, the real task was what to do therapeutically with Alex while he was in that dissociated state. It is here that individuals and schools of therapy differ the most. It is also here that it should be underscored that hypnosis was only one element in Alex's therapy.

In many ways, Alex was an ideal case, since many important therapeutic elements were already in place before I became involved. First, and most important, he was removed from the abusive situations and relationships. No therapy for abuse can proceed successfully without that step being taken. Secondly, Carole was and is a good parent, with both intelligence and good instincts. It was often painful to see her input ignored or denigrated by staff members at other facilities who deluded themselves into believing that they knew better just because they were professionals and had known Alex for a few days. A third factor was the large contribution of Bill, his primary psychotherapist when I worked with Alex. Bill's hard and excellent work freed me to be a consultant able to distance myself from some of the administrative nitty-gritty like limit-setting, which sometimes interferes with doing the therapeutic work necessary.

Even with all of these fortuitous factors present, I still believe that hypnosis has a central place in such cases as Alex's. Put most simply, Alex was going in and out of hypnotic states before I met him. My task was to help him gain better control of this switching of states, not to "help" him remember trauma. If people are unable to access traumatic memories, then the reasons for not remembering should be respected, and addressed.

Although undoubtedly very dramatic, this wrenching out of dissociated memories while the patient is in a directed trance strikes me as a kind of secondary abuse perpetrated by some professionals. Taking people who feel a severe loss of control and forcing memories upon them before they are ready typically interferes with therapy rather than facilitating it.

On the other hand, working with the reasons for not being able to remember, when successful, allows the person to confront the painful memories without decompensating. Therefore, with Alex, we worked on his establishing greater senses of control and safety. As his sense of self-control and his felt safety increased, often terrible memories came out, many times without the unraveling of his personal functioning that had occurred before the hypnotic work.

This is how the image of the castle was used, as a special place of safety. Castles have a prominent place in many fairy tales, as a place of magic, and they also have a special place in history as a fortress for protection. Everyone is familiar with the image of a moat and a drawbridge that can be raised to separate the castle from what is occurring outside. It is also easy to conjure up such touches as secret passages, treasure rooms, and other rooms deep inside that contain hidden secrets behind heavy doors. Alex was also able to avail himself of a handy magic suit of armor, which he could don at times for further protection when meeting an alter personality.

Perhaps most important in the castle were secret rooms found by Alex while traversing hidden passages to find peace, quiet, and a place to reflect. Using this magic, special castle of his own creation, Alex was able to do much of the therapeutic work by himself, as well as to calm himself while increasing his controls. Thanks to his highly developed skills of self-hypnosis, teaching him to use hypnosis adaptively involved little more than guiding him into safer, more useful images and places in his mind.

The fact is that any human who has survived to Alex's age must have some positive, somewhat nurturing memories. Admittedly, such good times may have been few and doled out in a totally unpredictable manner. Such early positive memories may also be totally denied by someone like Alex as incompatible with his memories of abuse and torture, but they are there, allowing the eventual slow building of trust.

Feeling in control of his dissociation and meeting his alters were the main goals of the hypnosis. In sessions in which he came feeling plagued by amnesic gaps or behavior he felt was out of his control, meetings were set up with the alters to learn about them. Alex was instructed not to quiz the alters concerning their memories but rather to inquire about their needs, wishes, and goals. Neither was he pushed to attempt integration. Rather, he was instructed to seek communication, and to attempt to learn from these parts, just as he was also instructed to share with them and help them understand the favorable circumstances of his present life.

Typically, this communication led to learning about episodes of abuse, which, once learned from the "other," became integrated as part of Alex's own personal history. Not surprisingly, as Alex increased his ability to make himself feel safe, he was able to face more and more profound abuse episodes. Some workers in the field have compared this to an onion, stating that as one peels away each level of the onion, more awful, "deeper" trauma awaits. This appears to be a useful metaphor in my experience.

Yet, even with all these explanations, there seems no definite way to convince another person of what happened. I know of at least several cases in which mental health workers, skeptical of the existence of multiple personality disorder despite reading reports and even viewing videotapes, came to accept the diagnosis only after witnessing an interview with an actual multiple. Obviously, this route is not available to most readers of this book.

Another element of this story that is controversial is the specter of satanic worship and satanic cults, topics leading to strong debates even in the professional literature. There could be several explanations for Alex's memories, even when one excludes the possibilities of overwrought imaginations. One possibility is that there was indeed a satanic cult, which may or may not have been connected with other cult groups. Secondly, there may have been a sadistic, perverted group of individuals who, for "fun," cloaked their activities in the mantle of satanism, but had no true allegiance to any of its central beliefs, such as the belief in the existence and power of the devil.

Beyond the question of the beliefs of the group is the question of its activities, such as the murder of infants. Again, it may be that there were such murders, but it may instead be that some or all of the horrible events were a type of stage show in which sleight of hand and substitutions (for example, of animal parts) convinced Alex that events occurred although they actually did not. Even if the latter explanation is correct for some or all of the events that Alex finally remembered, the reality for him was that they did happen. The horror and fear would be the same.

No book or scientific paper will resolve these important debates. It is clear from the evidence that Alex was repeatedly abused while he was very young. It is also clear that he was extremely dysfunctional when he came to Carole's home. Beyond those facts is the ordering of the data that is called explanation in the social sciences. We state that the abuse led to the dysfunction, based upon the study of others who have been abused. Similarly, some state that this dysfunction is caused by a process called dissociation. Others go further and state that this dysfunction results in multiple personality disorder. All this can be interesting, but the ultimate purpose is to develop a coherent story to guide the therapist and help the patient develop some order and control out of the felt chaos.

I believe this story combined with the theories I have mentioned was useful to both Alex and to me. This does not make it "truer," only more useful. It is hoped that this ordering of events is also useful for the reader of this book.